Church Ethics and Its Organizational Context

BOSTON COLLEGE CHURCH IN THE 21ST CENTURY SERIES

MISSION STATEMENT

As a Catholic university, Boston College seeks to be a bridge between Catholicism and contemporary society. The Church in the 21st Century initiative proposes to assist the Catholic Church in exploring the issues emerging from the clerical sexual abuse crisis that has shaken the trust of many Catholics and non-Catholics in the Catholic Church. The project has three foci: first, understanding more clearly the roles and relationships of lay men and women, priests, and bishops in the Church of the 21st century; second, identifying and exploring the critical issues that Catholics face in living, deepening, and handing on the faith to succeeding generations; and third, developing a contemporary understanding of sexuality in the light of Catholic tradition and beliefs. The Church in the 21st Century does not intend to take the place of those in the Church ultimately responsible for resolving these issues, but rather to fulfill the role of a Catholic university in providing a forum and resources to help the Catholic community—lay men and women, priests, and bishops—transform the current crisis into an opportunity for renewal.

SERIES EDITORS
Patricia De Leeuw and James F. Keenan

TITLES
Church Ethics and its Organizational Context:
Learning from the Sex Abuse Scandal in the Catholic Church
edited by Jean M. Bartunek, Mary Ann Hinsdale, and James F. Keenan

Church Ethics and Its Organizational Context

Learning from the Sex Abuse Scandal in the Catholic Church

Edited by
Jean M. Bartunek,
Mary Ann Hinsdale,
and
James F. Keenan

A SHEED & WARD BOOK

ROWMAN & LITTLEFIELD PUBLISHERS, INC.
Lanham • Boulder • New York • Toronto • Oxford

A SHEED & WARD BOOK

ROWMAN & LITTLEFIELD PUBLISHERS, INC.

Published in the United States of America
by Rowman & Littlefield Publishers, Inc.
A wholly owned subsidiary of The Rowman & Littlefield Publishing Group, Inc.
4501 Forbes Boulevard, Suite 200, Lanham, Maryland 20706
www.rowmanlittlefield.com

PO Box 317
Oxford
OX2 9RU, UK

British Library Cataloguing in Publication Information Available

Library of Congress Cataloging-in-Publication Data

Church ethics and its organizational context : learning from the sex abuse scandal
in the Catholic Church / edited by Jean M. Bartunek, Mary Ann Hinsdale, and James
F. Keenan.
    p. cm. — (Boston College church in the 21st century series)
Includes bibliographical references and index.
ISBN 0-7425-3247-X (cloth : alk. paper) — ISBN 0-7425-3248-8 (pbk. : alk. paper)
1. Child sexual abuse by clergy. 2. Christian ethics—Catholic authors.
3. Celibacy—Catholic Church. 4. Catholic Church—Discipline. 5. Authority—
Religious aspects—Catholic Church. 6. Church discipline. 7. Church polity.
I. Bartunek, Jean. II. Hinsdale, Mary Ann. III. Keenan, James F. IV. Series.
BX1912.9.C49 2005
261.8'3272'088282—dc22   2005014499

Printed in the United States of America

♾™ The paper used in this publication meets the minimum requirements of
American National Standard for Information Sciences—Permanence of Paper
for Printed Library Materials, ANSI/NISO Z39.48-1992.

To the memory of Father Bob Bullock,
Priest of the Archdiocese of Boston
1929–2004

CONTENTS

ABBREVIATIONS

AG	Ad gentes, Decree on the Missionary Activity of the Church
AAS	Acta Apostolicae Sedis
ES	Ecclesiam suam, Encyclical Letter on the Ways in which the Church Must Carry out Its Mission in the Contemporary World
GS	Gaudium et spes, Pastoral Constitution on the Church in the Modern World
HV	Humanae vitae, Encyclical Letter on Human Life
JW	Justice in the World, Document of World Synod of Catholic Bishops
LE	Laborem exercens, Encyclical Letter on Human Work
LG	Lumen Gentium, Dogmatic Constitution on the Church
PG	Pastores Gregis, Apostolic Exhortation on the Bishop
RM	Redemptoris missio, Encyclical Letter on the Permanent Validity of the Church's Missionary Mandate
QA	Quadragesimo anno, Encyclical Letter on Reconstruction of the Social Order
SC	Sacrosanctum concilium, Constitution on the Sacred Liturgy
UR	Unitatis redintegratio, Decree on Ecumenism

INTRODUCTION

Jean M. Bartunek and James F. Keenan

The church historian John O'Malley notes that the first characteristic of the sexual abuse crisis in the Catholic Church is its extent. Though well publicized in Boston, the crisis has multitudinous expressions throughout the world. As a result, theologians of every kind—systematicians, historians, canonists, and ethicists—have written articles, essays, and books recognizing that the scandal arose from what O'Malley has called a "crisis of authority."[1]

Other writers have addressed the topic as well: Sociologists such as Katerina Schuth and Andrew Greeley, church historians such as Brian Tierney and Francis Oakley, and journalists such as Peter Steinfels and David Gibson have all weighed in with their distinctive competencies. In one noteworthy instance, a major Catholic center, the Saint Thomas More Chapel and Center at Yale University, hosted such speakers to address the crisis of authority and published their papers written from their diverse church historical, canonical, and theological perspectives on the crisis.[2]

Boston College, under the leadership of its President Fr. William P. Leahy, SJ, has addressed the sexual abuse crisis in an extended, scholarly way that aims not only to shed light on the immediate circumstances and experiences of those involved, but also to study and address them in a broader, scholarly way that can make evident their importance not only for the Catholic Church but for the larger society as well.

By means of a large-scale initiative entitled "The Church in the 21st Century" (www.bc.edu/church21/), Boston College has become the only university to commit its many resources toward envisioning the church for future generations. Through the initiative, Boston College, as its initiative's mission statement affirms, explores the issues underlying the clerical sexual abuse crisis in the Catholic Church by providing a forum and resources to assist the Catholic community in transforming the current situation into an opportunity for renewal. For this reason, for the past three years, the Church 21 Project (as it is now called) has held literally hundreds of lectures, panels, forums, and meetings to better understand and respond to these issues of significant import.

Among these events was one planned by a committee of the initiative, named to analyze the "roles and responsibilities" proper to church leadership. This committee, chaired by Mary Ann Hinsdale, Francis Sullivan, and Jean Bartunek, worked for nearly eighteen months to bring together a group of scholars to foster the development of an ecclesial professional ethics for the church.

Development of such an ecclesial professional ethics was an entirely new undertaking. While others, individually and collectively, had addressed problems of governance, authority, accountability, and transparency, no one had specifically studied whether and how professional ethics could shape the identity and actions of church leaders, ministers, and their congregations. Almost fifteen years ago, a group of theologians looked at the question of clergy ethics per se, but not for any practical purpose of implementation.[3] That prior academic investigation was not confronted with the urgency of the crisis of authority now facing the church universal.

To accomplish its purpose, the subcommittee realized it needed to expand the types of conversation partners beyond theology. Thus, they designed a conference in which "the usual suspects," whose work focused somewhat explicitly on the church, would be in conversation with newcomers to the conversation: scholars from other disciplines whose research does not typically address church-related issues but does address crucial issues pertinent to institutional and professional ethics. These newcomers included scholars in organization studies, law, and other social science disciplines.

The planners also wanted to include people who were actually in the trenches of church formation and leadership. To this end, we invited the Most Reverend John R. Quinn, retired archbishop of San Francisco; Dr. James Post, president of Voice of the Faithful (VOTF); Monsignor Dennis Sheehan, board member of the Boston Priest Forum; Father Richard Gula, SS, professor of moral theology and noted instructor on clergy ethics; and Dr. Francis Butler, president of Fundraisers and Donors Interested in Catholic Apostolates (FADICA).

Since the topic—ecclesial professional ethics—was so new, it allowed everyone to discuss on the same level of competency. Yet, precisely because it was in these other disciplines that professional ethics had received the most attention, the newcomers brought a degree of experience and expertise that the usual suspects, more familiar with the church and its history, lacked.

In the end, the conference, chaired by Mary Ann Hinsdale, included forty-five participants. Its three constituencies, scholars reflecting on the life of the church; academicians from the fields of law, organization studies, and multiple social sciences; and representatives of the different forms of leadership within the church, met at Boston College for two days, February 14 and 15, 2004, to present, discuss, and explore a variety of issues associated with the possibility of a professional ethics for the church.

Several of the invited participants presented papers on the topic of ecclesial professional ethics, all of which had been posted on the conference website in advance, to further discussion at the meeting. These presentations, the diversity of the constituencies present, the level of discourse, and the importance and uniqueness of the topic occasioned a truly formidable conference.

At the end of the conference the planning committee met again, discussed publishing the papers, and decided on three of us (Jean M. Bartunek, Mary Ann Hinsdale, and James F. Keenan) to be the collection's editors. We in turn asked our contributors for revisions and found in Mr. Jeremy Langford of the Sheed & Ward division of Rowman & Littlefield a creative and engaging publisher.

As we finish editing the collection we are indebted to all of the conference participants and especially to the presenters, whose contributions are uniformly thoughtful and thought provoking. We acknowledge with gratitude the additional long-standing committee members (Patricia Chang, James O'Toole, and Francis Sullivan, SJ) who met tirelessly to realize this event and do initial planning for this book. We are especially grateful to Rose Mary Donahue, assistant to Father Leahy, and Michael Boland, administrative coordinator of the Church in the 21st Century initiative, who organized all the logistics for the conference and made it a very hospitable event. Finally, we give special thanks to Lawrence Manfredi for his skilled copyediting and to Jonathon Sage for all the audiovisual arrangement at the conference.

We present these essays so as to further the discourse that the conference helped initiate last February. We believe that they represent a singular contribution, one that can broaden significantly the understanding and appreciation of the range of issues associated with an ethics that is ecclesial and professional. We also believe that this contribution raises issues that, while evoked by the sex abuse scandal in the church, have implications far beyond it, to much broader issues such as the role of professionalism in ethics and what it means for an organization to act morally.

Finally, we dedicate these essays to the memory of Fr. Bob Bullock, a beloved pastor, who throughout the crisis led us by example and by dialogue to envision a church rooted in the Gospels, serving the contemporary world.

NOTES

1. John O'Malley, "The Scandal: A Historian's Perspective," *America* 186 (27 May 2002): 14–17.

2. Francis Oakley and Bruce Russett, eds., *Governance, Accountabilty, and the Future of the Catholic Church* (New York: Continuum, 2004).

3. James P. Wind, Dennis McCann, and Russell Burck, eds., *Clergy Ethics in a Changing Society: Mapping the Terrain* (Chicago: Park Ridge Center, 1991).

I

NEW WAYS OF UNDERSTANDING
THE CRISIS

1: UNDERSTANDING THE CRISIS IN THE CHURCH

Paul Lakeland

> "Is it wise, is it prudent, that those whose voice is law in everything else, should be made to feel, that in that very thing, in which they are most deeply interested, they have no voice at all?"

> —Anonymous early nineteenth-century Philadelphia Catholic[1]

Rather than offer a blow-by-blow account of the crisis, this paper will approach it in three ways, each of which takes a somewhat different approach to the same essential question: What, in essence, *is* the crisis? The first and most pedestrian step is to look at it as a series of concentric circles around the anything-but-still point of child sexual abuse by some clergy. The second step will shift the metaphor slightly, from concentric circles to layers, moving from the shallower to the deeper layer, in search of what is at the core of the problem. And the third and final method, mixing theology and history, will be to ask, in effect, just how new this crisis is. The suggestion will be that the more widely we traverse the concentric circles, and the deeper we dig in the layers, the more evident it becomes that the crisis is not new at all, indeed it is almost as old as the hills, and that it is anything but what on the surface it appears to be.

PHASE ONE: THE SCOPE OF THE CRISIS

No one would argue with the statement that at the heart of the sex abuse scandal that has been front and center for the past two years stands a sizeable number of victims of abuse. Just how many there are, no one will ever know. Those who came forward may be most of the victims, but they cannot be all. Moreover, just as a large number of the abusers are deceased, so there must have been many victims who died unknown, and a church that takes seriously the communion of saints and the resurrection of the body must be ready to recognize that solidarity with victims extends especially to those who died unrequited. Whatever we go on to say, however much the focus seemingly shifts from victims, the value of what in the end we do here can be simply measured. Have we made it at least a little less likely that people will be victimized and suffer injustice at the hands of the church?

The response to victims and abusers alike must be marked by justice, mercy, and sound pastoral practice. Obviously this means somewhat different things for the two groups. The church has made some progress in the last few years in bringing justice and mercy to the victims, though it is saddening to see that the greatest progress seems to have been made under the threat of litigation. Justice for the victims requires appropriate redress of their grievances, whether that means financial compensation or the provision of therapy or the prosecution of their abusers, or all of the above. Mercy for victims translates into compassionate reception of their complaints. And sound pastoral practice goes beyond this to an effort to draw them back into the community of faith from which they may have become alienated through no fault of their own. This last is the most difficult, perhaps the most important, and has thus far been least attended to. When we turn to the abusers, we can readily see that justice is most directly going to mean bringing them to account for their crimes. However, justice does not stop there. Justice for abusers needs to go on to ask to what degree their criminal behavior was facilitated by the church itself. A dysfunctional family can all too readily be in denial about the failings of its members, and moving them from parish to parish or diocese to diocese is as plain a case of enabling as I can imagine. Then justice may also lead into mercy, and we face the need for rehabilitation of the abusers. Obviously, this is a sensitive point. "Rehabilitation" of a kind has been one of the most scandalous failings uncovered in the last couple of years, as abusers have been pronounced cured and released once again upon the unsuspecting children. But it is not crystal clear that the mercy and compassion that must accompany the necessary and rigorous insistence on justice is visible in the simplistic expediency of the so-called "zero tolerance" policy, any more than it is certain that the abusers are the only church personnel who deserve to stand in the dock.

Once we step beyond the central circle in a schema of concentric circles, the picture can be completed in a number of different ways depending on what we imagine we are depicting or, perhaps, who is doing the drawing. Looked at as a map of responsibility for the scandal, the central circle would be occupied by the abusers alone. The next circle must be the episcopacy, followed by the Vatican, then the parochial clergy, and after them the laity.

- responsibility
- has been hurt
- " benefitted

Beyond that, perhaps, we could find a place for contemporary American culture and even the press. The only ones who must be pronounced innocent and without any responsibility for the scandal are, of course, the victims. But this is a liberal drawing of the picture. If George Weigel sketched it,[2] he would probably agree that the bishops occupy the second circle, but then our diagrams would differ: next would surely come the permissive culture of America since the sixties, then the press, and only after that a minor place for Vatican, clergy, and laity. I am not sure where Weigel himself would stand, but some conservative commentators would want the victims occupying a circle of responsibility somewhat closer to the center than more liberal visions. After all, weren't at least some of them responsible to some degree, and hasn't their litigiousness been a major contributor to the crisis? And more than one individual has tried to lay the blame on parents for putting their children in harm's way!

If we adopt a different approach and draw the circles as a measure of who is hurt most by the scandal, the picture is not the same. The group most hurt—after the victims of course—would be the parochial clergy, followed closely by the laity. Next, if hurt means "caused to suffer" rather than simply "damaged," would have to come American society, which surely needs the perspective and priorities that a vigorous Catholicism can bring to the public forum. However, if we stress the element of damage, particularly damage to their credibility, then perhaps next would come bishops and the Vatican, both of whom seem to have isolated themselves fairly successfully from serious psychological trauma, if not systemic harm.

As a third way, we might ask who has benefited from the scandal. Then we have to draw a very different kind of picture. Most people would put the lawyers and the press at the center here, though it might be better to put the victims first, since the crisis is fundamentally about redressing rather than creating their problems. After that, who benefits most depends on how we see the crisis having salutary effects. Perhaps it might be the bishops, whom public scrutiny has forced into action. But a better answer might be the church as a whole and particularly the laity. Large sections of the laity have been scandalized and energized, and a more adult laity can only be to the benefit of the church. Or can it? Obviously, the question of who benefits can only be answered relative to a vision of the good, in this case, the good of the church. How do we envisage the good of the church? There is no consensus on this. Ecclesiologies are deeply and increasingly reflective of positions drawn on the ideological battle lines of the liberals and the (neo)conservatives. To the latter, the liberals are using the crisis to benefit a vision of the church as just another liberal Protestant denomination, "Catholic Lite" if you will (Weigel's phrase), and we all know what is happening to liberal Protestantism. To the liberals, more conservative types see the crisis as a chance to reassert a preconciliar vision of the church. Both the liberals and

Previous ecclesio
drives perception of scandal

the conservatives, of course, would counter these arguments in a similar way. Both would claim to be in defense of a legitimate understanding of Vatican II's ecclesiology. Who isn't, outside of Lincoln, Nebraska?

It is pretty clear, then, that if we stay with the story of the scandal as it has unfolded, without going into questions of meaning, there are too many ends of the stick to get hold of. We can read the crisis in so many different ways, and most of them—liberal or conservative—will tend to confirm our own vision of what the church should be and where it ought to be going if it would only listen to us. Worst of all, and perhaps this is the greatest danger at the present time, we can look at the crisis divorced from issues of deeper meaning, perhaps hypnotized by the evil at its heart, and understand it bureaucratically. Then we draw up report cards for the bishops and check on how they are doing at meeting the standards they wrote for themselves. But if there is one thing we can be clear about, it is that the presenting problem is not in the end successfully addressed unless it is placed in the larger context of systemic issues. Get to the systemic issues and the presenting problem will be dealt with. Don't get to the systemic issues and even if the presenting problem goes away, some other will appear to take its place.

PHASE TWO: THE DEPTHS OF THE CRISIS

Let us be clear. There is no sex abuse crisis in the church. What the church suffers from is a crisis issuing from the real problem of clerical sexual abuse of minors. Sex abuse itself is a heinous crime and a scandal in the church of the highest order of magnitude. But it isn't in itself a crisis. First, the numbers of abusers are not inordinately large, as far as we can tell, and the statistical evidence puts the rate of abuse among clergy significantly below the rate of abuse by adult males as a whole. Of course, there are two corollaries that give cause for concern. One is that clergy are expected to stand in a particular relationship of trust toward laity and most especially toward children (though one cannot resist saying that parents—who statistically do most of the abusing—are also trampling on an equally solemn trust). And the other is that by far the majority of the victims have been postpubescent males, whereas in the population at large adolescent girls and young women are the preferred targets of the mostly male predators. Second, while one has to treat the statistics carefully, it seems as if the incidence of abuse has declined over the past ten to twenty years. Whether this is because traumatized victims have not (yet) come forward, or because there are simply fewer priests out there than there used to be, or because they are older, or because seminary training is better than it was, it is hard to say. Third, however late in the day, the bishops do seem to have made some efforts to address the scandal and to have had some success in dealing fairly with victims and perpetrators.

There is even, apparently, some restoration of confidence among sectors of the laity and the incidence of mass attendance is on the rise again, though for the first time in our history the percentage of Catholics at weekly worship is lower than that of their Protestant counterparts. how to define situatio

It is a much more accurate statement of the present reality, then, to say that the scandal of clerical sexual abuse of minors has thrown the church into crisis. It is also important to insist on describing the problem this way, and instructive to see that the Vatican and episcopate has a distinct preference for clinging to the language of the crisis of sexual abuse. The good work that the American bishops and the Lay Commission have done to address the problem of sex abuse will hopefully mean that this problem in its current dimensions will never trouble the church again. That would certainly be the hope of all of us. But if we call this "the crisis" and are able to declare it "solved" or at least taken seriously, then it is entirely probable that most church leaders will want to return to business as before. However, if we can be persuasive in the claim that the scandal has revealed a crisis, then the successful overcoming of the scandal is not at all the same thing as dealing with the crisis. Though, of course, the resolution of the true crisis will hopefully mean that such scandals will not occur again.

impt

Once we have determined that the crisis revealed by the scandal is a structural crisis in the church, then the process of identifying it is one of moving from the fairly obvious to the more fundamental levels. It is beyond dispute that the scandal pointed to a crisis in the episcopacy. Poor leadership in dealing with the scandal has led to the kind of public scrutiny to which bishops are not accustomed. The precise nature of the crisis is not something that all will agree upon, but its elements are pretty evident. To name them is not to accuse every American bishop of all the elements, but to point to systemic dysfunctionalities to which all American bishops must attend. Among the charges that have been made over the past couple of years are the following: a faulty understanding of what it is to be a leader on the part of those who select bishops, and a consequent lack of good leaders within the episcopacy; bad judgment about how the good name of the church can best be assured; secrecy; isolation; ambition and careerism; poor theology; too centralized an understanding of the church, with a concomitant overdeference to the Roman Curia; and excessive bureaucratization of the role of the bishop. Some or all of these may be accurate, but not all qualify as systemic issues. Inappropriate ambition, for example, is something that systemic problems can foster, but in itself it is personal rather than structural sin.

The structural problems to which we can point as the primary causes of the problems of the episcopate are the following: a fundamental imbalance in power relations between the Vatican and the national bishops' conferences; a poor theology of the episcopate; and a deeply flawed process for the selection of bishops. The seeds of a healthier understanding of all three are to be found in the documents of Vatican II, but sadly and confusingly interwoven with that far more traditional approach that has stymied genuine theological development of the council's teaching. In *Lumen Gentium*, for example, you find both a vision of the church in which the Vatican is the head office of a major corporation and the bishops are managers of local branch offices, together with a profound insistence on the local church as the whole church that verges on a federalist understanding of the Roman communion. In the years since the council, unfortunately, power has intervened to assert the essential character of what is in truth only a relatively recent historical accident of autocratic centralization, to see to it that bishops act and even think as agents of the Vatican, and to make sure that only those willing to do so will even be considered for episcopal appointment. No wonder that collectively the American bishops have shown weak leadership. They were selected to be weak leaders, to be middle managers in a centralized transnational organization.

Beyond the crisis in the episcopate there is a deeper ecclesiological crisis that is at the same time a cultural crisis. A number of the church historians to whom all of us who try to do ecclesiology today are deeply indebted have pointed out not only that the structures of government in the church have changed over time, and have indeed always been changing, but more importantly that these changes have accompanied changes in secular understandings of government. They have usually needed to stress this in the teeth of those who see the first and last word on ecclesiology to be that "the church is not a democracy." Thus Bishop Donald Wuerl's opening address, in the spring of 2003 at the Yale Conference on Governance and Accountability in the Church, was startlingly and tellingly at variance with the approach of the many distinguished scholars whose presentations followed his. Ah, if only he had stayed to hear Francine Cardman challenge the proponents of what she called "default ecclesiology" to recognize that the church is not monolithic but "a dynamic, evolving, diverse movement," or Brian Tierney explain that "within the Catholic church there have always been these three, Peter, the apostles, and the people of God, but the constitutional relationships between them have been defined differently in different ages," or Marcia Colish point out that while secular governments have continued to change throughout history, becoming constitutional monarchies and then representative democracies with no kings or queens, "the church remained trapped in the absolute monarchy time warp of the early modern period," or Frank Oakley offering up the conciliarist movement as a phenomenon that has much still to teach us, though it has been consigned to the garbage heap of church history by what Oakley calls "an ultramontane politics of oblivion," or John Beal's eloquent call for a canon law that restores the balance between *communio* and juridic ecclesiologies.[3] Now is surely the time to the answer the question with which Oakley ended his presenta-

(Margin notes: "(3) power"; "(4) cultural change ↓ towards democ but not in RCC")

tion: "With what confidence, after all, can we Catholics hope to erect a future capable of enduring if, for ideological reasons, we persist in trying to do so on the foundation of a past that never truly was?"[4]

The weight of the historical evidence would strongly suggest that it is quite appropriate to ask how democratic sensibilities might have something important to offer to the church today, and that it is entirely probable that the church will evolve, willy-nilly, to incorporate some genuine role for the voice of the whole community into its structures of governance. It has been so in the church's past, most recently in the American church of the eighteenth and early nineteenth century, and it could be so again. The lessons of history also teach us, however, that it is exceedingly rare that an elite in any society will freely give up its own hold on power. And this brings us to what may be a yet deeper level of the crisis, namely, an ecclesiology and a polity that gives no formal role to the voice of laypeople in the church to which they belong, buttressed by the sorry history of theological reflection upon the laity. Here is where the discussion of clericalism belongs.[5] Clericalism can be damaging and can be petty. It can be ridiculous and it can be scandalous. It can be as sinister as it is in John Gregory Dunne's *True Confessions* and as comic as it is in J. F. Powers's incomparable stories of the lives of clergy. But in the end it is always epiphenomenal to the real issue that for at least three-quarters of the church's life the best theological definition the church could offer of the layperson was "not clergy."

Because we have no serious theological vision of what it is to be a layperson, there is no chance that structures could develop through which the laity could have an appropriate active if not passive voice in church affairs. Any such suggestion arouses the specter of the Great Terror in the minds of some ecclesiastics and some conservative laity attached to the cozy caste system prevalent currently. Restive laity are seen as a species of *sans-culottes*, baying for blood and seeking to bring the ecclesiastical aristocrats to their knees, if not to the guillotine. Others not so fearful offer proposals like Brian Tierney's suggestion of a mixed constitution with monarchical, oligarchic, and democratic elements, or turn as Bruce Russett does to John Rawls's picture of a "decent consultation hierarchy." Any responsible hierarchy committed to a notion of the common good, suggests Russett, needs a process of consultation allowing for dissent and requiring official response to disputed points, in the context of an open-ended inquiry committed to the principle, as Ignatius of Loyola might have said, that "the truth shall appear, and not that we shall seem to get the upper hand." But such more liberal proposals are premature. The first step has to be to develop a theology of the laity. Theological reflection upon what it is to be a layperson implies a whole ecclesiology, and this in its turn will point the way toward developing appropriate structures. Right now, polity is the tail that wags the ecclesiological dog, and it has to change.

PHASE THREE: UNDERSTANDING THE CRISIS

In this last section, we need to examine three potentially helpful directions in which to turn in search of an ultimate explanation for the crisis. To do this, we need to ask a slightly different question: How new is the crisis? It is of course clear that we have begun to address the crisis in the church in consequence of the scandal of sexual abuse, which revealed some episcopal malfeasance, significant episcopal incompetence, and overwhelming poor leadership. This is a new scandal, but how long sex abuse has been a problem in the church is anyone's guess. However, the presenting problem of sexual abuse points to deeper systemic issues that are also much more longstanding. Do they in fact go back to the beginnings of the church itself? Are they merely a couple of hundred years old? Are they peculiar to the church or are they stresses that afflict all human communities?

The first resource at our disposal is the work of Yves Congar, especially his great book on the laity, *Lay People in the Church*.[6] Congar's wisdom would be reason enough to read him. Additionally, however, he is a theologian who appeals to both the conservative and liberal temperament. One of the most extensive recent treatments of his work is by a priest of Opus Dei.[7] More importantly, perhaps, in Congar's work more than that of Schillebeeckx or Rahner, one can see the development of his thought, as he goes from a very moderate position in his writings of the '40s and '50s—though not moderate enough to save him from Roman suspicion and exile to Cambridge, England—on to rehabilitation, the great work he did at Vatican II, and work in his later years that adds considerable audacity and creativity to what was always solid historical scholarship. From defining the laity in relation to the clergy and so stressing their "secularity" in *Lay People in the Church*, thus unintentionally perpetuating the problem he set out to solve, he comes to the point twenty years later where he can announce that "from now on, the priest must be defined in relation to the laity." Symbolically, too, he is significant. There can be few, if any, other church figures who were silenced by Pius XII and given a red hat by John Paul II.

Congar's great book draws attention to the distinction between two constitutive principles that together make up a living church, the principle of structure and the principle of life. At times he also calls these the hierarchical and the communitarian principles. In *Lay People in the Church* he discusses the role of lay involvement in authority in the church under the rubric of "kingship as power." Here he is adamant that throughout the history of the church the laity have never legitimately exercised any ecclesiastical rule. It is the bishops' job to give the church "her structure as church." But at the same time Congar stresses that an excessive focus on this truth has occluded the real role of the laity, which resides "in the principle . . . of consent, as a principle not of structure but of life, as a concrete law of all the great acts of

② role of laity

ecclesiastical life, beginning with that of designation to the highest offices."[8] A healthy ecclesial life, thinks Congar, will be one that balances the hierarchical constitution of the church with the cooperation of the faithful, through which life is breathed into the otherwise true but sterile structure. Unfortunately, the church has tended to overstress the communion of the parts *with* the hierarchy as the principle of structure, instead of the communion *between* the parts, namely, between the hierarchical ministry and the community of the faithful within which all, clergy and laity together, exist. Catholic unity resides above all in the will of the parts to behave as members of one body, regulated by the power of the Holy Spirit. Because this pneumatological emphasis has been played down in the post-Reformation church, omitted entirely from Robert Bellarmine's influential definition of the church, the faithful are unaware of their responsibility to make the church. The passivity of the laity, in other words, often passed off as the historical accident of an unlettered people, is a result of conscious choices on the part of the leadership. The principle of structure, it would seem, does not easily warm to the Spirit that blows where it will.

Congar's later views, where he turns more to the language of "different ministries," only serve to strengthen his case that the church is healthy when it balances the roles of clergy and laity, and not when power interferes to damage this equilibrium. Like many others, Congar brings his vast historical erudition to bear and singles out the juridicization of the church in the Middle Ages as the primary culprit, since it enshrined into law an already disturbed equilibrium. It is one thing, however, to explain the structures that need to be balanced, quite another to show the convergence of forces that have led in recent centuries to an even more autocratic situation and a corresponding reaction.

③ Habermas – 1. lifeworld + system

A second helpful direction in which to search for answers can be found in the insights of systems theory, in particular the communicative action theory of Jürgen Habermas.[9] Habermas has drawn attention to the ways in which in modernity the two basic components of all societies become uncoupled from one another in potentially damaging ways. An integrated and successful community, he seems to say, would be marked by cooperation and a common purpose between what he calls the "lifeworld," or the human community in all its specifically human interactions, and the "system" of means/ends rationality by which the community manages the whole panoply of its non-human interactions (science, technology, the everyday manipulation of the environment). When, as in modernity, the system shakes off its human parent and, driven by imperatives of money, markets, and power, comes to have autonomous existence, even impinging on the specifically human, driving human interaction into purely private realms, and asserting the importance of action oriented to success over action oriented to understanding, pathologies arise. The system, in Habermas's challenging phraseology, has come to colonize the lifeworld. That which was an expression of the community has now made the community an expression of itself. The two spheres belong in an equilibrium in which the system is seen to serve the lifeworld. John Paul II came very close to this vision when in his 1982 encyclical *Laborem Exercens* (On Human Work) he referred critically to "the instrumentalization of labor to capital," insisting that a healthy society should show the reverse, the instrumentalization of capital to labor, of "stuff" to people. It is of course, in a parade of irony that we see so often in the life of the church, one thing to promote a democratic social order and quite another to extend it to the workings of the church.

Habermas's analysis of late capitalist society is relatively easily transferred to the church. The church is a community of faithful people, equal in virtue of their baptism, ordered toward truth that emerges in noncoercive interactions. But, like any human community that will perdure in time, it has a public, institutional face. The institutional superstructure or system exists to aid the functioning of the community as what it is, in this case, a faith-community that believes in Jesus Christ. Of itself, the institution/system employs forms of rationality that could be described as instrumental or means/ends, but only legitimately if they are employed in the service of the lifeworld/community. Unfortunately, the institution has become uncoupled from the community and has come to colonize it, to extend the realm of actions oriented toward success, or means/ends rationality, into the essentially communicative, understanding-oriented rationality of the community itself. So the open communication that should mark human interactions is replaced by more manipulative practices. One particularly clear sign of such an event in Habermas's view is the replacement of the authority of prestige by that of the authority of influence. The former is leadership based upon fundamental commitment to the communicative character of the lifeworld. The latter is rule by those whose principal tool is power. Prestige is related to "personal attributes," while influence stems from "disposition over resources." Thus, we can explain the often-noted ambiguity of our collective response to John Paul II. He had enormous personal attributes that inspired great respect and caused him in many ways to be an extraordinary leader. At the same time, he often seemed to lead in an authoritarian fashion, or in virtue of his "disposition over resources." The more critical judgments made of his pontificate as a whole are rarely if ever challenging his legitimate prestige, but rather pointing to the exercise of influence. His own pontificate, they are saying, had too often placed the prestige at the service of the influence, in order to shore up the preeminence of the system over the lifeworld.

A third and final resource, drawn this time from church history, supports the application of Habermas's theories to ecclesiology. In an article titled "Modernity and the Construction of Roman Catholicism,"[10] Joseph Komonchak argues that the form of the church that prevailed in the century and a half before Vatican II was developed in conscious reaction to the Enlightenment and out of fear of modernity. Nothing new there. But he goes on to suggest that the church very consciously drew on elements of modernity itself in order to create this "counter-modern" church. The authority that it exercised, he says, "represents a classic illustration of that self-conscious, rationalized, and bureaucratized mode of thought in which Max Weber saw the distinctive mark of modernity." "This anti-modern Roman Catholicism," he adds, "was very modern indeed."[11] In other words, in order to protect a premodern view of the church against the normal processes of historical development to which the ecclesial lifeworld, like others, is subject, the institution adopted the mechanisms of modernity. History was to be managed in the service of an elite whose very continued existence depended upon persuading the community to accept an ahistorical essentialism. The ghost of Karl Marx himself cannot be far from this test case in the construction of a hegemony.

When we place the insights of Komonchak in the context of Habermas's thought about late capitalist society, even without the overtones of Marxist analysis, we come up with a pretty persuasive explanation of the growth of a centralized bureaucratic Catholicism. It additionally strengthens the story, told so well by Jay Dolan in his most recent book,[12] of how the remarkably liberal American Catholicism of the late eighteenth century was transformed into the ultramontane empire of the nineteenth. As Dolan charts the story, when the papacy begins to revive in the first quarter of the nineteenth century it increasingly insists on dismantling the American system in favor of a Roman model. But why it does this, and especially why it can enlist the help of so many American churchmen in the execution of its policies, is not satisfactorily explained solely in terms of European lack of sympathy for American culture. When we add the insights of Komonchak and Habermas to the mix, we get a much more persuasive picture that puts the American experience in the context of a worldwide effort at centralization.

Komonchak's theory extends to an interpretation of Vatican II that also has considerable explanatory potential in our present crisis. As he sees it, the council's challenge was to the modern centralized and bureaucratized Catholicism that had emerged in the course of the nineteenth century and had become entrenched during the reigns of the three Piuses. It consisted in suspicion of intellectual modernity, controls over the community through the promotion of forms of devotion and worship that had their origins in baroque European piety, and centralized control of the universal church. But the council produced a much more positive evaluation of modernity; it sought to reform Catholic worship, devotion, and practice; and it encouraged "culturally distinct and relevant realizations of Catholicism" in different parts of the world. Though Komonchak does not say it in this article, John Paul II's reign was marked by efforts to undo precisely these three developments. His writings grew more and more suspicious of contemporary culture and in particular of the so-called hedonism and ethical relativism of American society. He advocated traditional forms of piety, especially Marian piety and Eucharistic adoration, in ways that we have not seen since Pius X, and he showed considerable suspicion of liturgical variations that reflect local cultures. And, above all, he sought to recentralize the church by, among other things, promoting the quasi-infallibility of the ordinary magisterium and undermining the authority of national bishops' conferences.

In conclusion, we need to return to John Beal's call for balance and Cardinal Bernardin's hope for common ground. The problem is not that the institution is bad and the faith-community is good. The faith-community will always have an institutional face. The problem is that too much power has shifted to the institution and the church is in consequence off-center. That this has happened because of the church's suspicion of modernity seems very likely. The result of the imbalance is certainly bad. The historical chickens have come home to roost, and in the end it is not surprising that the center of the crisis is the American church. On the one hand, it remains the most vibrant of churches in the so-called developed world. On the other, its increasingly vocal and well-educated laity, roused to action by the scandal of sexual abuse, represent a movement for potential reform that cannot be controlled in the ways the clergy can, and that is feeding off two centuries of the American experiment in democracy. An open society is always better than a closed society. This is the unshakable conviction of thinking people in a society that strives to be democratic. The crisis in the church will not go away until we find ways to make the church into the open society that, at the present time, it is certainly not.

In sum, the history of the church has shown a tension between the institutional and the charismatic, juridical and *communio* ecclesiologies, the principle of structure and the principle of life, Christology and pneumatology. This is unproblematic until serious imbalances arise, and when they do we have an ecclesiological crisis on our hands. The latest crisis has been brewing for two hundred years, as the church bureaucratized and centralized itself in a defensive reaction to modernity. Oblivious to the role of the Spirit and the principle of life, in the name of defending faith the institution has only defended itself. It has created a professional class, self-perpetuating and self-policing, insulated from the people by lifestyle and the possession of all executive and legislative authority. The evils of sexual abuse are a direct but epiphenomenal consequence of this bureaucratic blindness. But cultural forces cannot be indefinitely withstood, particularly not if they are of the Spirit. The increasingly loud voice of faithful, well-educated lay Catholics demanding a role in the church that, even when they are unaware of it, has a long historical pedigree and considerable theological justification would seem to be just such a Spirit-inspired initiative.

NOTES

1. Quoted in Jay Dolan, *In Search of American Catholicism: A History of Religion and Culture in Tension* (New York: Oxford University Press, 2002), 33–34.

2. Along the lines of his recent conservative treatment of the crisis, *The Courage to Be Catholic* (New York: Basic Books, 2002).

3. The papers delivered at this very important conference have recently been published as *Governance, Accountability, and the Future of the Catholic Church*, ed. Francis Oakley and Bruce Russett (New York and London: Continuum, 2004).

4. Oakley and Russett, *Governance, Accountability, and the Future*, 87.

5. Handled best by Donald Cozzens, *Sacred Silence: Denial and the Crisis in the Church* (Collegeville, Minn.: Liturgical Press, 2002).

6. Yves Congar, *Lay People in the Church*, rev. ed. (Westminster, Md.: Newman Press, 1957).

7. Ramiro Pellitero, *La teología del laicado en la obra de Yves Congar* (Pamplona: Servicio de Publicaciones de la Universidad de Navarra, 1996).

8. Congar, *Lay People*, 247.

9. I wrote a whole book on Habermas's value for ecclesiology that was published in 1990 and sank without a trace just a year later, but as I return to it now, I still think that Habermas has much to offer us. His theories are complex and his language is sometimes close to impenetrable, so I don't suppose I will need forgiveness for an effort to paraphrase some of what he has to say that seems significant. For anyone who would like to see the argument in its full complexity, see *Theology and Critical Theory: The Discourse of the Church* (Nashville, Tenn.: Abingdon, 1990).

10. Joseph Komonchak, "Modernity and the Construction of Roman Catholicism," *Cristianismo nella storia* 18 (1997): 353–85.

11. Komonchak, "Modernity," 383.

12. See note 1.

2: THE SEXUAL ABUSE SCANDAL AS SOCIAL DRAMA

Jean M. Bartunek

In this paper I describe social dynamics that typically accompany serious large-scale crises such as revelation of the decades-long cover-up of the child sexual abuse scandal in the Catholic Church in Boston and elsewhere. These dynamics center on the fact that revelations of the cover-up of sex abuse by priests created a serious disruption in the perception of church officials' behavior as exemplifying high moral standards. This disruption has evoked considerable discomfort and outrage, in part because it has exposed a large gulf between church officials' actions and the ways they had portrayed themselves and had been perceived.

Social science research has repeatedly demonstrated that when a significant discrepancy between perception and behavior is revealed people try to understand what happened and to restore or create some new type of congruence.[1] In this paper I will describe how some of these congruence-seeking processes have occurred and suggest a step, based on them, toward addressing the crisis. I will do so by listing and then fleshing out seven statements that indicate some of the social dynamics present in how the sex abuse scandal has unfolded.

First, events out of the ordinary trigger sensemaking, action that encompasses sensing, constructing, and then attributing meaning to various aspects of the world.[2] Second, the sense that people and groups make of particular phenomena is affected by the cultural context in which they understand the phenomena. Third, when people and groups make sense of particular phenomena, they do so in ways that are related to and motivated by their particular concerns, interests, and aspirations. Fourth, sensemaking is intimately linked with affective responses to a situation. Fifth, the sense people and groups make of any situation, along with their affective responses to it, impacts how they act there. Sixth, all of these statements are particularly true in situations that Victor Turner labeled a "social drama."[3] Seventh, the long-term outcome of a social drama depends to a considerable degree on how the tensions and contradictions inevitably unearthed by it are handled.

EVENTS OUT OF THE ORDINARY TRIGGER SENSEMAKING

It is not unusual during routine times for people to operate on something like "automatic pilot," not paying close attention to what they are doing. We know how to use a copy machine, how to place phone calls, how to order from a restaurant menu, and so forth, and so we often do not attend very much to these activities when we carry them out. But something that we do not expect, that is very much out of the ordinary, evokes conscious, active efforts to make sense, to understand what is going on and, often, to convey this understanding to others.[4] When there are revelations that sex abuse in the Catholic Church was systematically covered up for several decades, especially when these revelations as presented in as dramatic a way as was the case in the *Boston Globe* and other media, the scandal evokes for just about everyone directly or indirectly touched by it the need to make sense of how this could have happened.

Sometimes a single individual tries to understand why events have happened as they have. In many social settings, however, the sensemaking is collective.[5] Groups of people work to develop a shared understanding of the phenomenon, and/or members of a social setting may interpret an event for others. In the case of the sex abuse scandal, for example, the lay Catholic group Voice of the Faithful (VOTF) began as a small group of members of one parish trying to understand together how the sexual abuse of children by priests could have occurred for so long and been so covered up.[6] The investigative staff of the *Boston Globe* interpreted the sex abuse scandal for the *Globe*'s readers, as did other media.[7]

CULTURAL CONTEXTS AFFECT SENSEMAKING

Second, the sense that people and groups make of a particular phenomenon is affected by their cultural context, the shared, sometimes implicit, norms of their social setting. For example, faculty in a theology department sometimes understand particular phenomena in a different way than faculty in a business school do, in part because of the different disciplinary emphases that help create their cultural contexts.

Two types of cultural contexts are particularly salient to discussion of the sex abuse scandal. First, Pratt has described how organizations, particularly religious organizations, sometimes use spiritual values and beliefs to create an "ideological fortress, a worldview that is seemingly impervious to attack by those who might oppose it."[8] This term refers to strong and shared ways of understanding that bind people to their organization and foster ways of perceiving particular events, even events apparently detrimental to the organization, in ways that reinforce the organization's belief system. Thus, for example, when the Vatican and Cardinal Law interpreted the considerable media attention to the sex abuse scandal in the *Boston Globe* as an example of anti-Catholic bias, they were reinforcing a worldview that made the Catholic Church somewhat impervious to external challenge.[9] They were treating some journalistic coverage of the sex abuse scandal as an illustration of the bigotry and bias against which the Catholic Church in the United States had often had to defend itself.[10]

In addition, Morrison and Milliken have described the concept of "organizational silence."[11] By this they mean that some organizations strongly emphasize that lower-level members should "withhold their opinions and concerns about organizational problems."[12] The only organizational members allowed to surface problems are higher-level officials. Morrison and Milliken suggest that organizational silence is particularly prevalent in organizations that are very hierarchically structured.[13] When a cultural context of organizational silence is present, there is likely to be an exaggerated perception on the part of lower-level members of the riskiness and futility of speaking up when they encounter problems. Thus, top leaders may not recognize that they lack important information, while lower-level members believe that their feelings are not valued and that they have very little control.

From written reports of the sex abuse scandal it seems quite likely that organizational silence has characterized the church and affected the sensemaking of its members. The investigative staff of the *Boston Globe* reported that priests who were aware of particular instances of child sexual abuse sometimes did nothing about it.[14] Muller and Kenney described how church officials in Boston rebuffed VOTF and told its members that the hierarchy had sole authority to make decisions.[15] In an e-mail to the leaders of VOTF a priest wrote that "I am going to raise the question as to why we as a priest group are remaining so silent. If one or two speak out, they are immediately confronted by (a bishop)." The investigative staff of the *Boston Globe* referred to the "extraordinary cloak of secrecy under which the Archdiocese of Boston had settled child abuse claims."[16]

Such a combination of organizational patterns—an ideological fortress reinforced by characteristics of organizational silence—makes it very difficult for leaders of an organization, in the case of the Catholic Church its bishops, to perceive accurately that there are serious problems to be confronted. Problems are less likely to be noted or registered at all by priests and others who are not high in the hierarchy. Those problems that are reported are

analyzing the ch. as any other social institution, using tools from secular sciences likely to be recast to some extent to fit the organization's—the church's—already established worldview.

THE MOTIVATIONAL BASIS OF SENSEMAKING

Third, when people make sense of particular phenomena, they do so in ways that are motivated by their individual and group-based concerns, interests, and aspirations. There are a wide range of possible concerns, interests, and aspirations that may motivate sensemaking. For example, Weick and Suls, among others, suggest that one frequent motive for sensemaking is the need to construct or maintain a positive self-concept, one that affirms the self, especially in the face of threats.[17] Some other motives for sensemaking include the need to accomplish particular goals with respect to some event, the need to maintain authority over appropriate interpretations of an event, and the need to be accurate in understanding what happened in a given situation.[18] There are multiple other possible motives as well.

For example, organizational leaders concerned about maintaining an "ideological fortress" may be motivated to perceive a potentially damaging event in a way that supports their worldview and enables them to serve as the primary interpreter of the event for others. The motives of people who have been severely harmed by the event, or people who stand to gain from it, are likely to be very different.

The fact that different individuals and groups have different motives for making sense of a particular situation, especially one associated with a crisis, means that these different individuals and groups are likely to attend to and notice diverse aspects of it and/or interpret the same aspects differently.[19] Members of the church hierarchy, for example, may perceive some decisions about transferring the priests who were abusing children to different parishes as based on the advice they were given by physicians and may only later perceive their actions as an error in judgment. Others may first attend to the actions of the abusing priests and the impacts of these actions, and perceive the bishops' decisions as sinful or, perhaps, criminal. In a situation like the sex abuse scandal in the Catholic Church, not only will many people, groups, and organizations need to make sense of what is happening, but the motivations underlying their need, and thus the features of the situation to which they attend, are likely to differ.

Table 2.1 (columns 1 and 2) lists some needs and aspirations regarding the sex abuse scandal and its cover-up that may motivate sensemaking on the part of the groups of people affected by the scandal. The table also lists (column 3) some ways these groups may understand the scandal based on what motivates their understanding. This table just begins to suggest the varied motivations for making sense of the scandal; there are many others as well.

Table 2.1. Sensemaking—Needs and Motives, Groups Motivated, Types of Sense Made, Accompanying Affect, and Actions Taken

1. Some needs that may motivate sensemaking	2. Some individuals/groups that may be motivated by these needs	3. Some sense that may be made or rationalized through these needs	4. Some possible accompanying affects	5. Some possible accompanying actions
Need to recover emotionally	Victims of abuse and their families	"The sexual abuse and cover-up were grievously wrong."	Traumatized, depressed, emotionally and physically scarred	Protection of their children, protesting against the church, serious emotional illness
Protect or restore self-esteem	Clergy	"Just because I'm a clergyman doesn't mean I'm bad."	Anger, fear	Denunciations of the media, audit of compliance with guidelines for treatment of children and young people
Concern to protect children	Parents, legislature, clergy	"How could anyone act like this toward children or allow it to happen?"	Disgust, anger, outrage	Reduced donations to the church, reduced attendance at mass.
Desire to understand what is happening	Groups of lay Catholics, the general public	"How in the world could this have happened in a church I respect?"	Concern, upset, anguish	Formation of VOTF, Church in the 21st Century initiative at BC
Anxiety about being discovered	Unnamed perpetrators	"How do I keep this low key and a secret?"	Fear	Make secret arrangements to avoid discovery
Opportunity for gain	Attorneys, some who may need land	"I can gain from this."	Anticipation	Attempt to solicit cases, attempt not to alienate the hierarchy
Desire to retain power/image	Church hierarchy	"How do we keep our position and power?"	Denial, defensiveness, threatened	Refusal to collaborate with the laity (e.g., VOTF)
Desire to preserve the church	Church hierarchy	"These revelations are terrible. We need to preserve the church."	Anguish	Try to create reform from within the hierarchy

Moreover, some people's and groups' sensemaking may be based on multiple motives, and these motives may evolve over time.

SENSEMAKING AND AFFECT

Fourth, sensemaking is intimately linked with affect. People do not simply make cognitive sense of events. Rather, the discrepancies and surprise that lead to sensemaking also stimulate emotional reactions. In fact, it is these emotional reactions that may trigger the sensemaking.[20]

In a situation such as the sex abuse scandal, the various types of sense made by different actors typically include and are stimulated by strong emotions, including anger, fear, anxiety, love, hatred, outrage, concern, excitement, and revulsion. At the first discussion by members of the group that became VOTF, for example, those present expressed confusion, distress, anger, and outrage.[21] The investigative staff of the *Boston Globe* reported that many of the abuse victims and their families felt abused again, traumatized, depressed, and emotionally scarred by the response of the archdiocese to their claims.[22] Many priests who were not abusers and many other people were scandalized by what had occurred.

Feelings give energy to the attempts to make sense of the situation, and they are, in turn, affected by the sense made. Thus, to understand sensemaking adequately it is necessary also to understand the emotional reactions of those who are doing the sensemaking. The fourth column in table 2.1 includes some of the emotional reactions that may be accompanying the sense being made by some of those involved in the sex abuse scandal.

SENSEMAKING, AFFECT, AND ACTION

Fifth, the sense people make of an event and the feelings that stimulate their sensemaking affect the actions they take in response. The sense they make and their feelings also affect the actions they believe that others should take.

As I noted above, it is uncomfortable for people to experience significant discrepancies between perceptions and actions, their own or others'.[23] For example, when people experience strong discrepancies between others' self-portrayal and their actions, they may feel betrayed and lose trust in and respect for these persons.[24] The actions people take are often motivated by discrepancies like this and are often aimed at reducing the discrepancy experienced. When someone feels betrayed, for example, they are likely to take actions against those who have betrayed them.

Thus, sensemaking and its associated affect often lead to actions aimed at making the various aspects of a situation "fit" better. People may change their earlier perceptions to correspond with their recent experience (e.g., "I had high regard for bishops before, but now I know they are frauds"), and/or they may take more active initiative such as protesting. For example, VOTF members' perceptions that some clergy and bishops had betrayed their trust led to several efforts to protest official church actions and to show support for victims of clergy sexual abuse.[25] When church officials sensed that the church was under attack, the actions they took were aimed at warding off the threats. Muller and Kenney described some of the actions of the bishop with whom VOTF representatives met, sometimes apparently misleading them about the release of particular documents, sometimes insisting that the hierarchy should make the decisions.[26] These actions seemed aimed more at protecting the church hierarchy from threat than responding to the victims of abuse or collaborating with laypeople trying to attain some voice in the church. The fifth column of table 2.1 suggests some of the actions that might be taken, based on the sense people and groups make and their accompanying feelings.

SOCIAL DRAMA

Sixth, the impact of all of these statements is amplified when what is being made sense of is a social drama, as Victor Turner defined and developed this term.[27] On the basis of extensive anthropological research, Turner defined a social drama as an event that revolves around a breach of group or societal norms or rules in some important public manner. It is a volatile episode that interrupts the otherwise smooth surface of routine life in a social setting and reveals underlying tensions there, and it represents a potential turning point in which a particular social order may become transformed.[28]

Social dramas occur in a wide variety of arenas, both large and small. These arenas include some identified by Turner, such as Watergate, the Dreyfus affair, and Thomas Beckett's confrontation of Henry II.[29] Beeman identified the crisis associated with tabulating the final results of the 2000 presidential election in the United States as a social drama, and McFarland has shown how acts of resistance by high school students against their teachers may illustrate this phenomenon.[30]

As Turner defined them, social dramas encompass four stages. The first stage is a public *breach* of important social norms, perhaps through a societal conflict, perhaps by lawbreaking or some other means. The second stage is a *crisis* caused by the breach in which societal conflicts and tensions become visible and public, sides are taken, and the breach is widened to include multiple members of a social group. The third stage involves some type of *redressive action* aimed at limiting the spread and impact of the breach and conflict. The redressive action may include legal processes, arbitration, or rituals that include some kind of recompense for the original breach, such as resignation or punishment of a key figure. The final stage is *reintegration* or *schism*. This stage involves the integration of the disturbed social group back into society or recognition of an unbridgeable divide between the party and society.

Although clerical sexual abuse of children had occurred in the church for some time, the extent of its cover-up was not widely known until publication of the *Boston Globe* articles began in early 2002. When it was revealed, the extent to which the cover-up was not only a disruption of expectations but also a serious *breach* of societal norms became very evident.

The revelation of the extent of sexual abuse and its cover-up soon became a *crisis* for the church, in Boston and elsewhere. Several aspects of the crisis were reported by the investigative staff of the *Boston Globe*.[31] In the Boston archdiocese alone there were ongoing revelations of child molestation, public protests were mounted against the church and especially Cardinal Law and other bishops, the cardinal was forced to backtrack on statements he had made, the Vatican summoned him to Rome and felt a need to take a stance on sexual abuse, the Massachusetts legal system ceased protecting the church and the cardinal in ways it had before, VOTF was formed and soon found itself in conflict with church officials, and many other actions were taken.

This crisis prompted both tensions and contradictions to become visible and public. Just a few of the tensions evoked by the crisis include the comparative responsibility of priests and bishops, the applicability of canon and civil law, the sexual orientation of aspiring clergy, the roles and authority of laypeople in the church in relation to the hierarchy, and the (largely missing) roles of women in the events related to the scandal, even though some nuns had raised questions about clerical sex abuse for decades. Some contradictions have also become evident.[32] One is that priests, bishops, and others who in many ways appear to be good and caring people with high moral standards may at the same time be abusive or totally insensitive to the victims of abuse. Another is that the Catholic Church, which sets for itself a higher moral standard than many business organizations, did not immediately respond to the scandal in ways that seemed to differ significantly from business organizations' responses to their own corporate scandals being unveiled at about the same time. Finally, many of the attorneys seeking public redress for their clients had previously colluded with church officials in keeping the sex abuse quiet. Many other contradictions have surfaced as well.

As I noted above, almost any disruption or jarring event leads to sensemaking and its associated motives, feelings, and actions. However, the disruptions, tensions, and conflict that are surfaced by a social drama are much more severe and evoke more extreme responses than is the case with most disruptions or surprises.

Very strong, or highly "activated," feelings carry considerable energy and mobilize people to act.[33] Tensions and contradictions, especially during a time of crisis, are often accompanied by very strong feelings and a narrowed range of sensemaking.[34] Thus, they often lead to polarization, to taking sides, to a perception that one side in a dispute is correct and that the other is wrong. In a social drama such as the sex abuse scandal, strong feelings are likely to lead to people identifying themselves strongly with or against the church, with or against the news media, with or against attorneys, and so forth. The expressions of these tensions may be found in assertions such as the following: bishops and priests are moral *or not*; the church is just like a business *or not*; the hierarchy should be totally in charge *or not*; attorneys are out *either* for their own benefit *or* for their clients'; and so forth. While these expressions are one-sided, they signal the existence of tensions that have multiple sides.

The church and others are taking multiple steps to redress the sex abuse and its cover-up. Within the Boston archdiocese these steps have included, among others, the resignation of Cardinal Law and the appointment of Archbishop Seán O'Malley, removing priests who have been credibly accused of sexual abuse, and the settlement of several claims. Additional steps such as an audit of sex abuse policies have been taken by the U.S. Bishops' Conference.[35] New state laws are being enacted that will make cover-up of sexual abuse more difficult. These will, along with other actions, respond to some extent to the breach of societal norms that has occurred.

Nevertheless, few would claim that as of this writing the sex abuse scandal has been settled. There are some continuing revelations of sexual abuse, including against a bishop of the Springfield, Massachusetts, diocese. There have been additional claims of sexual abuse in the Boston archdiocese, and the archdiocese has been forced to sell some of its land to pay some of the claims. New conflicts between the laity and the hierarchy of the church are surfacing as the church is attempting to close several parishes in the Boston archdiocese. Many of the tensions and contradictions that have surfaced have not been resolved.

THE OUTCOME OF THE SOCIAL DRAMA WILL DEPEND ON HOW ITS TENSIONS AND CONTRADICTIONS ARE HANDLED

The seventh and final statement is that the outcomes of the social drama will depend to a considerable extent on how the tensions and contradictions unearthed by the scandal, such as those indicated in section 6, are addressed. I have indicated some actions being taken to resolve the crisis, such as new laws. Such actions are necessary but not sufficient for the crisis truly to be resolved. Rather, the tensions and contradictions that have been surfaced and their expression in the various participants' affect, perceptions, and actions also need to be understood and addressed for more full resolution. Dealing adequately with these tensions requires appreciation of how they are experienced by all those involved in the social drama.

Turner suggested that there are two primary ways a social drama may be concluded, through reintegration of the offending party or schism.[36] McFarland has recently shown that there are additional ways a social drama may be resolved, including ways that lead to a larger transformation than simply reintegration of an offending party.[37]

Given the redressive actions that are being taken, such as the new statutes and policies, the church is clearly being "reintegrated" into prevailing social norms. A more fundamental resolution would include a transformation in understanding, a reframing, of the sexual abuse scandal and its multiple tensions in a way that is sensitive to and incorporates the perspectives of all of the constituencies involved in the scandal.[38]

Experiencing tensions in either-or fashion, and perceiving them only from one's own viewpoint—the type of approach that typically emerges in conjunction with the high feeling states associated with a social drama—provides people with cognitive and affective clarity and congruence in the short run. It is comparatively easy to be on one side of the crisis and to interpret events from the perspective of that one side. But taking only one side interferes with achieving the energy and creativity essential for truly moving participants in a social drama beyond their original positions and creating the possibility for a new type of relationship that takes each others' perspectives into account.

Attempts to take the perspective of many parties is more likely to enable recognition and acknowledgment of the full range of ways the sex abuse scandal is being experienced.[39] For example, there may be recognition that bishops, priests, and others act both morally and immorally. The church lives according to high ethical standards in some ways but not others. The authority of the hierarchy of the church may be both valuable and problematic. Attorneys may be out for their own gains and also care about their clients.

Recognizing the validity of the multiple, conflicting perspectives on this crisis sounds counterintuitive. It is difficult to accomplish, especially at times of high tension.[40] The various components do not "fit" together, and taking each others' conflicting perspectives is very uncomfortable.

But it is also important. As Seo, Putnam, and Bartunek note, acknowledging the validity of two (or more) sides of a tension or contradiction, which includes acknowledgment of the different perspectives, actions, and feelings that embody it, enables construction of a more realistic picture of the complex and dynamic nature of the tension or contradiction (e.g., the church may appear as both moral and immoral to different groups, and these perceptions carry strong, conflicting emotions) and the unfolding events associated with it.[41] It also helps provide energy for movement.

In practice, acknowledging the validity of two or more sides of a tension might imply something like building on table 2.1. It might mean developing as complete a depiction as possible of the multiple motives, perceptions, actions, and feelings of all those involved in some way in the sex abuse scandal, including bishops, clergy, lay groups, attorneys, abuse victims and their families, and so on, one that recognizes the various motives, perceptions, emotions, and actions of the different groups. Developing a complex understanding such as this has the potential over time to enable those involved in the scandal to have a better chance of working together to make significant progress on addressing fundamental causes of the scandal and decreasing the chances that something like it will take place again.

A task like this is extraordinarily difficult for those directly involved in the scandal. But initial identification of the possible motives, perceptions, and emotions of the multiple actors and how these are enacted, such as was begun in table 2.1, may be easier for scholars who are less directly involved in the scandal and have some distance from it. Thus, one of the contributions that a chapter such as this one may make is to add to the recognition of and conversation about the multiple perspectives associated with the sex abuse scandal. To the extent that the chapter opens up awareness of ways of moving beyond one-sided perspectives to an appreciation of the complexity of the combined perspectives, it may contribute to movement in the social drama and may have consequences of importance for the Catholic Church and the larger society within which it exists.[42]

NOTES

1. For example, L. Festinger, *A Theory of Cognitive Dissonance* (Stanford, Calif.: Stanford University Press, 1957); K. E. Weick, *Sensemaking in Organizations* (Thousand Oaks, Calif.: Sage, 1995).

2. Weick, *Sensemaking in Organizations.*

3. V. Turner, "Social Dramas and Stories about Them," *Critical Inquiry* 7 (1980): 141–68; and elsewhere.

4. For example, M. R. Louis and R. I. Sutton, "Switching Cognitive Gears: From Habits of Mind to Active Thinking," *Human Relations* 44 (1991): 55–76; M. G. Pratt, "Building an Ideological Fortress: The Role of Spirituality, Encapsulation and Sensemaking," *Studies in Culture, Organizations, and Society* 6 (2000): 35–69; Weick, *Sensemaking in Organizations.*

5. W. Ocasio, "How Do Organizations Think?" in *Organizational Cognition: Computation and Interpretation*, ed. T. K. Lant and Z. Shapira (Mahwah, N.J.: Lawrence Erlbaum Associates, 2001), 39–60; K. E. Weick and K. H. Roberts, "Collective Mind in

Organizations: Heedful Interrelating in Flight Decks," *Administrative Science Quarterly* 38 (1993): 257–381.

6. James E. Muller and Charles Kenney, *Keep the Faith, Change the Church: The Battle by Catholics for the Soul of Their Church* (Emmaus, Pa.: Rodale Books, 2004).

7. Investigative staff of the *Boston Globe, Betrayal: The Crisis in the Catholic Church* (New York: Little Brown and Co., 2002).

8. Pratt, "Ideological Fortress," 35.

9. K. Kay, "US Media "Hounding" Vatican over Sex," *London Times*, 10 June 2002, 6(A); M. McGrory, "Overdue Penance," *Washington Post*, 17 Feb. 2002, 7(B); Archdiocese of Boston, "Sex Abuse Scandals Give Rise to Distorted Attacks," <www.rcab.org/News/releases/zenit020420.html> (20 April 2002).

10. A. Greeley, "Scandal Brings Out the Bigots," *Chicago Sun Times*, 12 Apr. 2002, 45.

11. E. W. Morrison and F. J. Milliken, "Organizational Silence: A Barrier to Change and Development in a Pluralistic World," *Academy of Management Review* 25 (2000): 706–25.

12. Morrison and Milliken, "Organizational Silence," 707.

13. Morrison and Milliken, "Organizational Silence."

14. Staff of *Globe, Betrayal*, chap. 4.

15. Muller and Kenney, *Keep the Faith*, 110.

16. Staff of *Globe, Betrayal*, 100.

17. Weick, *Sensemaking in Organizations*; J. Suls, "The Importance of the Question in Motivated Cognition and Social Comparison," *Psychological Inquiry* 10 (1999): 73–75.

18. S. Chen, K. Duckworth, and S. Chaiken, "Motivated Heuristic and Systematic Processing," *Psychological Inquiry* 10 (1999): 44–49; D. Dunning, Z. Kunda, and S. L. Murray, "What the Commentators Motivated Us to Think About," *Psychological Inquiry* 10 (1999): 79–82; Suls, "Importance of the Question."

19. B. Vidaillet, "Cognitive Processes and Decision Making in a Crisis Situation: A Case Study," in *Organizational Cognition: Computation and Interpretation*, ed. T. K. Lant and Z. Shapira (Mahwah, N.J.: Lawrence Erlbaum Associates, 2001), 241–63; Weick, *Sensemaking in Organizations*.

20. J. M. George and G. R. Jones, "Towards a Process Model of Individual Change in Organizations," *Human Relations* 54 (2001): 419–44; M. Seo, L. Barrett, and J. Bartunek, "The Role of Affective Experience in Work Motivation," *Academy of Management Review* 29 (2004): 423–39.

21. Muller and Kenney, *Keep the Faith*, chap. 1.

22. Staff of *Globe, Betrayal*.

23. Festinger, *Cognitive Dissonance*.

24. A. D. Brown and M. Jones, "Honourable Members and Dishonourable Deeds: Sensemaking, Impression Management and Legitimation in the 'Arms to Iraq Affair,'" *Human Relations* 53 (2000): 655–89.

25. Muller and Kenney, *Keep the Faith*.

26. Muller and Kenney, *Keep the Faith*.

27. V. Turner, *Dramas, Fields, and Metaphors: Symbolic Action in Human Society* (Ithaca, N.Y.: Cornell University Press, 1974); Turner, "Social Dramas"; V. Turner,

On the Edge of the Bush: Anthropology as Experience, ed. Edith L. B. Turner (Tucson: University of Arizona Press, 1985).

28. D. A. McFarland, "Resistance as a Social Drama: A Study of Change-Oriented Encounters," *American Sociological Review* 109 (2004): 1249–1318.

29. Turner, *Dramas, Fields*.

30. W. O. Beeman, "Social Drama of Election Deadlock Points to a True American Culture," *JINN Magazine*, no. 6.25 (2000) <www.pacificnews.org/jinn/toc/6.25.html>; McFarland, "Change-Oriented Encounters."

31. Staff of *Globe*, *Betrayal*.

32. See M. Seo, L. Putnam, and J. Bartunek, "Dualities and Tensions in Planned Organizational Change," in *Handbook of Organizational Change and Innovation*, ed. M. S. Poole and A. H. Van de Ven (New York: Oxford, 2004), 73–107.

33. Seo, Barrett, and Bartunek, "Affective Experience."

34. C. M. Pearson and J. A. Clair, "Reframing Crisis Management," *Academy of Management Review* 23 (1998): 59–76; Vidaillet, "Cognitive Processes."

35. M. Paulsen, "Audit Finds Safeguards Working in US Dioceses," *Boston Globe*, 7 Jan. 2004, 1(A), 6(B).

36. Turner, *Dramas, Fields*.

37. McFarland, "Change-Oriented Encounters."

38. J. Bartunek, "The Dynamics of Personal and Organizational Reframing," in *Paradox and Transformation: Toward a Theory of Change in Organization and Management*, ed. R. E. Quinn and K. S. Cameron (Cambridge, Mass.: Ballinger, 1988), 137–62.

39. Seo, Putnam, and Bartunek, "Dualities and Tensions."

40. Pearson and Clair, "Reframing Crisis Management."

41. Seo, Putnam, and Bartunek, "Dualities and Tensions."

42. I am very grateful to Meg Guider, Jane Maltby, and Frank Sullivan for their helpful comments.

3: THE SIX AGES OF CATHOLICISM IN AMERICA

James M. O'Toole

The story of American Catholic history seems a familiar one. It tells of pioneer bishops, priests, and nuns who built an impressive array of churches and schools, often in the face of vigorous opposition. But what would the history of the Catholic Church in the United States look like if we tried to see it not through its leaders and institutions, but rather through its people? How have the laity—ordinary Catholics; the men, women, and children in the pews—defined themselves as members of their church? When looked at from this perspective, it becomes clear that their ways of being Catholic have changed markedly over time. No single experience has been *the* American Catholic experience, and the experience that any of us remembers (or thinks we remember) is not the only possible one. Rather, the history of the church in this country falls into six distinct ages, each with its own characteristics.

1. THE PRIESTLESS CHURCH

It is only a slight exaggeration to say that, for its first three centuries, Catholicism in the territory that subsequently became the United States was a church without priests. That sounds anomalous, perhaps even oxymoronic, but for more than half of its entire historical experience, the church had an insufficient number of clergy to meet the most minimal religious demands of its people. From the time of European contact at the end of the fifteenth century until the Revolution at the end of the eighteenth, native and European Catholics in America always outnumbered, by a wide margin, the priests available to provide them with the sacraments and services of religion. In seventeenth-century New Mexico, for instance, thirty-two Franciscans were available to serve about three thousand Spaniards and probably thirty-five thousand Christian Indians scattered across hundreds of trackless miles. In Maryland at the same time, the numbers were not much different. Two Jesuits had accompanied the two hundred original settlers there, but the ratio got steadily worse thereafter. Just before his designation as the first bishop in the United States in 1789, John Carroll reported to Rome that there were about twenty-five thousand Catholics in the new nation (less than 1 percent of the population) but only twenty-four priests, of whom several were "approaching seventy years, and thus they are incapable of sustaining the labor necessary for cultivating the vineyard of the Lord." In such cases, each priest had to travel a wide circuit. Carroll himself had care of "a very large cong[re-gatio]n" in Baltimore, he told an English friend, but he also had "to ride 25 or 30 miles to the sick; besides which I go once a month between 50 & sixty miles to another cong[regatio]n in Virginia."[1]

With infrequent connection to the institutions of their church, ordinary believers had to find other, self-defined and self-directed ways of sustaining their identity as Catholics. Where a priest might say mass in a given locality at best once a month, the laity took responsibility for organizing their own ad hoc worship, with families gathering on Sunday in one another's homes. Publishers produced manuals and prayerbooks, most of them reprints of English models, to be used in such circumstances. One spiritual guidebook suggested that three-quarters of an hour be set aside for a service led by "the head of the family, or any other who reads freely and distinctly; and let all others who are present join in answering." The service might begin with a psalm and then proceed to the prayers assigned for that particular Sunday, followed by "the thanksgiving and examination of conscience. The service may conclude with reading a chapter or two out of the gospels, the abridgment of the old and new Testament, or of some other approved book of instruction or meditation."[2]

For all its lay initiative, we should not idealize this period as a "golden age" of the American Catholic laity. Those who gathered for these impromptu services always thought that they were merely making do, so long as the religious "real thing" (that is, regular Sunday mass) was unavailable; whenever it was, they happily abandoned home worship for communal liturgy. Indeed, one of the principal benefits of private lay gatherings, a priest from Boston told an isolated Catholic family in northern Maine in 1797, was to prepare them for confession, mass, and communion "the next time that you will have a priest with you."[3] These Catholics had no thought of constructing an independent, lay-run church. Priestlessness was a constraint they accepted, not a goal they embraced. Moreover, the very irregularity of home-based worship led to a high rate of what would later be called "leakage" from the church. Many who had been baptized as infants found it impossible or undesirable to sustain a connection to so remote a church, and they joined nearby Protestant congregations, or they slipped off into the great body of the unchurched, particularly on the frontier. Even so, what is striking from our perspective is the responsibility that laypeople in the age of the priestless church took for the maintenance of their religious identity. They would clearly have preferred to have more of an institutional setting for their faith, but in its absence they built their own supports.

2. THE CHURCH IN THE DEMOCRATIC REPUBLIC

However reluctantly they may come to it, revolutionaries usually think that they are beginning the world over again, and those who first made the American Revolution and then formed a government were no exceptions. This heady sense of new beginning applied equally to those who were, at precisely the same historical moment, organizing the Catholic Church in the new nation. John Carroll became the bishop of Baltimore in the very year that George Washington became president, and the coincidence seemed hardly coincidental. Carroll feared that a church that was too monarchical would be unacceptable in a nation that had just spent more than a decade overthrowing a monarch. Thus, he sought to limit the role of the pope—who was, after all, still the king of his own nation, the Papal States—in American church affairs. "I am and ever shall be opposed . . . to the pope's having the nomination" of bishops in the United States, Carroll wrote; this might suggest that American Catholics had divided loyalties. The "interference of any foreign jurisdiction" was "incompatible with the independence of a sovereign state" and would be the cause of "continual anxiety." Better, Carroll thought, to apply the political principles of the emerging American system and to have bishops here elected by the clergy, just as presidents, governors, and legislators were elected. Nothing in this was incompatible with Catholic doctrine, Carroll was sure, for Catholics would always acknowledge the "spiritual supremacy" of the pope as head of the church and "center of ecclesiastical unity." The idea that the pope or his Roman departments would have administrative supervision over the church in this country, however, seemed a dangerous innovation and contrary to the American spirit.[4]

Carroll lost the battle to have bishops elected by the nation's clergy, but other leaders of the church in the democratic republic continued to hope for a genuinely American approach to the structure and functioning of the church. John England, bishop of Charleston, South Carolina, from 1820 to 1842, was an Irish immigrant who fell deeply in love with America, and he sought to apply its political ideas to the governance of the church. This meant that every diocese should have its own written constitution and that representative bodies of priests and laypeople should work with the bishop in managing the practical affairs of the fledgling church. England published and implemented his "Constitution for the Diocese of Charleston" shortly after arriving there. The scattered Catholic congregations in the diocese elected representatives to an annual convention, which was in essence a bicameral legislature, with a house of clergy and a house of laity. The convention met annually to discuss the needs of the diocese: funding the education of seminarians, building churches, helping form new parishes in outlying districts, publishing a newspaper to counteract nativist hostility toward Catholics, and other matters. Each house deliberated, passed resolutions, and then submitted them to the bishop for his approval and action. The system was admirably "well adapted to the attainment of its ends," a contemporary observed. "The utmost harmony subsists between the clergy and the lay delegates, . . . and the welfare of the church [is] ensured."[5]

England's constitutional system did not survive him; his successor discontinued the annual conventions and no other American bishop ever took them up. While it lasted, however, it bound together the leaders and the led, committing them to work toward common goals. To be sure, these were of the most elemental kind: the mere survival of the church in unfamiliar territory, efforts to reduce the impact of priestlessness, and so on. Moreover, the convention itself was always small—the house of the clergy was never much more than half a dozen, and the house of the laity only about twice that—and this made it unlikely that rancor would develop or fester. But later characterizations of this system, or of the similar "trustee" systems at the parish level elsewhere, as somehow "un-Catholic" would have surprised Bishop England and his people. It is often said that the church is not a democracy. Perhaps not; but Catholics living in South Carolina in the 1820s and 1830s certainly thought that the church could profit from emulating the institutionalized participation inherent in democratic republicanism.

3. THE IMMIGRANT CHURCH

The Catholic population of the United States grew at an astonishing—to some, an alarming—rate in the nineteenth century, increasing tenfold between 1800 and 1850 and twelvefold again between then and the end of the century, mostly through immigration from Europe. No wonder observers often described this as an immigrant "flood" or "tidal wave," images that hardly spoke of welcome. As with the biblical flood, this one eradicated the antediluvian world: The small, scattered church of earlier years became a large and constantly expanding institution. Especially in the cities of the East and upper Midwest, Catholicism was overwhelmingly a church of the working class, often self-segregated internally into distinct ethnic "leagues." The church's expansion was impressive by any measure. In Detroit, for instance, the number of parishes grew from 11 to 73 between 1870 and 1920; in

Chicago, delayed only temporarily by the great fire of 1871, the number of parishes grew from 25 to 227 in the same period.[6]

This was a "brick-and-mortar" Catholicism, with all energy seemingly turned toward building an infrastructure of which earlier priests and laypeople could only have dreamed. Churches, schools, hospitals, orphanages, and social service agencies went up everywhere, funded by large numbers of small contributions (rather than the other way around). Seminaries were opened to train American-born clergy, and their cavernous corridors filled up with young men, genuinely eager to be of service and, perhaps, to enhance the standing of their own families in the process. Young women entered vowed religious communities in even greater numbers, in many places outnumbering priests by factors of four and five to one. These sisters often found within the apparently confining walls of the convent the chance for higher education and professional careers foreclosed to them outside. In a way that they had not previously, Catholic laypeople came to depend on these "religious professionals" to define the church. Clerical standards of what constituted faithful Catholic practice became the operative ones, internalized by the laity: weekly mass, monthly confession, participation in the devotional societies of the parish, attendance at periodic retreats or missions, and the education of their children in the parish school. This was the Catholic world that was later romanticized on film by Spencer Tracy and Bing Crosby—a kind of Catholic ghetto but, as Garry Wills noted long ago, "not a bad ghetto to grow up in."[7]

A new passivity of the laity came to mark this age of the immigrant church. Religious commitment was expressed through routine practice, not through any sort of personal quest or effort. Catholics felt little need to wrestle with the great questions of faith themselves; trying to determine "what Jesus means to me" would have struck them as peculiar and unnecessary. Such matters had already been settled by the church and its leaders, and the answers had an unassailable authority. The sacraments worked objectively, *ex opere operato* ("out of the work worked"): Something real happened at baptism, confirmation, and communion, and it happened simply by saying the right words, by doing the right things, and by the participants' having the right intentions, however incapable they might be of articulating them in much detail. Personal qualities had little to do with it all. "Protestants are so accustomed to depend on a personality [of a minister] for continued interest in their religious life," one Boston priest complained to his diary in 1899, and his future archbishop made the same point a few years later: "There is no such thing as the personality of . . . a parish priest," Cardinal William O'Connell said.[8] In a sense, a priest did not need one; religion "worked" perfectly well without it. From the perspective of today, this approach to faith can seem hollow, but it was no less genuine than later experiences. Lay Catholics, slowly making their way amid difficult economic circumstances, had little time for the luxury of personal theological reflection. Their regular presence in the pews was a sufficient measure of their commitment. The hold of this immigrant church on the Catholic imagination has been powerful, and it is often thought of as being somehow the most genuine way of being an American Catholic. It is, rather, merely one of several, no more permanently normative than any other.

4. THE CHURCH OF CATHOLIC ACTION

Beginning in the early twentieth century, a more active role for the laity began to reemerge. This was the age of Catholic Action. That phrase had long been used in a variety of contexts—in Europe it might connote a confessional political party—but it was put into common American usage after the encyclical *Quadragesimo Anno* (1931), in which Pope Pius XI summarized and extended the social teachings of his predecessors. In this vision of its role, the church was not merely a religious institution, concerned with the otherworldly salvation of individual souls; it was also a this-worldly organization, the members of which were required to try to put its teachings into practice in the social, political, and economic spheres of life. That duty fell to laypeople no less than to the clergy and hierarchy. Their task was to "Catholicize the Fatherland," as the somewhat archaic phrase had it, by applying religious principles in literally mundane circumstances. It was understood that the laity were always to be guided in this by the authority of the hierarchy, not striking out on their own, but the message was still clear. They, as much as priests and sisters, bore the burden of the church's work.[9]

A host of organizations and movements sprang into being under the broad banner of Catholic Action. The Catholic Workers, founded in 1933, were probably the most famous, marked by a radical commitment to serving the urban poor, but they were not alone. The Association of Catholic Trade Unionists (1937) coordinated the work of Catholics in organized labor, and the Catholic School of Social Service was opened at Catholic University in 1934 to train social workers imbued with church principles. For those living outside the cities, the Catholic Rural Life Movement (1923) promoted back-to-the-land efforts and worked to improve farm conditions during the Great Depression. Occupational and professional associations for Catholics came together in virtually every walk of life: doctors, lawyers, dentists, nurses, psychologists, even telephone operators. Beginning in the early 1930s a Catholic Youth Organization was devoted to addressing "the youth problem," and their parents were not left out either. Married couples in the Christian Family Movement (1949) studied Catholic social teachings in one another's living rooms and then worked to put them into practice. Almost everywhere, Catholics began to assert themselves as Catholics. The Legion of Decency (1936) promoted quality—and still more vigorously tried to suppress vice—in the popular new medium of motion pictures. Rating movies on a scale that ranged from "unobjectionable" (the slightly skeptical term for the best classification) to "condemned" (the unambiguous designation for the worst), the Legion even reviewed scripts in advance, as producers learned to avoid its wrath and the box-office failure that usually followed. There were no actual political parties that formed with the call to Catholic Action—the Democratic Party served the purpose well enough—but Catholic strength was marshaled unapologetically at the polls. In Massachusetts in the 1940s, Catholic voters were twice mobilized by their bishops to defeat referenda liberalizing the state's birth-control laws. A bloc of Catholic voters and legislators prevented similar changes in Connecticut, driving reformers to the courts, which, in the case of *Griswold v. Connecticut* (1965), paved the way for recognizing a constitutional right to privacy and finally to the legalization of abortion in *Roe v. Wade* (1973).[10]

The two decades after the Second World War are often characterized as a period of quiescence, in the church no less than in American society at large. This was the time, it is said, when Catholics were expected merely to "pray, pay, and obey"—to use that offensive phrase. The legendary calm of the 1950s is more apparent than real, however, when this period is reimagined as the age of Catholic Action. Lay Catholics might seem to have been sitting quietly in their pews, but they were also doing many other things besides, becoming accustomed to taking personal responsibility for the church and its work. The governing metaphor for the church at the time was that it constituted the "Mystical Body of Christ," an image many found difficult to grasp. Insofar as they did, they were increasingly comfortable picturing themselves as God's arms, hands, and tongues in this world.

5. THE CHURCH OF VATICAN II

For that reason, the historical break represented by the reforms of the Second Vatican Council (1962–1965) seems less sharp, less out of the blue than is usually thought. The church of Vatican II was believed at the time, and has generally been regarded since, as representing a radical departure from what the church had "always" been. There certainly is evidence for discontinuity. In parish churches, the altar was moved away from the back wall, and the priest turned around to face the congregation as he said mass. More surprising yet, he was speaking clearly in the vernacular language of the people, who were expected to respond to him by reciting portions of the liturgy previously entrusted only to altar boys. To the dismay of some parishioners, they were even expected to sing. Many popular devotional practices, such as Sunday evening vespers and benediction, effectively disappeared, and sacraments were significantly reconfigured without much fanfare or resistance. Whereas reception of the Eucharist had once been an occasional (monthly, at most) thing, now the majority of churchgoing Catholics took the sacrament every time they went to mass. The sacrament of "extreme unction" was completely recast from an anointing of the dying immediately before death (and thus something to be put off as long as possible, lest it hasten the end) to a general spiritual encouragement of the sick.[11]

For all the obvious differences between pre–Vatican II and post–Vatican II American Catholicism, we can now see more clearly the continuities linking one to the other. The best metaphor for the change wrought by the council is probably that of water coming to a boil: The water does indeed boil at some point, but not until after it has gone through a process of coming to boil. So it was with American Catholics, who had been prepared by decades of Catholic Action finally to embrace the notion that *they* were the church— not the hierarchy, not the institutions, not the clergy. They themselves were indeed the "People of God," the new image for the church. This "coming to boil" had been apparent in the various Catholic Action movements, but it was no less significant in Catholic devotional life. Even when participating in such apparently old-fashioned exercises as praying Father Patrick Peyton's "family rosary," lay Catholics were becoming used to the idea that they had the capacity to determine the course of their own spiritual lives. The laity increasingly heeded encouragements from the clergy that they work toward genuinely personal experiences of prayer, beginning with the lay retreat movement earlier in the century, proceeding through increasingly popular Cursillo, charismatic, Bible study, and other groups, and leading eventually to the practice of individual laypeople acquiring spiritual directors. Dozens of new church ministries opened to laypeople. Married men were ordained as "permanent" deacons, assigned to perform many of the pastoral duties formerly carried out only by priests; lay eucharistic ministers, religious education directors, youth ministers, and others soon came to outnumber priests on parish staffs.[12]

Underlying all this was a heightened sense among laypeople that they were indeed ready to take such roles in the church, a feeling that was often expressed in the language of growth from childhood into thoughtful adulthood. "When will the Church start a sincere effort to appeal to the faithful as rational beings rather than just a herd of followers who are told what to do?" a layman wrote to Washington's Cardinal Patrick O'Boyle in 1968, taking sharp exception to the cardinal's endorsement of Pope Paul VI's controversial encyclical *Humanae Vitae*, which restated the church's opposition to so-called artificial contraception. "We are adults and as such we would like to have some open discussion on such questions," a laywoman told Detroit's Cardinal John Dearden at the same time. "As adults, with all that term implies, we can make moral decisions," yet another man said.[13] "Adults, with all that term implies"—the words encapsulate a fundamental shift in Catholic thinking. More than anything else, here was the essence of the church in the age of Vatican II.

6. THE CHURCH IN THE TWENTY-FIRST CENTURY

Contributors to this collection will forgive me for borrowing the general title of the current initiative at Boston College to designate the last of my six ages of American Catholicism. They will also, I hope, forgive me for saying less about this one than the others: The twenty-first century has, after all, just begun. While historians are rightly cautious when speaking of the future rather than the past, four features of this new age already seem apparent.

First, all the data suggest that American Catholicism is becoming once again a priestless church. New ordinations to the priesthood have long since fallen below the replacement rate of those who die, retire, or resign the ministry, and the average age of active priests climbs toward sixty. Demography alone will force change.

Second, the broader institutional infrastructure of Catholicism is contracting for the first time in its history. Boston's archbishop, for example, is closing about one-fifth of the parishes in his eastern Massachusetts diocese; his predecessor had already closed approximately 10 percent of the parishes there in the eighteen years of his tenure. This same pattern is being replicated elsewhere, even as the Catholic population increases. The Catholic people continue to grow more numerous, but the institutions of their church are becoming fewer and more scattered.

Third, the loss of confidence in the hierarchy that came with the sexual abuse crisis has been deep and, for the foreseeable future, irremediable. Where bishops were once important civic as well as religious leaders, they are now suspect and ignored. Whether it is on sexual issues (homosexuality and gay marriage, for instance) or on foreign affairs (the war in Iraq, for instance), the bishops have collectively lost the capacity to influence public policy. The American church is for the time being essentially leaderless.

Finally, the twenty-first century began with a burst of independent organizational activity among the laity, organizations that have consciously defined themselves as distinct from the hierarchy. The four thousand people from around the country who attended the ad hoc convention of Voice of the Faithful in Boston in July 2002 rallied to the group's slogan "Keep the faith, change the church," a phrase that presupposes divergent interests between the laity and the bishops. This dynamic has also been evident at the local level. In 2004, parishioners at a church on Long Island organized resistance to their new pastor, a former diocesan official implicated in the mishandling of clergy sexual abuse. They were quoted in the newspapers as referring to the unwanted priest contemptuously as "this guy."[14] The staying power of any of these groups is by no means certain, but it does seem clear that independent lay voices will continue to be heard in church affairs. Perhaps, in combination with the gradual disappearance of the clergy, laypeople will again become the principal sustainers of their own religious identity, thereby leading the American Catholic church back to the future.

NOTES

1. On New Mexico, see James J. Hennesey, *American Catholics* (New York: Oxford University Press, 1981), 17; on early Maryland, see Thomas Spalding, *The Premier See: A History of the Archdiocese of Baltimore, 1789–1989* (Baltimore: Johns Hopkins University Press, 1989); for Carroll's descriptions, see Carroll to Antonelli, 1 Mar. 1785, *Papers of John Carroll*, ed. Thomas O'Brien Hanley, 3 vols. (Notre Dame, Ind.: University of Notre Dame Press, 1976), 1:179–80, and Carroll to Plowden, 28 Feb. 1779, *Carroll Papers*, 1:53.

2. *Grother's Prayers for Sundays and Festivals, Adapted to the Use of Private Families or Congregations* (Wolverhampton: J. Smart, 1800), vi–vii. Also popular in America were editions of Richard Challoner's *The Garden of the Soul; or, a Manual of Spiritual Exercises and Instructions for Christians, Who Living the World Aspire to Devotion*, which went through a variety of editions in the late eighteenth and early nineteenth centuries. For a general discussion of these manuals, see Joseph P. Chinnici, *Living Stones: The History and Structure of Catholic Spiritual Life in the United States* (New York: Macmillan, 1989), esp. Part I.

3. Cheverus to Roger Hanly and family, 4 Aug. 1797, quoted in Robert Howard Lord et al., *History of the Archdiocese of Boston*, 3 vols. (Boston: Pilot Publishing Company, 1944), 1: 540–41; original in Archives, Archdiocese of Boston.

4. Carroll to Ashton, 18 Apr. 1790, *Carroll Papers*, 1:436; Carroll to Farmer, December 1784, *Carroll Papers*, 1:156; Carroll to Doria Pamphili, 26 Nov. 1784, *Carroll Papers*, 1:153.

5. *United States Catholic Miscellany*, 17 Nov. 1827. On England and his constitutional system, see Patrick W. Carey, *Immigrant Bishop: John England's Adaptation of Irish Catholicism to American Republicanism* (Yonkers, N.Y.: U.S. Catholic Historical Society, 1982), and Patrick W. Carey, *People, Priests, and Prelates: Ecclesiastical Democracy and the Tensions of Trusteeism* (Notre Dame, Ind.: University of Notre Dame Press, 1987).

6. This story was repeated practically everywhere in Catholic America and is told in virtually every diocesan history. Two of the best of that genre are Leslie Woodcock Tentler, *Seasons of Grace: A History of the Catholic Archdiocese of Detroit* (Detroit: Wayne State University Press, 1990), and Ellen Skerrett et al., *Catholicism, Chicago Style* (Chicago: Loyola University Press, 1993); see especially Skerrett's own essay, "Sacred Space: Parish and Neighborhood in Chicago," 137–69.

7. Garry Wills, *Bare Ruined Choirs: Doubt, Prophecy, and Radical Religion* (Garden City, N.Y.: Doubleday, 1972), 37.

8. Both quotes in Robert E. Sullivan, "Beneficial Relations: Toward a Social History of the Diocesan Priests of Boston, 1875–1944," in *Catholic Boston: Studies in Religion and Community, 1870–1970*, ed. Robert E. Sullivan and James M. O'Toole (Boston: Archdiocese of Boston, 1985), 219.

9. One of the clearest theoretical statements of these positions came from John J. Wright, *National Patriotism in Papal Teaching* (Boston: Stratford, 1942).

10. There is no good general history of Catholic Action, but for many of these movements and their meaning, see David J. O'Brien, *Public Catholicism* (New York: Macmillan, 1989), esp. chaps. 6 and 7.

11. For a discussion of some of these practices before and after Vatican II, see James M. O'Toole, ed., *Habits of Devotion: Catholic Religious Practice in Twentieth Century America* (Ithaca, N.Y.: Cornell University Press, 2004).

12. For the growth of the laity's sense of responsibility for its own spiritual welfare, see James P. McCartin's very insightful "'The Love of Things Unseen': Catholic Prayer and Moral Imagination in the Twentieth-Century United States" (Ph.D. diss., University of Notre Dame, 2003). On lay small faith groups, see Alan Wolfe, *The Transformation of American Religion: How We Actually Live Our Faith* (New York: Free Press, 2003), 15–16. I have shamelessly stolen the boiling water metaphor from Joseph P. Chinnici, OFM, of the Franciscan School of Theology, Berkeley, California, and I thank him for it.

13. Meister to O'Boyle, 10 Oct. 1968, and Burkard to Dearden, 30 Oct. 1968, copies in Lawrence Sheehan Papers ("Humanae Vitae"), Archives, Archdiocese of Baltimore; layman comments in *U.S. Catholic* Surveys, 24/16, Archives, University of Notre Dame.

14. "Pastor Controversy Goes Public," *Newsday,* 19 Apr. 2004.

4: THE STRUGGLE TO PRESERVE RELIGIOUS CAPITAL: A SOCIOLOGICAL PERSPECTIVE ON THE CATHOLIC CHURCH IN THE UNITED STATES

Michele Dillon

The Catholic Church's recent sex abuse scandal—a term inclusively used to refer both to the incidents of priest sex abuse as well as the response of bishops and church officials to those incidents—severely challenged the public credibility of the church in American society. Even more consequential, it destabilized the religious and social identity of large numbers of American Catholics. Thus with good reason, many media commentators, scholars, and laity alike refer to the scandal using the language of crisis. Legitimation crises arise when the collective trust critical to maintaining belief in an institution—in its purpose and mission and in the processes it uses to realize its mission—are called into question, not by outsiders, but by the very community of individuals whose voluntary participation in the institution rests on their belief in its overall goodness or integrity.[1] Such crises are exacerbated when an institution's own resources are discounted in efforts toward institutional recovery or problem solving.

INSTITUTIONAL IDENTITY AND CULTURAL LEGITIMATION

Like all institutions, religious institutions exist and function within particular and necessarily changing sociohistorical and cultural contexts. As such they invariably encounter legitimation dilemmas that routinely challenge how they articulate their institutional identity—their structure, beliefs, and practices—to their diverse institutional constituencies and to the society at large. Even the most cursory review of the Catholic Church's history will attest to its cultural and institutional resourcefulness, underscored by the complex and multifaceted identity it has carved out across time and space.

43

Certainly, the Catholic Church's trajectory in American society indicates that it can successfully confront legitimation challenges. As an immigrant church, a theological and cultural outsider, the Catholic Church had to forge its legitimacy vis-à-vis the dominant Protestant churches and the Protestant values embedded in the culture as a whole.

Theologically, the church confronted the task of adapting a universal, "one true church" to a denominational society that affirmed the existence of many pathways to God/religious truth. Organizationally, the American context of religious pluralism and religious freedom meant that the church had to adjust its way of relating to other institutions such as the state; unlike in many European countries it did not enjoy any formally acknowledged privileged place in the political arena. It also had to adjust how it related to its own segmented Catholic constituency—an impoverished substratum of the new nation rather than the dominant majority the European church was accustomed to leading. And, in building and encompassing a wide range of strong working-class, ethnic subcultures, the church further distanced itself from mainstream Protestant middle-class culture while simultaneously being the object of prejudicial discrimination and violence. This cultural gap was further accentuated because Catholics' participation in a global transnational institution has meant that collective affiliation to the Vatican, rather than being a source of pride as was true in countries where the church was an insider (e.g., Ireland, Poland), has long been a source of (continuing) tension in the American polity. Yet the church's history in America, its successful negotiation of these diverse theological, organizational, and cultural challenges, attests to its resourcefulness and adaptability.

As part of the post–World War II economic boom and the upward social mobility it provided many Americans, Catholics transcended their immigrant, ethnic, and working-class status to become full participants in all sectors of American society. Catholics' socioeconomic success was also of course in large part due to the Catholic educational and other institutions that were so critical to their parents' and grandparents' assimilation, and which in turn enabled them to take advantage of the expanded structural opportunities in the economy and society in the 1950s. As statistically documented by Andrew Greeley, Catholics' educational attainment, the social prestige of their occupations, and their family incomes are on a par with or greater than the levels characteristic of their more culturally elite Protestant neighbors.[2] Moreover, Catholics' political affiliations and their political and social attitudes, stereotypes of Catholic authoritarianism and intolerance notwithstanding, are "more likely than Protestants to fall on the liberal side of the political spectrum."[3]

Catholics' changing status in American society coincided, of course, with the transformative event in twentieth-century Catholic institutional history: the Second Vatican Council (1962–1965). Clearly, Vatican II provided the doctrinal blueprint for a broad array of changes in church practices and in Catholic identity. These multiple and far-reaching changes impacted the routines and experiences of ordinary Catholics as well as the ways the institutional church relates to other churches and to the state and other secular institutions. From a sociological perspective, the most significant changes had to do with Catholic identity, for the individual Catholic and for the Church as an institution. As I have elaborated elsewhere, Vatican II imposed new obligations on the church and on Catholics.[4] In particular, it expressed a highly agential view of the role of laity in the church and in society. The council stated, for instance, that the laity "should be given every opportunity to participate in the saving work of the church"; they should be permitted to express informed opinions on issues "pertaining to the good of the church"; and because men and women are "the authors and artisans of the culture of their community," "responsible for [its] progress," they look "anxiously upon the many contradictions which [they] will have to resolve" (*GS*, 55, 56).

Most notably, Vatican II shifted the understanding of authority in the church to impose a new ethic in which communal authority—the interpretive authority of Catholics as a whole, the "People of God" in informed conversation with the bishops and priests—would come to a reasoned, practical understanding of Catholicism. Certainly, Vatican II affirmed the importance of the church hierarchy; it reminded Catholic laity that they should give "close attention to the teaching authority of the Church." But it also explicitly affirmed the responsibility and reasoned interpretive authority of all church members. The council gave a clear and unequivocal endorsement to the authority of communal collaboration and privileged it over the bureaucratic authority that comes from the authority of office alone. The council stated:

> Laymen should also know that it is generally the function of their well-formed Christian conscience to see that the divine law is inscribed in the life of the earthly city. From priests they may look for spiritual light and nourishment. Let the layman not imagine that his pastors are always such experts, that to every problem which arises, however complicated, they can readily give him a concrete solution, or even that such is their mission . . . it happens rather frequently, and legitimately so, that with equal sincerity some of the faithful will disagree with others on a given matter . . . solutions proposed on one side or another may be easily confused by many people with the gospel message. Hence it is necessary for people to remember that no one is allowed in the aforementioned situations to appropriate the Church's authority for his opinion. They should always try to enlighten one another through honest discussion, preserving mutual charity and caring above all for the common good. (*GS*, 43)

> All the faithful, clerical and lay, possess a lawful freedom of inquiry and of thought, and the freedom to express their minds humbly and courageously about those matters in which they enjoy competence. (*GS*, 62)

In my assessment, this shift in doctrinal emphasis away from the unilateral exercise of hierarchical authority toward a reason-based and communal dialogue within the church—though it does not stand alone or exist in a socio-historical vacuum—is what is critical to the sociological context and understanding of contemporary Catholicism.

Vatican II's doctrinal and institutional changes, the changing socio-economic status and increased cultural confidence of American Catholics, and ongoing changes in American society as a whole—most notably the cultural transformation associated with the 1960s and 1970s—all converged to produce a different sociological reality than had characterized the Catholic experience in the late nineteenth century or indeed during the 1940s and 1950s. These shifts in the church–culture context and within the culture of Catholicism produced a new set of legitimation dilemmas for the Catholic Church. In view of the accented cultural emphasis on individual freedom in the post-1960s era—including freedom from the hold of external religious authority that for Catholics took on additional meaning in light of Vatican II's emphasis on personal conscience and freedom of dialogue—it is perhaps not surprising that the legitimation dilemma confronting the church in the latter decades of the twentieth century revolved around religious authority.

THE DILEMMA OF RELIGIOUS AUTHORITY

The sociological paradox presented by post–Vatican II Catholicism is that while the church hierarchy achieved a culturally legitimate voice in American civic society, its moral authority among Catholics has been severely attenuated. Indeed, it could well be argued that one of the clearest indicators of the Catholic Church's institutional success in America is its prominence as a public church. Notwithstanding the church's history as an institutional outsider, and as noted earlier, its attendant theological, organizational, and cultural dilemmas, the American Catholic bishops have solidly positioned the church in the public square of American life. Most notably, the church sponsors one of the nation's largest nongovernmental social services organizations (Catholic Charities), with close to fifteen hundred community branches and affiliates. A second significant aspect of the church's civic visibility is its active participation in state and national public policy debates since the 1970s. It has been most vocal on abortion but has also engaged debate on capital punishment, economic redistribution, war, welfare, and stem cell research, among other wide-ranging topics. In these public policy debates, the bishops use arguments that deftly blend scientific data and cultural themes rather than simply iterating Catholic tenets. Underscoring the church's institutional self-confidence, the bishops' public statements frequently invoke the words of John Winthrop and cultural motifs institutionalized by the founding fathers of the American Republic, by which to persuade all Americans, that is, "men and women of good will," of the moral virtue of their social teachings/policy stances.[5]

The bishops' carving of a culturally legitimate public church is quite an accomplishment because although Catholicism is the largest denomination in America, it nonetheless remains a minority religion vis-à-vis Protestantism. From a cultural perspective, this is additionally impressive because important strands in the Catholic doctrinal tradition are invariably in tension with the American cultural ethos, one that is thoroughly Protestant. Catholicism's emphasis on both hierarchy and community, for example, makes it at odds with American and Protestant emphases on individualism. The Catholic understanding of the mutuality of the relation between the individual and society, and thus of individuals' compassionate responsibility toward others, still presents somewhat as a foreign perspective in American politics. Andrew Greeley uses empirical research on social attitudes to illustrate David Tracy's elaboration of the differences reflective of the Catholic and Protestant imaginations.[6] Greeley shows that the Catholic understanding of God's presence in the world and the related view of the inherent goodness of human nature, social relations, and social institutions means that Catholics are significantly more likely than Protestants to have a benign or redemptive worldview. They tend to see the value of social and community-based solutions to poverty and other social ills, problems that the Protestant worldview would place squarely on the individual's shoulders. It is perhaps indicative of the extent to which the Catholic Church has overcome its outsider historical status in America that Robert Bellah, a sociologist deeply familiar with America's founding covenants, could recently argue that discourse about the American common good could well profit from greater attention to the Catholic ethos of community.[7]

But while the church's public or civic standing has substantially increased since the 1970s, its ability to constrain the opinions and behavior of its own adherents has dramatically fallen. The dominant trend is one of increasing Catholic disaffection with the reach of hierarchical authority. The laity's response to Pope Paul VI's birth-control encyclical, *Humanae Vitae* (1968), marked a watershed in American Catholicism. Its impact was reflected in national surveys showing a precipitous decline in church attendance for Catholics across all age groups. In 1968, 65 percent of American Catholics reported weekly mass attendance but in the ensuing years attendance declined steadily, so much so that by 1973 it was only 55 percent.[8] However, the decline in weekly mass attendance leveled off in 1975 at around 52 percent. Although not all lapsed Catholics resumed mass attendance, a substantial number did, and, importantly, this trend was not accompanied by a concomitant decline in Catholics' use of birth control, an outgrowth perhaps of Vatican II's affirmation of personal conscience as the individual's "most secret core and sanctuary" (*GS*, 16). In any case, as argued by Hout and Greeley, the return to church marked a significant transformation in Catholics' attitudes toward church authority: It signified ordinary Catholics' understanding that they could dissent from official church teaching and still be good Catholics.[9]

The laity's response to *Humanae Vitae* foreshadowed an accelerating decline in Catholics' acceptance of the church hierarchy's authority to demarcate the moral boundaries and content of Catholic identity. Almost all American Catholics think that a person who uses artificial contraception is still a good Catholic (89 percent) and that divorced Catholics should be allowed to remarry in the church (78 percent). The majority also believe that Catholic women who have an abortion are still good Catholics (62 percent), and close to half (47 percent) believe this is true of individuals who engage in same-sex sexual relations. There is also substantial Catholic divergence from Vatican teaching on specific church issues, with the majority of American Catholics agreeing that women should be eligible to be ordained priests (63 percent) and that priests should be allowed to marry (75 percent).[10]

Disaffection with church teaching on these various questions fueled a significant surge in lay activism among Catholics. Paralleling the emergence of secular social movements focused on greater equality for women and cultural minorities, several Catholic activist organizations were founded in the 1970s toward achieving changes in church doctrines and practices. Among these groups were Dignity, arguing for greater intrachurch acceptance of gay and lesbian Catholics; the Women's Ordination Conference, advocating for the ordination of women; and other Catholic organizations addressing a number of issues (e.g., Catholics Speak Out). These diverse groups are part of the Call to Action coalition whose annual conference articulates the reasons for a more participatory and egalitarian church. It is noteworthy that the arguments advanced by Catholics who favor changes in the church draw extensively on doctrinal reasoning from within Catholicism; these Catholics are committed to staying within the church while simultaneously pushing for institutional and doctrinal changes that more fully realize Catholic doctrinal ideals of equality and lay participation.[11]

THE IMPACT OF THE SEX ABUSE SCANDAL: DISRUPTING THE STATUS QUO

The sociological context defining Catholic culture and the church's place in American society prior to the sex abuse scandal was a fairly settled context. It was one in which the civic role of the church was strong and largely uncontested, and its interpretive authority among ordinary Catholics quite attenuated (e.g., on birth control) and publicly challenged by a significant but relatively narrow bloc of lay activism (and supported by many theologians).

This in essence was the status quo—an equilibrium in place whereby members of the church hierarchy were active participants in public policy debates and tacit acceptors of the doctrinal selectivity of American Catholic practices. Despite the disaffection caused by *Humanae Vitae* and its continuing impact on the church, the institutional crisis it provoked essentially vaporized; as the survey data above shows, many Catholics returned to the fold. Although there were episodic interruptions to the pragmatic consensus about what it meant to be Catholic—as for example when individual bishops periodically condemned pro-choice politicians or Call to Action activists—for the most part it was, in inelegantly phrased language, a "don't ask, don't tell" modus operandi. Bishops and priests did not make systematic recourse to their privileged status in the church and their ordained authority as interpreters of natural law to remind Catholics of the sinfulness of using artificial forms of birth control, for example; or to clarify, in the face of the increasing prevalence of annulments, the doctrinal grounds for nullifying sacramental marriages; or to encourage Catholics to make the sacrament of Penance a regular habit. In essence, the status quo was one in which church officials tacitly bowed to the interpretive authority and moral freedom of individual Catholics to remain Catholic and to determine their Catholic identity as lived in everyday life, while simultaneously giving public articulation to the boundaries demarcating a much more authoritative and narrowly drawn Catholic identity (cf. the Vatican's statements on homosexuality, women's ordination, divorce, sacramental participation).

As the chapters in this volume show, the sex abuse scandal can be analyzed in many ways—ranging from an episode of social drama[12] to providing material for reassessing the canon law definition of the priest–church relationship.[13] Few would disagree that the sex abuse scandal seriously disrupted the Catholic status quo. The scandal demonstrated that the collective trust in priests and bishops by virtue of their sacred authority, that is, their exclusive sacramental authority to access the sacred as in the celebration of the Mass, could no longer be vested beyond the altar to their nonsacramental functions. The sex abuse scandal forced collective awareness that priests and bishops have feet of clay, that they too, like the nonordained, are prone to the lure of profane sirens, whether the sirens of sexual impulse or of organizational legal-economic interests. The scandal thus created a legitimation crisis that was different from earlier legitimation dilemmas and crises; its object of focus was the behavior of priests and bishops, not lay Catholics or external forces.

The scandal and its aftermath turned the focus not on the church hierarchy's specialized doctrinal authority but on its weaker claim to sacred power—on its expertise in regard to everyday church structures rather than church doctrine (the power base challenged by individual dissent and previous lay activism). Prior to the sex abuse scandal Catholic dissent was largely confined to specific doctrinal issues (e.g., birth control, sexuality,

women's ordination) and by extension, the church hierarchy's monopoliza-
tion of doctrinal interpretive authority. What the sex abuse scandal accomplished was to energize ordinary churchgoing Catholics, many of whom
were relatively indifferent to doctrinal nuance, to do something that would
visibly impact how their church works, its everyday organizational structures. The depth of coverage provided by local and national media to the
many layers of evidence of priest sex abuse and its routinization within the
church unveiled for many Catholics a new knowledge of the church: a
knowledge of persistent wrongdoing by abusing priests and of cover-up by
their superiors; a knowledge that in turn directed attention to other aspects
of church practices and to the privileging of the church's legal and economic
interests over its core pastoral obligations.

The evidence of Catholic anomie, of a drift toward a disintegration of the
Catholic community in the wake of the scandal, was especially evident in
New England, its epicenter. Catholics' tendencies to reassess, if not disavow,
their Catholic identity were most visibly apparent in three ways: a decline in
their frequency of Mass attendance, a decline in financial donations, and an
increase in ordinary lay activism. Opinion poll data and the church's own
self-counting indicate that a substantial minority of Catholics have stopped
attending church since the scandal broke. National survey data (based on the
General Social Survey) prior to the scandal showed that New England
Catholics attended church as frequently as their coreligionists outside the re-
gion (44 percent). By comparison, a *Boston Globe* survey conducted in May
2003 found that 35 percent of Boston Catholics were currently attending
weekly Mass; 27 percent said the scandal had caused them to attend Mass
less regularly; and 18 percent said that it had made them less likely to encourage their children to practice Catholicism.

In an April 2002 poll conducted for the *Boston Globe*, a couple of months
after the sex abuse scandal became a topic of daily conversation, almost one-
third of Catholics in the Boston archdiocese said that the sex abuse scandal
had caused them to donate less money to the church. It is noteworthy that
this figure had increased to 44 percent in a poll conducted a year later (May
2003). This decline in financial support has been confirmed by church leaders who acknowledge that weekly and other donations to the church have
declined substantially—almost by half—since the scandal. It is estimated that
the Annual Cardinal's Appeal (now rebranded and depersonalized as the Annual Catholic Appeal) declined from 16 million dollars in 2001 to 8.8 million
dollars in 2002.

These downward trends have been complemented by a major increase in
lay activism, especially through Voice of the Faithful (VOTF), whose estimated twenty-five thousand nationwide members appear highly committed
to seeking specific changes in the church. VOTF's origins in the immediate
context of the eruption of the sex abuse scandal, its particular focus, its grass-

roots membership, and its media visibility give it a broader base of support and a greater proximity to mainstream Catholics and to local bishops and priests than longer established pro-change activist groups. Moreover, on the surface at least, VOTF would seem to have a relatively benign agenda. From the outset, VOTF has publicly and repeatedly insisted that it seeks only to change church "structures" and not church dogma. This avowal, presumably, is intended to communicate to church officials that VOTF is not interested in trying to challenge the privileged sacred authority of the bishops; it seeks merely to change or to have input into some of the routine and relatively mundane tasks that the church as an organization must do—for example, allocating money, assigning priests, reconfiguring parishes.

THE MONOPOLIZATION OF RELIGIOUS CAPITAL

In view of the new reality imposed on the church in the wake of the sex abuse scandal—its diminished trust and credibility and the more immediate crisis imposed by its declining churchgoing and financial base—it is of heightened sociological interest to inquire into the hierarchy's response to VOTF and lay activism. On the one hand, the hierarchy's response is remarkable for the extent to which it has resisted VOTF: prohibiting new chapters from meeting on parish/church property, being hesitant to accept donations to Catholic Charities, and generally avoiding dialogue with VOTF. Even more remarkable, perhaps, with the church trying to move forward from the sex abuse scandal, is the relative absence of lay involvement in the hierarchy's effort in the Boston archdiocese to reconfigure parishes.

On the face of it, the hierarchy's marginalization of VOTF and of the laity more generally seems puzzling, especially given the narrow structural concerns that VOTF articulates. The church's response to VOTF, however, and to the scandal more generally opens a door that unveils much about how the church functions. In particular it illuminates how the church hierarchy defines and seeks to preserve an expansive domain of power and expertise. In the modern world where institutional differentiation and specialization of function is normative, all institutions work to preserve their unique specialization, and so the church, too, seeks to preserve its sacredness. There is, however, greater ambiguity as to what comprises the church's expertise than there is in regard to Wall Street institutions or to the legal and medical professions. What is the church's specialty? On the one hand, the church, to use the economic language favored by the French sociologist Pierre Bourdieu, produces religious truth and sells access to the sacred via the sacraments.[14] Its main purpose is the production and the reproduction of religious capital. But this is not the only logic underlying church practices; religious capital is not the only capital the church produces.

The church produces capital across several institutional domains. Clearly, the church is an economic organization with economic interests; it is a major producer of economic capital, both directly and indirectly, as an employer, as a producer of an array of educational and social services, and as a consumer. The church also produces political capital; as a major actor in the policy-making arena it forms strategically advantageous alliances and coalitions with other religious actors and with diverse secular actors. Similarly, as a major institutional player in the fields of education and medicine, it forges alliances that advance the institutional capital of these respective fields. Finally, the church is a producer of legal capital; not only must it administer its own complex canon law but it also produces legal capital in its relation to civil law—the multiple civil law cases in which it participates either as a plaintiff, defendant, or friend of the court, as it weighs in and tries to advance its own institutional interests vis-à-vis a wide range of legal judgments (e.g., on abortion, prayer in school, employee discrimination). In sum, the church is a complex, multifaceted institution with many specialties; its diverse and wide-ranging practices produce many types of capital and rest on a number of different, at times contradictory, logics,[15] as for example, when its economic or legal interests take precedence over its pastoral obligations.

The multiplicity of the church's specializations, or the range of institutional fields in which it has a substantial stake, makes it difficult to articulate a meaningful "professional ecclesial ethic" for the church [the original aim of this volume's conference], because clearly, the church's "professionalism" subsumes several different professional ethics. In any given context, the multiple and potentially contradictory logics that underlie church practices tend to remain in the background or free from scrutiny. The sex abuse scandal brought them to the fore. Most visibly, the response of church officials to priest sex abuse (e.g., reassigning priests, having victims sign settlements promising not to disclose their abuse) pointed to a church that gave greater attention to the institution's strategic interests (e.g., administrative and legal maneuvers aimed at preserving the church's organizational resources) than to its religious values and the pastoral needs of victims, their families, and the common good of the parish communities of abusing priests. The collective knowledge that emerged from the sex abuse scandal thus highlighted a church committed to preserving its legal and economic capital rather than religious/moral/pastoral truth; and the shock imposed by this knowledge was severe because unlike economic corporations, the church is thought of by Catholics (and others) primarily in terms of its religious/pastoral truths and not in terms of its economic-legal identity.

Once the spotlight was focused on the church's legal and economic interests, it opened these aspects of the church to public scrutiny, and of particular import to hierarchical authority, it focused attention on management and control of those assets. The hierarchy derives its legitimacy from its religious capital; most especially, the sanctity of the bishops derives from the thesis linking them to apostolic succession. The inequality within the church between the ordained—who have privileged access to religious capital—and the laity means that many of the church's institutional practices are structured to remind the laity that they need special qualifications or special grace to allow them access to the religious capital held by church officials; this is most clearly seen in the delineation of the sacramental power of the priest.[16] Paralleling other professions, the specialized disciplinary training of priests culminating in their sacramental ordination legitimates their professional authority; it confers on them the power to execute priestly functions, that is, to access the sacred.

But in the church's everyday institutional practices there is quite a lot of ambiguity or fluidity between the church's sacred duties that require privileged religious capital and the maintenance of its economic and other organizational interests that do not require privileged access to the sacred. In any given parish, the priest celebrates the Mass and the sacraments; this sacramental power is what is legitimated by his ordination and what is special about his religious capital. Priests also, however, have several other functions in their parish/diocese—mundane functions—and even though many of these functions are independent of ordination, in practice, they get conflated with the priest's sacred authority. Church officials do not draw attention to this ambiguous conflation; instead, church structures and everyday practices reproduce the fluidity between the priest's sacred authority and his assumed authority to also control nonordained functions.

VOTF's advocacy of a greater participatory role for the laity in the church's structure directed attention to the conflation between the church's sacred, sacramental functions and its mundane organizational duties, the control of its organizational and economic capital. The focus on the church's structure begged the question: What is sacred and what is not sacred about what the church does? VOTF does not challenge the church's religious capital, its sacred (doctrinal or dogma-based) authority, but it does challenge the ambiguous connection between the church's religious capital and its nonreligious capital. Accordingly, VOTF has challenged the power of the church to administer church finances and make personnel decisions (among other functions), tasks that, a priori, are not dependent on the sacramental power of priests. These functions, as VOTF contends, are bureaucratic functions dependent on expert knowledge, but not on knowledge that is uniquely grounded in sacramental authority. VOTF, therefore, has disrupted the status quo in the church. It has done so not by challenging the church's doctrinal and sacramental authority but by challenging its monopoly of control over the church's nonreligious capital.

The negative response of church officials to VOTF can be seen as an attempt by the hierarchy to maintain the institutional ambiguity between

sacred, or religious, capital and priests' hold over the church's nonsacred
functions and material resources. From a sociological perspective, there are
at least three interrelated reasons that shed light on the resistance of the
church hierarchy to lay involvement in regard to any aspect of the church,
either dogma or structure. First, notwithstanding VOTF's emphasis that it
wants to change structures and not doctrine or dogma, the distinction between structure and doctrine is not so clear-cut and is in fact an artificial, pos-
itivistic distinction. Doctrine and structure mutually inform each other in a di-
alectical manner such that the church's structures reflect the Catholic
tradition's doctrinal understanding of the origins and mission of the church.
Accordingly, the hierarchical structure developed by the church attests to the
church's theology of authority and of social and institutional relations.

Second, the church is a deeply cultured organization whose long history
and geographical breadth have encrusted it with several pronounced motifs;
most notably, that of hierarchical organization. For all the talk of hierarchy
and community that Vatican II unleashed, much of the church's history is a
history that affirms, to a greater or lesser extent, a culture of hierarchy; indeed, some would argue that the concept of hierarchy is inscribed in the
Catholic imagination.[17] Structurally and culturally, the church is a hierarchical organization and this truth is crystallized as much by the local parish as
by the Vatican. Indicative of this truth, it is instructive to bear in mind that the
hierarchy, at least since the Counter-Reformation, has never been very re-
sponsive to lay concerns; consequently, perhaps, we should not be so surprised that church officials are so resistant to lay input and opinion during
the present moment. The papacy of John Paul II would certainly seem to
represent an accentuation of the church's emphasis on hierarchical authority, but, in any case, it simply makes it all the more difficult for lay voices to
be included in church deliberations about any matter and at any level.

Third, for church officials to acknowledge the reasonableness of VOTF's
interest in participating in routine church practices such as financial decision-
making would be to concede that not every church function is necessarily
sacred and demanding of specialized religious charisma. This however
would demand a transformation in the worldview that both priests and laity
alike have long shared. The laity may have come to a new knowledge of the
church, but church officials have not. The new knowledge that the sex abuse
scandal unveiled to the laity about church practices was, apparently, already
well-known and routinized among (many) priests and bishops. But even if
priests and bishops are, like the laity, shocked by the scandal, a lag in understanding between the laity and the ordained is to be expected. Priests and
bishops have been socialized into a professional church culture that has
given them ownership not just of the church's sacramental functions but of
many other of its functions; ownership, therefore, of the church's religious
and its economic/organizational capital. Indeed, for church officials, reli-

gious capital subsumes economic and administrative capital; that is, they are sanctified to celebrate the Mass and to reconfigure parishes. The church hierarchy thus resists lay attempts to demystify the symbolic ambiguity and institutional practices that enable it to maintain control of the church's capital.

For these reasons, the resistance of the hierarchy against the laity is understandable, but it nevertheless has a spiraling impact on the very legitimation crisis that threatens the church. It causes further disaffection among the laity whose moral and financial support the church needs. Thus the institutional viability of the church and the collective trust necessary to its functioning is threatened less by lay activism than by the hierarchy's response to that activism: its denial of a legitimate role for the laity in the administrative and other structural and doctrinal work of the church. Contravening the church's own doctrinal ethics, the hierarchy's marginalization of the imperatives of cooperative responsibility and communal dialogue with the laity dismisses a critical resource within the church. The denial of the possibility of participative intrachurch dialogue, most evident in the non-communicative attitude of church officials toward VOTF and parish laity, forecloses a priori the possibility that Catholic laity and bishops can collectively collaborate in dialogue toward identifying solutions that can likely move the church forward from its current crisis and restore the solidarity of the Catholic community.

As elaborated elsewhere, the realization of reasoned communicative interaction between church officials and the laity (as articulated by Vatican II) is not an easy task.[18] It demands that all parties to the conversation must be sincerely open to the possibility, if sufficiently good reasons are adduced, of changing their assumptions and ideas about each other, about their understanding of the concepts of hierarchy and community, and about how the church works; in this regard, no one has an a priori monopoly on problem-solving strategies. In this challenging venture, however, church officials and lay Catholics alike can be guided by their shared doctrinal tradition as they move forward in narrowing the gaps between church ideals, the sociohistorical forces that currently shape both church and culture, and the human imperfections of those to whom the gospel is entrusted.

NOTES

1. See Jurgen Habermas, *Legitimation Crisis* (Boston: Beacon Press, 1975).
2. Andrew Greeley, *The American Catholic and Religious Change in America* (Cambridge, Mass.: Harvard University Press, 1989).
3. Greeley, *Social Portrait*, 93*ff.*
4. Michele Dillon, *Catholic Identity: Balancing Reason, Faith, and Power* (New York: Cambridge University Press, 1999), 45–53.

5. For example, Michele Dillon, "Religion and Culture in Tension: The Abortion Discourses of the U.S. Catholic Bishops and the Southern Baptist Convention," *Religion and American Culture* 5 (1995): 159–180.

6. Andrew Greeley, "Protestant and Catholic: Is the Analogical Imagination Extinct?" *American Sociological Review* 54 (1989): 485–502.

7. Robert N. Bellah, "Religion and the Shaping of National Culture," *America* 181 (31 July–7 Aug. 1999): 9–14.

8. Andrew Greeley, *American Catholics since the Council* (Chicago: Thomas More Press, 1985), 53–55.

9. Michael Hout and Andrew Greeley, "The Center Doesn't Hold: Church Attendance in the United States, 1940–1984" *American Sociological Review* 52 (1987): 325–45.

10. George Gallup and D. Michael Lindsay, *Surveying the Religious Landscape* (Harrisburgh, Pa.: Morehouse, 1999), 85–87.

11. See Dillon, *Catholic Identity*.

12. See Jean Bartunek's essay in this volume.

13. See John Beal's essay in this volume.

14. Pierre Bourdieu, "Genesis and Structure of the Religious Field," *Comparative Social Research* 13 (1991): 1–44.

15. Bourdieu, "Genesis and Structure."

16. See Bourdieu, "Genesis and Structure"; Michele Dillon, "Pierre Bourdieu, Religion, and Cultural Production," *Cultural Studies: Critical Methodologies* 1 (2001): 411–29.

17. John Coleman, "Raison D'Eglise: Organizational Imperatives of the Church in the Political Order," in *Secularization and Fundamentalism Reconsidered*, ed. J. Hadden and A. Shupe (New York: Paragon House, 1989), 252–75.

18. Michele Dillon, "The Authority of the Holy Revisited: Habermas, Religion, and Emancipatory Possibilities," *Sociological Theory* 17 (1999): 290–306.

5: ECCLESIOLOGICAL PERSPECTIVES ON CHURCH REFORM

Richard R. Gaillardetz

- Ch as sacrament & sign of Kingdom (LG)
- Justice in the World — est applied
   within to church

In the last four centuries of Roman Catholicism, questions of church reform and renewal have been tainted by Catholic–Protestant polemics. Luther's vigorous assertion that the church was an *ecclesia semper reformanda* led to Catholic counterassertions regarding the church as a *societas perfecta* possessing an indefectible holiness. Though important exceptions would emerge over the next four centuries,[1] the dominant Catholic Counter-Reformation ecclesiology that emerged in response to the reformers seemed to preclude any consideration of church reform beyond that of its individual members. In 1950 the Dominican theologian Yves Congar published his controversial study on the possibility of reform in the church, *Vrai et fausse réforme dans l'Église*.[2] In spite of the fact that the Vatican intervened to prevent future translations of this work, the book's central theme became an important topic at Vatican II. Pope John XXIII placed the topic at the forefront of conciliar reflection when he explicitly called for an *aggiornamento*, bringing the church "up-to-date," in his address at the opening of the council.[3]

A fresh consideration of the possibility of substantive church reform was made possible by fundamental shifts in Catholic ecclesiology that found their way into the conciliar documents: First, a heightened appreciation for the eschatological dimension of the church as not just a church of pilgrims but a pilgrim church made it easier to suggest that if the church does not "achieve its perfection until the glory of heaven" (*LG*, 48) then substantive ecclesial reform must be possible. Second, the recovery of the pneumatological foundations of the church furthered this development by viewing institutional change as potentially the work of the Spirit and not necessarily a departure from immutable ecclesial structures. Third, in 1964 Pope Paul VI issued his first encyclical, *Ecclesiam suam*, in which he encouraged the value of respectful dialogue both within the church and between the church and the world. This theme would be adopted in the council's *Pastoral Constitution on the Church in the Modern World*. These new perspectives allowed the council to address the possibility of church reform within an alternative theological framework. In their *Decree on Ecumenism*, the council bishops wrote:

> Christ summons the church, as she goes her pilgrim way, to that continual reformation of which she always has need, insofar as she is a human institution here on earth. Consequently, if, in various times and circumstances, there have been deficiencies in moral conduct or in church discipline, or even in the way that church teaching has been formulated—to be carefully distinguished from the deposit of faith itself—these should be set right at the opportune moment and in the proper way. (*UR*, 6)

Since the council, there has been widespread agreement among theologians and church leaders regarding the necessity and value of the reforms called for by the council and enacted, with varying degrees of success, in the fundamental revision of the church's sacramental rites, the creation of the world synod of bishops, the suppression of minor orders, the restoration of the permanent diaconate, the encouragement of lay ministries, and the promulgation of both the new *Code of Canon Law* and the *Catechism of the Catholic Church*.

Some church commentators suggest that these reforms represent, in many instances, only compromise developments. They insist that the postconciliar reforms have not gone far enough and that, particularly in the face of the recent clerical sexual abuse scandal exacerbated by the gross malfeasance of church leadership, further structural or organizational reform is still needed. This collection's focus on the merits of developing a professional ethic in the church is, I believe, largely in keeping with this viewpoint. However, others in the church, including some influential bishops and Vatican officials, have questioned the continued focus on institutional or organizational reform, contending that the energy of the church today needs to be redirected from structural church reform to the church's mission to be an evangelizing presence in the world.[4]

It is my contention that it is an error to place in opposition the two imperatives of church reform and church mission. In the first part of this chapter I will argue that an understanding of the church as a universal sacrament of salvation and the church as seed of the kingdom of God presupposes an intrinsic connection between the church's own structural reality and its mission in the world. Structural church reform cannot be dismissed as a mere left wing agenda, nor can it be placed in opposition to the church's mission in the world. Structural church reform is essential precisely in order that the church might better fulfill its mission in the world. In the second part I will propose that since justice is constitutive of the church's mission, the church's reality as sacrament of salvation and seed of the kingdom demands that the church's teaching on social justice be applied to the church itself as the basis for ongoing structural church reform.

RETRIEVING KEY CONCILIAR TEACHINGS ON THE NATURE AND MISSION OF THE CHURCH

As a way of developing the ecclesiological connections between church reform and church mission I would like to highlight two themes found in the *Dogmatic Constitution on the Church, Lumen gentium*: the church as universal sacrament of salvation and the church as seed of the kingdom of God.

The Church as Sacrament   *Schillebeeckx, church*

Catholicism has a long tradition of theological reflection on the place of the sacraments in the life of the church. The council, however, recovered a more ancient Christian conviction that the church not only administered the sacraments, it was itself a kind of sacrament.[5] Already in the first document considered by the council, the *Constitution on the Sacred Liturgy*, we find this statement:

> This work of human redemption and perfect glorification of God, foreshadowed by the wonders which God performed among the people of the Old Testament, Christ the Lord completed principally in the paschal mystery of his blessed passion, resurrection from the dead, and glorious ascension, whereby "dying, he destroyed our death and rising, restored our life." For it was from the side of Christ as he slept the sleep of death upon the cross that there came forth the wondrous sacrament of the whole church. (*SC*, 5)

This passage highlights the paschal mystery and thus already suggests the council's consistent emphasis on the church as a sacrament of salvation. In article 9 of *Lumen gentium* the council notes that God ". . . has, however, willed to make women and men holy and to save them, not as individuals without any bond between them, but rather to make them into a people who might acknowledge him and serve him in holiness." It is in this corporate work of salvation that the church can be a sign to the world:

> All those, who in faith look towards Jesus, the author of salvation and the source of unity and peace, God has gathered together and established as the church, that it may be for each and everyone the visible sacrament of saving unity. In order to extend to all regions of the earth, it enters into human history, though it transcends at once all time and all boundaries between peoples. (*LG*, 9)

Later in article 48 the church is referred to as the "universal sacrament of salvation" (cf. *AG*, 1, 5). This theme would be carried forward in the *Pastoral Constitution on the Church in the Modern World*. That remarkable document firmly situated the church within the world as a sign to the world of God's redemptive love.

Wherein lies the sacramentality of the church? If bread and wine are essential to the sacrament of the Eucharist because they serve as efficacious signs of a new sacramental reality, then what is it in the church that functions as an efficacious sign? The answer can only be, everything that comprises the church in its visible reality. The church certainly serves as a sacrament before the world in its members' ordinary life-witness to the values of the gospel, but also in its church law, offices, and ecclesial practices—all of these visible manifestations of the church participate in the church's sacramental reality. This leads to a second question: If the whole of the church's visible reality participates in the church's sacramentality, what does this visible reality actually signify, that is, what does the church as sacrament "make present" to the world? In the language of scholastic sacramental theology, what is the *res* of the church as sacrament? Seeking an answer to this question leads us to a second conciliar theme, the relationship between the church and the kingdom of God.

The Church and the Kingdom of God

At a relatively late stage in the history of *Lumen gentium*, a proposal was made by several Latin American bishops to incorporate into the document the biblical metaphor of the reign or kingdom of God. Although this proposal came too late to allow the theme to be integrated into the whole of the document, it does appear in several significant passages. For example, in article 5 of *Lumen gentium* the council asserted boldly that the church does not exist for its own sake but in service of the coming reign of God: "Henceforward the church, equipped with the gifts of its founder and faithfully observing his precepts of charity, humility and self-denial, receives the mission of proclaiming and establishing among all peoples the kingdom of Christ and of God, and is, on earth, the seed and the beginning of that kingdom" (*LG*, 5). Later in that same document the council refers to the church as a "messianic people" and asserts that as such the church's destiny is realized in that "kingdom of God which has been begun by God himself on earth and which must be further extended until it is brought to perfection by him at the end of time when Christ our life, will appear and 'creation itself also will be delivered from its slavery to corruption into the freedom of the glory of the sons and daughters of God'" (*LG*, 9). Here again the power of the biblical image of the kingdom of God, an image that so dominated Jesus' own preaching, is evoked. In the teaching of the council, the kingdom of God, which was manifested in human history as Jesus Christ, continues as a force in history and will find its consummation only in the eschaton. The church exists in human history as "the seed" and beginning of this kingdom.

Pope John Paul II, in his encyclical *Redemptoris missio*, gave this theme a much fuller exposition. The pope stresses the inseparability of Jesus and the kingdom of God. He begins by developing the biblical image of the kingdom of God in the teaching and ministry of Jesus, noting that the "proclamation and establishment of God's kingdom" constituted the essential purpose of Jesus' mission (*RM*, 13). Jesus revealed the kingdom, not just in his teaching but "in his actions and his own person" (*RM*, 14). Central to the manifestation of the kingdom of God are Jesus' ministries of healing and forgiving, ministries that result in transformed human relationships. The kingdom thereby grows "as people slowly learn to love, forgive and serve one another" (*RM*, 15).

> The kingdom's nature, therefore, is one of communion among all human beings—with one another and with God. The kingdom is the concern of everyone: individuals, society, and the world. Working for the kingdom means acknowledging and promoting God's activity, which is present in human history and transforms it. Building the kingdom means working for liberation from evil in all its forms. In a word, the kingdom of God is the manifestation and the realization of God's plan of salvation in all its fullness. (*RM*, 15)

The pope warns against overly reductive interpretations of the kingdom of God that focus exclusively on the socioeconomic and political spheres of human existence without reference to their transcendent horizon. This last point is crucial; the pope does not deny the social and political dimensions of the kingdom of God but only the removal of any transcendent reference (*RM*, 17). At the same time he warns against completely severing the relationship between the kingdom of God, Christ, and the church (*RM*, 18).

As the pope looks to the origins of Christianity, he sees service to the kingdom of God as the "very raison d'être" of the early church. He reiterates the teaching of the council, affirming that the church is a seed of the kingdom to the extent that it preaches Christ and promotes gospel values.

The Church as Sacrament of the Kingdom

In his encyclical on mission, the pope went beyond the conciliar documents by explicitly considering the relationship between these two themes, the church as sacrament and the church as seed of the kingdom of God. He wrote:

> The many dimensions of the kingdom of God do not weaken the foundations and purposes of missionary activity, but rather strengthen and extend them. The

> Church is the sacrament of salvation for all humankind, and her activity is not limited only to those who accept her message. She is a dynamic force in mankind's journey toward the eschatological kingdom, and is the sign and promoter of gospel values. (*RM*, 20)

Combining the two themes of church as sacrament of salvation and church as seed and sign of the kingdom, it is possible to speak of the church as a sacrament of the kingdom of God. As such the church must be vigilant to insure that its whole visible reality—its institutions, offices, and practices—functions as an effective sign of that kingdom.

By means of this somewhat lengthy excursus on the teaching of the council and John Paul II, I have tried to lay out the theological foundations for what follows: a theological argument for the necessity of ongoing structural church reform. The argument proceeds in several steps. First, we begin with the kingdom of God as a divine, historical dynamism, fully manifest in Christ, which works toward the transformation of all human relationships. It is evident wherever people "learn to love, forgive, and serve one another." This transformative divine presence in history can never be captured in any one ideology, for it will find its final consummation only in the eternity of divine communion. Second, the church is an efficacious sign or sacrament of this kingdom. It serves the liberative presence of God in history. Third, the church's status as sacrament and seed of God's reign is grounded in its total visible reality; it is only as a visible, historical reality that the church can be sacrament of salvation and seed of the kingdom. Fourth, this visible reality, as the indispensable basis of the church's status as sacrament and seed of the kingdom, is comprised of the church's teaching, institutional structures, communal practices and policies, and the witness to holiness of its members. In other words, to assert the sacramentality of the church is to assert that all things pertaining to the church's visibility matter. Church structures and policies can never be merely functional, merely "in-house" realities for a church that claims to be itself a sacrament of the kingdom. Any aspect of the church that makes it present to the world shares in its sacramentality. To the extent that these visible ecclesial realities are in keeping with the values of the kingdom of God, they share in the church's sacramentality. To the extent that any church structure, teaching, or policy is counter to the kingdom, it diminishes the church's sacramentality.

It is the commitment to the sacramentality of the church that renders questions of institutional/structural church reform more than a matter of church housekeeping or the rearrangement of ecclesiastical furniture. For the church to be an effective sacrament of the kingdom of God one must be able to see in the whole visible reality of the church a "seed and sign" of that kingdom. When the visage of the church before the world reflects instead values and practices counter to the kingdom of God, the church's sacramentality is thereby compromised, and its mission undermined.

A fifth step in this argument moves from the common teaching of both Vatican II and Pope John Paul II that the church is a sacrament of salvation, a sign and seed of the kingdom, to an important development in the teaching of the 1971 world synod of bishops. In the introduction to their statement, *Justice in the World*,[6] the bishops wrote that "action on behalf of justice and participation in the transformation of the world fully appear to us as a constitutive dimension of the preaching of the Gospel, or, in other words, of the Church's mission for the redemption of the human race and its liberation from every oppressive situation." In that document the bishops boldly claimed that the church must not only offer to the world its rich social teaching, it must embody that teaching in its structures and practices: "While the Church is bound to give witness to justice, she recognizes that anyone who ventures to speak to people about justice must first be just in their eyes. Hence we must undertake an examination of the modes of acting and of the possessions and life style found within the Church itself" (*JW*, 3). This passage suggests that one way to enhance the church's mission as a sacrament of the kingdom of God in the world is for the church to embody in its own structures and practices the very gospel values it wishes to offer to modern society.

THE CHURCH AS VISIBLE SIGN OF GOSPEL JUSTICE

Following the lead of the 1971 synodal document, let us consider some applications of Catholic social teaching to the life of the church that might serve as the basis for church reform.

Solidarity with the Poor

Justice in the World dared to apply the church's developed social teaching on economic justice to its own policies and procedures for the administration of the temporal goods of the church as an expression of its solidarity with the poor. At the minimum, this solidarity with the poor would challenge the sometimes-affluent lifestyle of the "leadership class" in the church. In an era of unfortunate church closings in diocese after diocese, ostentatious church offices and episcopal residences often appear as a scandalous countersign to the church's commitment to the poor. In the face of a U.S. economy that was sent reeling just two years ago by a series of corporate scandals in which dubious accounting practices proliferated, the effective witness of the church would also seem to require a much greater transparency and accountability in its own financial affairs. The church's administration of its temporal goods must be a witness to the world of what responsible stewardship of financial resources might mean.

Labor Rights

Justice in the World applied the Catholic teaching on the laborer's right to a just wage to its own treatment of those who work for the church. Far too many Catholic employees in diocesan offices, parishes, and schools receive considerably less than a fair wage and often work without the kind of basic contractual protection and benefits assumed for commensurate positions in the private sector. The unionization of church employees is frequently discouraged as employees are told that their work should be viewed as a "vocation" or "ministry" that therefore cannot be compared to correlative positions in the secular business world. This avoids the fact, however, that many of these church employees, unlike the clergy who often hire them, have families to provide for. Moreover, while women constitute the majority of lay church employees in both schools and parishes, they often encounter a church version of the "glass ceiling" as regards key positions for which they are canonically eligible. Standardized personnel policies, such as established procedures for job performance reviews or the adjudication of employee grievances, are still the exception rather than the norm.

Respectful Relationships — *compare to Buckley*

Catholic social teaching has consistently emphasized the importance of encouraging authentic forms of community constituted by relationships and institutional structures predicated on the dignity of each human person. Social and political relationships, as those between government officials and the governed, must be characterized by dialogue and mutual respect. The gospel would seem to challenge any social relationships based on a social stratification or elitism that would undermine the dignity of all persons.

In the light of this teaching the Catholic church must seriously examine its own tendency to apply titles and other ecclesiastical honorifics to those called to church service, much as it must concern itself with the real dangers of ecclesiastical careerism. When diplomats and curial officials are given episcopal titles without authentic pastoral charges to living communities of faith, when loyal priests are made "monsignor" in recognition of service and/or church loyalty, ordained ministries of service risk losing their evangelical character and the conditions are created for a kind of ecclesial elitism or clericalism. The practice of transferring bishops from diocese to diocese, a practice roundly condemned in the early church as constituting an ecclesiastical "divorce" between a bishop and his church, encourages bishops in "minor sees" to make decisions with an eye toward, not the needs of their flock, but the possibility of ecclesiastical advancement.

Participation and Dialogue

Catholic social teaching stresses the value of political participation and need for open civic discourse. The United States was built on a tradition of civil discourse. Yet this discourse has been corrupted in the last few decades by what can only be called the "politics of demonization." This failure of conversation is often played out on various cable news networks and talk radio stations where the demonizing of one's opponents and the imputation of ill will to those with whom one disagrees substitutes for respectful public conversation. When serious public debate fails to go beyond petty name-calling and the application of "spin" to every partisan issue, our country moves another step further away from the participatory democracy that our founders had in mind.

This crisis of civil discourse makes it all the more important that the church, in its structures and practices, embody another form of discourse, one characterized by open and charitable dialogue. The Second Vatican Council, recognizing that Christians of good will may at times disagree with one another regarding the demands of the gospel, exhorted Christians to "try to guide each other by sincere dialogue in a spirit of mutual charity and with a genuine concern for the common good above all" (*GS*, 43). Authentic dialogue means neither demonizing opposing views nor granting the equal truth of all possible positions. Authentic dialogue does not mean compromising one's convictions; it presumes that one will give an impassioned account of one's convictions, of what one holds to be true. But authentic dialogue does demand the courage to genuinely hear the other and to be open to the possibility that one's conversation partner may bring new insight, and perhaps even expose flaws in one's own position. When bishops refuse to meet with church groups who may be critical of church policies or even its doctrine, they offer a clear counterexample of the failure of church leadership to heed the demands of open and charitable dialogue.

The 1971 synod also called for greater participation of the laity in church decision-making. In the recent postsynodal exhortation, *Pastores Gregis*, on the office of the bishop, Pope John Paul II considers the exercise of church governance within the framework of communion.[7] The document advocates "open collaboration" and "a type of reciprocal interplay between what a bishop is called to decide with personal responsibility for the good of the church entrusted to his care and the contribution that the faithful can offer him through consultative bodies such as the diocesan synod, the presbyteral council, the episcopal council and the pastoral council" (*PG*, 44). The pope asserts that

the church is an organically structured community which finds expression in the coordination of different charisms, ministries and services for the sake of attaining the common end, which is salvation. The bishop is responsible for bringing about this unity in diversity by promoting, as was stated in the synodal assembly, a collaborative effort which makes it possible for all to journey together along the common path of faith and mission. (*PG*, 44)

Yet further on he states that

> if communion expresses the church's essence, then it is normal that the spirituality of communion will tend to manifest itself in both the personal and community spheres, awakening ever new forms of participation and shared responsibility in the faithful of every category. Consequently, the bishop will make every effort to develop within his particular church structures of communion and participation which make it possible to listen to the Spirit, who lives and speaks in the faithful, in whatever the same Spirit suggests for the true good of the church. (*PG*, 44)

One often hears the slogan, "the church is not a democracy," yet almost never does one hear its necessary ecclesiological correlate, "neither is the church a monarchy or an oligarchy." In fact, the church cannot be compared to any single political model for it is, uniquely, a spiritual communion constituted as such by the power of the Holy Spirit. Within the life of the church, unlike an oligarchy, power is not to be located in a select few. Ecclesiologically, power proceeds from baptism as a gift of the Spirit and can be defined as *the capacity to fulfill one's baptismal call and engage in effective action in service of the church's life and mission.* The power we receive through Christian initiation enables us to fulfill our calling as disciples of Jesus. We are empowered to share the good news of Jesus Christ, to pursue holiness, to love our neighbor, to care for the least, to work for justice, and to build up the body of Christ through the exercise of our particular gifts in service of the church. Power cannot be considered apart from a concrete ecclesial relationship, whether that relationship is constituted by sacramental initiation or ordination.

If the church is not an oligarchy, it is also not a liberal democratic polity; the church does not, and ought not, make decisions based on the aggregate majority of private opinions on a given matter. As a spiritual communion bound to discern the will of God, the church should avoid any kind of majoritarianism. Its task is to cultivate a "holy conversation" in which each participant actualizes the *sensus fidei* (supernatural instinct for the faith) they received at baptism in order to discern the will of God rather than their private desires or preferences. These ecclesial discernment processes will acknowledge the indispensable role of ordained church leadership as unique guardians of the apostolic faith while also remaining open to the prophetic voice that so often emerges outside of established institutional structures.

Subsidiarity

Finally, the demand for structural reform in the church would seem to require a thorough implementation of the principle of subsidiarity that first appeared in Catholic social teaching in *Quadragesimo anno*. Put simply, the principle of subsidiarity holds that higher levels of a society should not take on tasks and functions that can be accomplished better at lower levels. Pope Pius XII extended the sphere of application of this principle to the church when he observed in 1946 that this principle, "valid for social life in all its grades," was valid "also for the life of the church without prejudice to its hierarchical structure."[8] The principle was not explicitly mentioned in the documents of Vatican II, though several commentators believe it is implicit in several passages.[9]

The application of subsidiarity to the life of the church requires that we transpose the sociopolitical principle into the ecclesiological framework determined by the integrity of the local church "in and out of which" the universal church is manifested (*LG*, 8). If we admit that, at least analogically, it can be applied to the church, we might reformulate that principle as follows: *The pastoral authority with direct responsibility for a local community must have primary responsibility for pastoral ministry within that community and is expected to address, without external intervention, the pastoral issues that emerge there. Only when these issues appear insoluble at the local level and/or threaten the faith and unity of the church universal should one expect the intervention of "higher authority."*

Sound ecclesiology demands the preservation of the full integrity of the local church as the concrete presence of the one church of Christ in that place. Any exercise of authority at a level beyond the local can never be undertaken in a way that undermines that local church's integrity. The exercise of "higher authority" must always be a means toward preserving the integrity of the local church and its communion with the other churches.

Richard McBrien once observed that one of the most significant features of Vatican II's important document, *Gaudium et spes*, was that it shifted Catholic social teaching from the framework of moral theology and the virtue of "justice" to that of ecclesiology and the church's mission in the world.[10] While the claim might be overstated, it is essentially valid. The call for justice is indeed a constitutive dimension of the church's mission to be a universal sacrament of salvation and a first seed and sign of the kingdom of God before the world. To the extent that the church's own structures and practices are viewed as unjust, its mission is compromised. The statement of the bishops in *Justice in the World* over thirty years ago remains valid: "anyone who ventures to speak to people about justice must first be just in their eyes" (*JW*, 3).

NOTES

1. I have in mind such important figures as Jacques Bossuet, Johann Adam Möhler, John Henry Newman, Adrién Gréa, and Hermann Schell.

2. Yves Congar, *Vrai et fausse réforme dans l'Église* (Paris: Cerf, 1969, originally published in 1950).

3. For the English translation of the pope's opening address see Walter M. Abbott, ed., *The Documents of Vatican II* (New York: Crossroad, 1989), 5: 710–19.

4. See for example, Joseph Ratzinger, "A Company in Constant Renewal" in *Called to Communion: Understanding the Church Today* (San Francisco: Ignatius, 1996), 133–56. According to Peter Feuerherd, this viewpoint is held by the influential American Cardinal Archbishop of Chicago, Francis George. Feuerherd writes: "One of George's favorite themes is that the church has spent enough time focusing on itself and now must spend more time on the work of conversion. He sees evangelization as the solution to perennial problems such as the looming priest shortage." See Peter Feuerherd, "Chicago Catholic: A Profile of Cardinal Francis George," *Commonweal* 131, <http://69.93.235.8/article.php?id_article=826> (14 Jan. 2004).

5. The retrieval of this insight was accomplished by a number of important theological works being published just prior to or during the council itself. See Edward Schillebeeckx, *Christ the Sacrament of the Encounter with God* (Kansas City: Sheed & Ward, 1963); Otto Semmelroth, *Church and Sacrament* (Notre Dame: Fides, 1965); Karl Rahner, *The Church and the Sacraments* (New York: Crossroad, 1963).

6. In *Catholic Social Thought: The Documentary Heritage*, ed. David J. O'Brien and Thomas Shannon (Maryknoll: Orbis, 1992).

7. Pope John Paul II, *Pastores Gregis, Origins* 33 (November 6, 2003): 353–92.

8. Pope Pius XII made this statement in an address to newly created cardinals, *AAS* 38 (1946): 144–45. He reaffirmed the ecclesial implications of the principle of subsidiarity in an address to the Second World Congress of the Lay Apostolate in 1957. See *AAS* 49 (1957): 926–28.

9. Joseph Komonchak, "Subsidiarity and the Church: The State of the Question," *Jurist* 48 (1988): 298–349, at 309–12. It is disappointing that *Pastores Gregis* referred to the ecclesial application of this principle as "ambiguous" (*PG* 56).

10. Richard McBrien, "Catholic Social Action," *National Catholic Reporter* (3 Mar. 1987): 7–8.

6: LOOKING GOOD VS. BEING GOOD: PITFALLS OF MAINTAINING PERCEPTIONS OF STRONG LEADERSHIP FOLLOWING ORGANIZATIONAL SCANDALS

Kimberly D. Elsbach

Our perceptions about what "good leaders" look like (e.g., what they say, what they do) are shaped by a number of stereotypical traits that we assign to leaders. I discuss how maintaining perceptions of each of these traits may actually hinder effective leadership in the wake of corporate scandals. I illustrate these pitfalls of "looking like a strong leader" with the case of the 2001–2002 sex abuse scandal in the U.S. Roman Catholic Church. Then, I present some guidelines for effective perception management following organizational scandals, and I conclude with an example of this form of management.

Consider the following events: the disclosure that auto corporation executives had driven over sixty thousand cars with unhooked odometers before selling them as new; the revelation that corporate accountants had kept millions of dollars of losses off the books to improve performance indicators; and the reporting of widespread overcharging of auto repair customers linked to an organizational quota system for selling brakes and other common parts. These are all examples of organizational scandals that, all too commonly, threaten the legitimacy and trustworthiness of the associated organization.

Most audiences view such scandals as the result of avarice by top managers of the organization and, thus, perceive them as high in preventability.[1] As a result, organizational audiences are typically critical of organizational scandals, even if they are not personally harmed by the events themselves. This critical judgment commonly affects organizational images of legitimacy and trustworthiness, as well as long-standing organizational reputations for integrity (i.e., audiences feel that past, reputation-enhancing events are suspect and that the organization may not deserve its enduring categorization as a high-status company).[2]

Because of their perceived central role in organizational scandals, organizational leaders are expected to carry out perception management tasks, that is, actions designed to protect or repair audiences' perceptions of the organization, in the wake of these types of crises.[3] Researchers suggest that audiences focus centrally on the actions and accounts of organizational leaders when things go badly, at least in part, because of their romanticized notions of leadership.[4] Such romanticized notions include a number of stereotypical traits that we ascribe to "good leaders" and that help us trust what leaders say and do following crisis events.[5] These stereotypic traits include: (1) *control* (i.e., the belief that leaders have the final say in important decisions and that they are in charge of what happens), (2) *competence* and *consistency* (i.e., the beliefs that leaders will make the right decisions and will remain consistent in the thinking that guides those decisions over time), and (3) absolute *certainty* (i.e., the belief that leaders are completely certain about the things they say and do).

At the same time, social-psychological research suggests that maintaining such stereotypical images may require leaders to engage in behaviors that counter what scholars know about effective leadership.[6] That is, most laypersons' stereotypic conceptions of strong leadership may be inconsistent with what effective leaders actually do. These paradoxes or "stereotype traps" may mean that short-term gains in leadership images (and repair of organizational images) may, ultimately, give way to long-term ineffectiveness in leadership performance. Further, it appears that maintaining the first of these traits (i.e., control) may produce a cascading effect in which the other traits (i.e., competence, consistency, and certainty) must also be maintained.

LEADERSHIP STEREOTYPE TRAPS

To explore these stereotype traps (i.e., traps that leaders find themselves in when they attempt to fit stereotypes of strong leadership) more fully, I discuss each of the leadership stereotypes described above and how leaders' maintenance of such stereotypes might undermine their leadership effectiveness in the wake of an organizational scandal. I illustrate these stereotype traps with evidence from a case study of the 2001–2002 sex abuse scandal in the U.S. Catholic Church (i.e., the scandal arising from the revelation that priests known to be pedophiles were repeatedly reassigned to new parishes where their abuse continued). Finally, I discuss how organizations and their leaders may engage in effective perception management (i.e., tactics designed to influence audience's perceptions of leaders) following organizational scandals.

The Control Trap

Probably the most common trait laypersons ascribe to "strong leadership" is control. We expect strong leaders to be "in charge" and running the show.[7] Our image of a strong leader includes a mental picture of former U.S. President Harry Truman, with his famous "the buck stops here" sign on his desk. We want to know that, when all is said and done, the person at the top has the final say.

Psychologists suggest that this need to have one person in control stems from our desires to reduce uncertainty and to have leaders fulfill our expectations about what strong leaders "look like."[8] That is, as humans, we like to be able to predict the events that may affect our lives. If we perceive that one person is in charge of these events (vs. numerous people) and that one person conforms to our prototype of a strong leader, then it is easier for us to predict what life-altering events might occur.

Yet, leaders who attempt to convince others that they have strong, central control over their organization may also convince audiences (and themselves) that the views and input of others are neither important, nor necessary for decision making. In turn, the *expertise of advisors may eventually be withdrawn*. Over time, leaders themselves may begin to believe their own perception management and fall prey to *illusions of control* (i.e., unrealistically high perceptions about their degree of control over the outcomes of events[9]) and *overconfidence* (i.e., unrealistically high perceptions about their likelihood of obtaining desired outcomes[10]). If such perceptions are contradictory to what the public sees (i.e., the public sees evidence that the leader actually lacks control), then continued expressions of control may be seen as both arrogance and hubris, and ultimately lead to loss of respect and trust for the leader.

Such mistaken confidence in one's own abilities can be seen over and over in Boston Archdiocese Cardinal Law's responses to the sex abuse issues in the Catholic Church. Given his high ranking in the U.S. Catholic Church, Cardinal Law became a central figure among church leaders. Yet, his overconfidence in his own abilities led him to discount the advice of others. For example, in response to early complaints of sex abuse by priests in the 1980s, many church members offered advice (based on scientific research) and service in helping the church to handle pedophiles. This advice was routinely discounted and ignored by Cardinal Law. As Reverend Thomas P. Doyle, a Catholic Air Force chaplain who had written a 1985 report on the problem of clergy sexual abuse while working as a canon lawyer at the Vatican Embassy in Washington, reported: "The Catholic hierarchy has stonewalled any attempts to do any kind of study on this issue, and they've had offers to do it."[11]

Later, following the publication of a *Boston Globe* opinion poll, which found that nearly half of all Boston-area Catholics wanted Cardinal Law to resign because of his poor handling of abusive priests, the cardinal resolutely announced that he had no intention of stepping down. Instead, he claimed that he, alone, would be the best person to guide the church through the current crisis. As he stated in a homily given the day after the opinion poll was published:

> I believe that, with regard to the issue at hand, that by the experience of being here when all of this was taking place, I have the ability to do something as bishop to make things better for the future, and I think that it would not serve that cause of protecting children if I were, at this point, to submit my resignation to the Holy Father. . . . Beyond that, it's important to remember that a bishop is not a corporate executive, is not a politician . . . the role of a bishop in relationship to the church he serves is something different. It's the role of a pastor, the role of a teacher, the role of a father.[12]

These comments suggest overconfidence and illusions of control by the cardinal, especially given the public sentiment at the time. As one victim of abuse stated, "I'm enraged at the arrogance and the hypocrisy of this leader who considers himself a father. A father doesn't trick or deceive his sons and daughters." Another protestor against Cardinal Law remarked, "It seems like he's intent on ignoring all of this."

As a result, there was evidence that even those Catholics who supported Cardinal Law were beginning to withdraw from the process and the dialogue. As one woman noted, "I think the anger is incredible—and there's a feeling of great helplessness. We don't know how to demand change because we have no power."[13]

Finally, months later, when the movement to remove him from his position had gained considerable momentum, the cardinal remained resolute in his place as the unquestioned leader in the Boston archdiocese. After meeting with other Catholic bishops for several days in April, the cardinal sent a letter to priests in his archdiocese stating that he would not step down. Because a majority of U.S. Catholics were now unsupportive of Cardinal Law's leadership, his continued affirmation of control over his archdiocese appeared to be both a sign of arrogance and a signal that the cardinal was still suffering from illusions of control and overconfidence. As one priest noted: "For him to think that he can be of any value in this role is proof in itself that he doesn't understand that he's a culprit, that what he's done is in many ways as damaging as what the priests have done. The very fact that he doesn't get that makes him incapable of participating in the solution."[14] An abuse victim echoed this sentiment: "This is like a criminal telling me, 'Listen, I am the best person to prevent break-ins because I've done them in the past.' This is a criminal activity, as far as I'm concerned. For him to even have the audacity to stay—he's operating in the surreal."[15]

This continued evidence of a "control" image presented by Cardinal Law and other top church leaders is important, not only because it reduced input by experts and appeared to support the cardinal's overconfidence and illu-

the best experts are plain Cath faithful

sions of control, but also because it appeared to induce a cascade of related perception management by church leaders. Specifically, in maintaining an image of control, the cardinal also made it important that he be seen as competent, consistent, and certain as a leader—since these traits were important to justifying his control over the Boston archdiocese. As I note below, these leadership stereotypes may have further hampered effective leadership by Cardinal Law.

The Competency and Consistency Trap

In addition to being in control, we like to think of our leaders as unfailingly competent at the jobs they do,[16] as well as consistent in the ideals that guide their actions.[17] We have chosen them, specifically, because we view them as competent decision-makers and policy implementers.[18] Further, we view leaders who change their minds to be untrustworthy and weak-minded.[19] We pick our leaders for the long term (years vs. days). If we cannot count on a leader to maintain a competent and consistent set of actions over this long-term period, we may be unwilling to support him or her in the first place.

Despite the apparent rationality of these perspectives, the requirement for competency and consistency in our leaders becomes troublesome when it causes those in leadership positions to view their own occasional human mistakes (e.g., misjudgments, biased information search, unscientific analysis) as unacceptable. In such cases, the need to appear unfailingly competent often causes leaders to deny making human mistakes and to defend previous actions that led to undesirable outcomes. When combined with the need to appear consistent over time, such a stance can lead to an *escalating commitment to a failing course of action*.[20]

For example, early on in the sex abuse scandal, Cardinal Law staunchly defended his reassignment of priests who had been accused of child molestation to other parishes after they had received psychological counseling.[21] When the first cases of child abuse began to be publicized in the 1980s the Catholic leaders stood firm on their approach of counseling and prayer within the church, rather than following the advice of emerging scientific research which suggested that pedophiles are rarely "cured" of their sexual preferences. As the sex abuse cases mounted, Law and other church leaders continued to defend their earlier decisions, it appears, as a means of maintaining the correctness of these decisions and supporting their own images of competence. As Cardinal Law's lawyer put it: "each assignment of [an abusive priest], subsequent to the first complaint of sexual misconduct, was incident to an independent medical evaluation advising that such assignment was appropriate and safe."[22] Yet, church leaders never acknowledged that these evaluations were largely performed by one institution, which later claimed that the church had concealed past information about priests' behaviors and had largely ignored its recommendations regarding reassignment of priests to new parishes.[23]

A second problem resulting from defending leadership competency and consistency is that if obviously wrong and recurrent actions cannot be attributed to incompetence, then the most likely alternative explanation is that they are due to a lack of integrity. This is because incompetence and lack of integrity are the most commonly found traits associated with untrustworthy behavior by leaders.[24] If Cardinal Law did not commit the untrustworthy behavior of reassigning abusive priests because he was incompetent (i.e., he wrongly discounted the research on pedophilia because he didn't understand it or know about it, or he failed to keep close watch on the actions of individual priests because he didn't think he had to), then he must have taken these wrong actions because he lacked integrity (e.g., he didn't want to bring attention to the problem and was protecting his own image at the cost of children's safety). Thus, in explaining the reasons for an untrustworthy action, leaders may trade a "violation of competency" for a "violation of integrity."[25] Yet, *such a trade-off can be even more damaging to a leader's effectiveness than the original bad act* because incompetence may be viewed as a trait that can be corrected (i.e., through training), while lack of integrity is typically viewed as a trait that is innate.

The Certainty Trap

Related to the stereotypic trait of leadership consistency is the trait of leadership certainty. Leaders are expected to speak in absolute terms with regard to their beliefs and intentions. This means that what they say can be trusted, and what they propose to do can be counted on to be done.[26]

Yet, certainty at one point in time may easily become uncertainty a few moments later. Information that was thought to be iron-clad can turn out to be incomplete or inaccurate. Data that were used to make predictions can be found to be unreliable or invalid due to the way they were collected or measured. As the saying goes, "the only things certain in life are death and taxes." Leaders who must backtrack on statements—especially statements made with expressions of certainty—may *lose the trust of audiences* regarding all future statements.

This need for absolute certainty caused problems for Cardinal Law in the wake of the sex abuse scandal. After finally admitting that rehabilitation of priests through counseling and prayer was not an effective approach, the cardinal moved to remove a large number of priests, who had been accused (but not convicted) of abuse, from contact with children. When asked if any priests who had committed sexual abuse of minors remained in active service, the cardinal repeatedly claimed that he was certain that none remained. As he asserted in a press conference on January 25, 2002:

There is no priest known to us to have been guilty of the sexual abuse of a minor holding any position in this archdiocese. . . . We cannot and we do not put people into positions now who have been guilty of sexual abuse. . . . I can tell you that there is no priest presently assigned anywhere who is, as far as we know, guilty of sexual abuse. . . . As I have indicated, there is no priest, or former priest, working in this archdiocese in any assignment whom we know to have been responsible for sexual abuse. I hope you get that straight.[27]

Yet, only eight days after making these assertions, Cardinal Law's archdiocese removed two more priests from Boston-area parishes, having discovered that both men had been accused of sexually abusing children in the past. These events caused church officials to admit that there might be priests guilty of molesting children who were still working in parishes and who would be removed as relevant evidence was uncovered.[28]

Not surprisingly, these comments further weakened the trust parishioners held for the leadership of the Catholic Church, including Cardinal Law. As the *Boston Globe* reported:

[Raymond L.] Flynn [former mayor of Boston and U.S. ambassador to the Vatican], like other Catholics interviewed in recent days, said he is increasingly making a distinction between his faith in God, which he said remains intact, and his attitude toward the church hierarchy. "I don't go to church because I pray to the priest or the bishop or the cardinal—I go to church because I pray to God to make me a better person," [Flynn] said.[29]

Similarly, another church member commented: "I'm a lifelong Catholic— I can show you the scars from Sister Gertrude's ruler in second grade—and I'm very much committed to the church. But to see the shortcomings of the leadership under this microscope is just very saddening. I'll be a Roman Catholic until the day I die, but I'm angry."[30]

The combined effects of the events described above appeared to critically damage audiences' trust in Cardinal Law. Over time, it became apparent to church leaders that this eroded trust could not be recovered with Law in his current position of leadership. On December 13, 2002, Cardinal Bernard F. Law resigned his post.

EFFECTIVE PERCEPTION MANAGEMENT FOLLOWING SCANDALS: ADMISSIONS OF INCOMPETENCE, CEDING CONTROL, AND DEVELOPING NEW LINES OF CONSISTENCY

In the wake of scandals, such as the one described above, effective perception management appears to require organizations and their leaders to resist inclinations to conform to stereotypes of strong leadership. Instead, the most effective words and deeds that organizations can use following scandals appear to run in the opposite direction, including admitting incompetence (at least in terms of human failings), ceding control (at least temporarily), and giving up traditional mantras in favor of new ideals.

First, it's important that leaders admit some incompetence in their initial accounts or explanations of the negative event.[31] Because scandals are typically shown to be the result of deliberate organizational actions, accounts that deny responsibility for them (e.g., excuses or denials) are not likely to be viewed as credible. Instead, apologies or justifications (which admit responsibility for the scandalous actions) are more likely to be accepted by audiences. Of these two types of accounts, apologies are often preferred following scandals that call into question an organization's integrity because such scandals often involve actions, such as criminal activities, that are hard to justify at any level.[32]

Effective apologies combine both an admission of blameworthiness and human failings ("we were wrong," "we made a human error") with a promise that the problem that led to the scandal has been isolated and resolved ("we won't let this happen again").[33] In this way, apologies are designed to convince the audience that the undesirable event should not be considered a "fair representation" of what the organization is really like or will be like in the future.[34] As Schlenker notes: "Blame must be attached to a 'self' that no longer exists or has changed sufficiently that audiences do not need to be concerned about a repeat of the offense. A current 'good' self is split off from the past 'bad' self that was responsible for the undesirable offense."[35]

Second, organizational leaders must, at least temporarily, cede control in the remaking of the organization. One of the most effective means of "proving" that an organization is currently distinct from the organization that caused a scandal is to take reparative actions that alter the organization's core structures or procedures (e.g., changing leadership). Such actions demonstrate a concern for the welfare of harmed audiences and provide "proof" of an organization's commitment to "righting the wrong" in situations where mere explanations and accounts would be met with suspicion.[36]

Finally, reparative actions that involve changes to fundamental organizational structures and practices—such as changing the nature of evaluation and training programs—help audiences focus on the future of the organization, rather than on its past. Such a focus allows organizational leaders to give up old mantras (e.g., counseling and prayer are enough to cure pedophiles) that have lost their credibility and concentrate on reestablishing a history of credible behavior and re-earning a reputation for integrity.

EXAMPLE: EFFECTIVE PERCEPTION
MANAGEMENT AT SOLOMON BROTHERS

An example of successful reputation management through the use of admissions of incompetence, ceding control, and reestablishing new lines of consistency involves the investment bank, Solomon Brothers, and the scandal over its illegal attempts to corner the Treasury securities market in 1991.[37] At the time of the scandal, Solomon Brothers was viewed as the most powerful and respected broker on Wall Street. Then, in August 1991, Solomon Brothers announced that it had committed, "irregularities and rule violations in connection with its submission of bids in certain auctions of Treasury securities."[38] By the end of the year, the company faced forty-six lawsuits over charges of fraud, price manipulation, and misrepresentation in its securities dealings. The company's shares lost almost $500 million in market value in the first week following the scandal, and credit regulators downgraded the bank's debt and stock ratings.[39] Shortly after the scandal broke, an editorial in the *New York Times* characterized Solomon Brothers as a company governed by "a culture of greed, contempt for government regulations, and a sneering attitude toward ethics or any other impediments to earning a buck."[40] Clearly, the bank had damaged its reputation for integrity.

In response to the scandal, Solomon Brothers carried out a textbook case of effective reputation management. In addition to accepting responsibility for their actions, the Solomon board undertook swift and sweeping reparative actions designed to correct the problems that led to the fraudulent bidding behavior and to prevent it from happening again.

First, the board appointed Warren Buffet as the interim chairman of the bank. Known as "Mr. Clean," Buffet maintained a personal reputation for integrity that sent a strong signal to outsiders about the bank's values. In turn, Buffet appointed another veteran officer of Solomon, Deryck Maughan, known as "Mr. Integrity," to act as chief operating officer. Second, Buffet cooperated fully and openly with the regulators who had been assigned to investigate the bank, and hired an outside firm, Coopers and Lybrand, to conduct an internal audit of the company's entire trading operations. Third, Buffet undertook a major restructuring of the corporation, including firing over 140 analysts, bankers, and traders; reducing the power of the investment banking subsidiary of the company; and revising the pay systems that been largely blamed as a motivator for fraudulent trading behavior.[41] These actions demonstrated that the company was committed, over the long run, to operating in a trustworthy and ethical manner—not just to overcoming the short-term obstacles that had resulted from the scandal. Such acts also helped focus audiences' attention on the future of Solomon Brothers, rather than on the past actions that led to the scandal. By 1996 Solomon Brothers had reemerged as Wall Street's largest and most influential banks.[42]

CONCLUSION

In sum, while the story of Cardinal Law and the Catholic Church reveals the stereotype traps that may hinder effective perception management (and organizational recovery) following a scandal, the Solomon Brothers case illustrates how effective responses to organizational scandals can repair even widespread damage. The lessons of Cardinal Law and Solomon Brothers suggest that organizational leaders need to resist desires to maintain stereotypic leadership perceptions, even when "strong" leadership is what appears to be needed most. While potentially damaging in the short term, actions that indicate that the leader is learning from past mistakes are most likely to lead audiences to respect and trust the leader over time. As presidential nominee John Kerry summed up in his response to questions about his own apparent inconsistency and uncertainty, "It's one thing to be certain, but you can be certain and be wrong."[43] In the end, it may be better for a leader to be, temporarily, uncertain, inconsistent, and lacking in complete control, but on the path to being right.

NOTES

1. A. A. Marcus and R. S. Goodman, "Victims and Shareholders: The Dilemmas of Presenting Corporate Policy During a Crisis," *Academy of Management Journal* 34 (1991): 281–305.

2. C. Fombrun, *Reputation* (Boston: Harvard Business School Press, 1996).

3. R. I. Sutton and D. C. Galunic, "Consequences of Public Scrutiny for Leaders and Their Organizations," in *Research in Organizational Behavior*, ed. B. M. Staw and L. L. Cummings, vol. 18 (Greenwich, Conn.: JAI Press, 1996), 201–50; Marcus and Goodman, "Victims and Shareholders."

4. J. R. Meindl, S. B. Ehrlich, and J. M. Dukerich, "The Romance of Leadership," *Administrative Science Quarterly* 30 (1985): 78–102.

5. R. G. Lord, C. L. de Vader, and G. M. Alliger, "A Meta-analysis of the Relation Between Personality Traits and Leadership Perceptions: An Application of Validity Generalization Procedures," *Journal of Applied Psychology* 71 (1986): 402–10.

6. R. B. Cialdini, *Influence: The New Psychology of Modern Persuasion* (New York: Quill, 1984); J. Greenberg, "Looking Fair vs. Being Fair: Managing Impressions of Organizational Justice," in *Organizational Behavior*, ed. Staw and Cummings, vol. 12 (1990): 111–57.

7. Sutton and Galunic, "Public Scrutiny."

8. M. A. Hogg, "A Social Identity Theory of Leadership," *Personality & Social Psychology Review* 5 (2001): 184–200.

9. E. J. Langer, "The Illusion of Control," *Journal of Personality and Social Psychology* 32 (1975): 311–28.

10. S. Oskamp, "Overconfidence in Case Study Judgments," *Journal of Consulting Psychology* 29 (1965): 261–65.

11. M. Paulson, "All Faiths Question Handling of Abuse. Debate Over Celibacy as Factor Is Rancorous," *Boston Globe*, 13 Mar. 2002, 1(A).

12. M. Paulson, "A Resolute Law Repeats He Won't Go; Vows to Focus on Protections for Children," *Boston Globe*, 11 Feb. 2002, 1(A).

13. S. S. Greenberger and M. Kurtz, "Outside Cardinal's Headquarters, Protestors Multiply," *Boston Globe*, 18 Feb. 2002, 1(B).

14. S. Pfeiffer, "Law's Decision to Remain/Victims Protest. Abuse Victims Decry Cardinal's Letter as Insult," *Boston Globe*, 13 Apr. 2002, 4(B).

15. Pfeiffer, "Law's Decision," 4(B).

16. J. R. Meindl and S. B. Ehrlich, "The Romance of Leadership and the Evaluation of Organizational Performance," *Academy of Management Journal* 30 (1987): 91–109.

17. Cialdini, *Influence*.

18. Lord, de Vader, and Alliger, "Meta-analysis."

19. Cialdini, *Influence*.

20. B. M. Staw, "Knee-deep in the Big Muddy—A Study of Escalating Commitment to a Chosen Course of Action," *Organizational Behavior & Human Performance* 16 (1976): 27–44; J. Brockner, "The Escalation of Commitment to a Failing Course of Action: Toward Theoretical Progress," *Academy of Management Review* 17 (1992): 39–61.

21. M. Paulson, "The Cardinal's Apology; Actions Follow an Established Course," *Boston Globe,* 10 Jan. 2002, 1(A).

22. M. Paulson, "Law Defends His Response in Clergy Sex Abuse Case," *Boston Globe*, 27 July 2001, 1(A).

23. E. Rich and E. Hamilton, "Clinic Says It Was Deceived by Church; Asserts Information Withheld on Priests and Past Complaints," *Boston Globe*, 24 Mar. 2002, 33(A).

24. M. C. Clark and R. L. Payne, "The Nature and Structure of Workers' Trust in Management," *Journal of Organizational Behavior* 18 (1997): 205–24.

25. Clark and Payne, "Worker's Trust."

26. Clark and Payne, "Worker's Trust."

27. M. Rezendes and W. V. Robinson, "Two Priests Ousted after Abuse Cited. DA to Get Data on Randolph, Quincy Pastors," *Boston Globe*, 3 Feb. 2002, 1(A).

28. Rezendes and Robinson, "Two Priests."

29. M. Paulson, "Stung By Sex-abuse Cases, Catholics Call for Reform," *Boston Globe*, 4 Feb. 2002, 1(A).

30. Paulson, "Catholics Call," 1(A).

31. C. M. Pearson and J. A. Clair, "Reframing Crisis Management," *Academy of Management Review* 23 (1998): 59–76; B. M. Staw, P. I. McKechnie, and S. M. Puffer, "The Justification of Organizational Performance," *Administrative Science Quarterly* 28 (1983): 582–600.

32. K. M. Hearit, "Apologies and Public Relations Crisis at Chrysler, Toshiba, and Volvo," *Public Relations Review* 20 (1994): 113–25.

33. Hearit, "Apologies."

34. B. R. Schlenker, *Impression Management: The Self-concept, Social Identity, and Interpersonal Relations* (Monterey, Calif.: Brooks/Cole, 1980), 154.

35. Schlenker, *Impression Management*, 154.

36. Marcus and Goodman, "Victims and Shareholders."

37. Fombrun, *Reputation*.

38. Quoted in Fombrun, *Reputation*, 365.

39. Fombrun, *Reputation*.

40. "Editorial," *New York Times*, 22 Aug. 1991, 26(A).

41. Fombrun, *Reputation*.

42. Fombrun, *Reputation*.

43. Associated Press, *Transcript of Thursday's Presidential Debate*, transcribed by e-Media Millworks, 1 Oct. 2004.

ETHICS, ORGANIZATIONS, AND CHURCH CULTURE

7: TOWARD AN ECCLESIAL PROFESSIONAL ETHICS

James F. Keenan

Clerical cultures, episcopal cultures, and the cultures of religious life do not regularly promote for their own members an awareness of the goods and benefits that are engaged by the practice of critical ethical thinking in routine decision-making. That is, unlike many other professions, religious leaders rarely turn to ethical norms to consider what constitutes right conduct in their field of leadership and service. I do not mean by this that religious leaders or their decisions are unethical. Rather, I mean that when religious, clergy, and bishops exercise routine decision-making, they turn to a multitude of considerations, but articulated ethical norms, their specific values and goods, the virtues, and the type of critical thinking that estimates the long-standing social claims these values, goods, and virtues have on us are not explicitly, professionally engaged. In a word, ethical norms and critical ethical reasoning, which frequently aid other professionals in their considerations, play a much less explicit role in ecclesial leadership practices.

I believe that this is in part because those who exercise leadership in communities of faith are not trained in the ethical issues relevant to matters that their leadership usually engages, and I believe that they ought to be trained in these matters. In this chapter, I focus my claim by arguing specifically that those who are trained for ministry (religious, clerical, hierarchical, or lay) in the Roman Catholic Church are not educated in the ethical issues relevant to their exercise of ministry and that they ought to be. I further believe that mandating ethical training and subsequent ethical accountability ought not be seen as inimical to the interests of the church or her mission, but rather constitutive of it. As Yale University's Wayne Meeks notes in *The Origins of Christian Morality: The First Two Centuries*: "Making morals means making community."[1]

I proceed in two steps: first, by stating fundamental insights necessary for establishing a consideration of ethics for ecclesial leadership; second, by making my argument that specific ethical norms and ethical reasoning are not explicitly engaged in exercising church leadership.

FUNDAMENTAL CLAIMS

I turn now to seven foundational presuppositions for considering the relationship between ecclesial leadership and professional ethical standards. First, what I say about the Roman Catholic Church applies to other communities of faith. I recall during a meeting at the Society of Christian Ethics, the professional organization of Christian ethicists, that I reported the fact that among religious orders, many require HIV testing as a condition for admission. It is worth noting that in the United States the only other persons who can be subjected to mandatory testing are prisoners and those who enter into the service of some areas of the defense and state departments.[2] Because of the separation of church and state, however, the state does not protect those candidates who voluntarily submit to church requirements. At the end of my report, one Protestant scholar shook his head in disbelief, muttering "you Catholics are incredible." An Episcopalian priest intervened and said, "Oh, we also have our share of unvalidated and unexamined practices. For instance, when I applied for ordination, my bishop required me to sign a release waiver to allow him to hire a private detective to investigate my past and present life. When the report was submitted, the bishop never let me see the document, but gave me the bill instead. I had no other choice. After all he was going to ordain me."

Second, those who study at seminaries, divinity schools, or schools of theology rarely receive the type of ethical training that those at most other professional schools receive. Persons admitted to business, medical, or law schools take ethics courses that address specifically the ethical issues that are relevant to their particular profession. The students are taught the responsibilities and rights specific to their profession, whether these deal with matters of representation, confidentiality, client expectations, privileges, promotions, evaluations, conflicts of interest, professional boundaries, and so forth. Their ethics courses in their professional schools aim to shape, if not the students' internal dispositions, then at least the students' external conduct so as to become acceptable colleagues in their particular professional field. Subsequent to this education, they join professional organizations that establish minimal codes of ethical conduct for their members.

This type of ethical training is generally not found at most seminaries, divinity schools, or schools of theology, even though many students take two, three, or four courses of Christian ethics. What we find, instead, are courses that deal with the sexual actions of the laity, the social ethics of businesses, and the medical ethics of physicians and nurses. That is, those in ministry are taught how to govern and make morally accountable the members of their congregations. Generally speaking, however, they are not taught by what ethical reasoning, insights, or norms they should be held themselves morally accountable.

On this point I need to mention a collection of essays that I edited with the Mennonite ethicist Joseph Kotva. Entitled *Practice What You Preach: Virtues, Ethics, and Power in the Lives of Pastoral Ministers and Their Congregations*,[3] the work held twenty-six essays by Christian ethicists from about a dozen denominations reflecting on the need, through lessons from the virtues, to develop more ethically accountable lives of service and leadership. The writers offered ethical guidance for both individual church leaders and for church institutions and dealt with issues such as disillusionment and deference in clerical life, their admissions' policies to seminaries, candidacy programs, pastoral assignments, staff salaries, liturgical celebrations, and the practices of collegiality and subsidiarity. The collection was very well reviewed and won the Catholic Press award for best work in pastoral ministry. I expected, given the dearth of books on this topic, that it would have multiple course adoptions and that Kotva and I would make a killing in sales. I was wrong. To this day, seminaries, schools of theology, and divinity schools rarely offer courses on the topic and rarely use our book.

Third, my proposal for training those aiming for professional service in church leadership is not singularly about observing sexual boundaries, though that subject would be evidently among the more important topics. Rather, I believe that, as the book itself suggested, there are many, many areas of church service that require ethical consideration and training. We should recognize, therefore, that this lack of training in ethics is not the result of the so-called scandal and crisis but rather a cause of it. Furthermore, it helps to explain—in part—why the judgments of both priests and bishops were so poor throughout the crisis. Not only were they poor in judging about sexual boundaries, but also about financial responsibility, personnel accountability, the limits of confidentiality, the importance of truth-telling, and so on.

Fourth, this is not, therefore, part of an ideological agenda. I am not recommending a progressive or a conservative series of courses. I am simply proposing that such formative courses in ethical reflection are necessary for those who exercise the various ministries of the church. More to the point, I am suggesting the need to hold formal public ecclesial discourses on the ethical dimensions of ordinary leadership decision-making.

Fifth, by speaking of "professional ethics" I mean the term in a very particular sense. Thirteen years ago, Chicago's Park Ridge Center published a collection of papers reflecting ecumenically on clergy and professional ethics, entitled *Clergy Ethics in a Changing Society: Mapping the Terrain*.

There, the University of Chicago's Martin Marty described the professional ethics of the clergy as "clergy ethics" but acknowledged that even that proposal confronts two enormous forces of resistance: The first is "the widespread belief that once upon a time, in the Good Old Days or Golden Age, ministers lived in a simple world and could more easily be good, or do good, or know what is good." The second is the "great reluctance to measure the clergy by formal legal norms" because "it is just about impossible to provide guidelines, principles, patterns, or laws for the clerical profession of the sort one finds in, say, the legal and medical professions."[4] Though Marty challenged that resistance, in the same collection Colgate University's Rebecca Chopp represented others by arguing that leadership in the church ought to be animated by a liberating spirit and that such a search for normative guidelines would inhibit that spirit.[5] DePaul University's Paul Camenisch, however, contended that

> the professional ethics model is useful and appropriate for the clergy as far as it goes. Seen positively as the standards that guide professionals in their relations to clients and the larger society in light of the special skills and knowledge they claim to have, the distinctive goal they pursue in their professional activity, and the atypical moral commitment they aspire to, professional ethics sets a floor below which the clergy ought not to fall.[6]

I agree with Camenisch but add that I mean not only the establishment of basic normative standards but more importantly the need both to design the courses and programs for the training of ethics that are relevant to ministerial training and to establish the governance structures and associations that could promote and guarantee adherence to those standards. In this broader sense of professional ethics, then, we would formulate the norms, the programs, and the structures within and not outside of the context of the life of the church, just as medical, business, and legal ethics are formulated in their own forms of life. As Marty wisely notes, "all ethics makes sense only in context."[7]

Sixth, as I will attempt to show, the lack of training in ethics has caused a greater vacuum than most laity, not involved in clergy, religious, or lay ministry, recognize. The laity, I believe, presume that we have attended to this training all along and that we routinely engage in professional ethical standards. Thus, for the most part, in the wake of the scandal the laity has rightfully insisted on talking about structures of governance. But aside from the Park Ridge collection, the one that Kotva and I edited, and the work of Richard Gula,[8] discussions about ethics and church leadership have been rare. This book generally and my proposal specifically concern establishing courses, programs, and workshops in professional, ecclesial, ethical reasoning that specifically aim at training, personally and collectively, those in church ministry.

Finally, we need to consider how this lack of critical ethical training applies not only to the ministerial decisions of those in church leadership but, I think, more importantly, how its absence shapes the practices internal to the clerical, religious, and episcopal cultures. That is, I think one reason why ethics is so rarely explicitly engaged in church ministry is that it is so rarely engaged in the formation and treatment of church ministers by church ministers. This possible corollary needs to be examined. Therefore, as I turn to the second part to argue that specific ethical norms and ethical reasoning are not explicitly engaged in exercising church leadership, I will highlight how church leaders exercise their judgment both externally in ministry and internally in their treatment of one another. In doing this I hope we recognize along the way that for the sake of the image and the mission of the church, men and women have sacrificed—to some degree—themselves and others, without, at times, significant critical ethical judgment.

MAKING THE CASE FOR PROFESSIONAL ETHICS IN CHURCH LEADERSHIP

In this part, I consider three issues and pair each with a different population in church leadership: confidentiality in religious life, due process in priestly life, and the ethics of discourse in episcopal life. In each instance I treat cases as found both in ministry and in the practices internal to that population.

Confidentiality in Religious Life

Confidentiality ought to be a question that religious, particularly religious priests, know something about. Movies like *I Confess* and *On the Waterfront* gave American cultures an appreciation of the extent to which priests protected the seal of the confessional. Many of us might recall how three years ago a New York Jesuit priest revealed the contents of a confidential conversation that, while it concluded with absolution, was not considered by the priest or by the New York archdiocesan offices to be an actual confession, even though the state attorney general's office originally excluded the testimony as confessional material.[9] The priest demonstrated from the conversation that his interlocutor and not the convicted was the guilty party. Subsequent discussions among Jesuits were vigorous and critical about the priest's disclosure. When it comes to confession, religious, clergy, and laity demonstrate a keen critical apprehension of the ethical goods at stake. But leave the clarity of the confessional and Catholic confidentiality becomes a bit of an ethical wasteland.

Consider the recent case of another Jesuit priest, the late Richard McSorley, who kept a typewritten diary that included his recollections of private conversations with Mrs. Jacqueline Kennedy, who in her grief over her husband's assassination sought the priest's counsel. The diary and private letters were among documents he left to Georgetown university's main library, which in turn made them available to researchers. Mrs. Kennedy's brother-in-law, Senator Edward Kennedy, responded that he was "deeply disappointed that the privacy of communications such as these—between a member of the clergy and his parishioner—would not be respected." In an interview with the Associated Press, however, a Holy Cross priest and theologian, the Reverend Michael Baxter, said the informal setting for the discussions complicates the matter. "If it was a clearly defined sacramental setting, it's hard and fast and clear" the conversations should be kept strictly private, Baxter said. "If it was a professional relationship, a formal counseling situation, that would be rather clear too. But, if it were something else, the situation changes."[10]

Granted "the situation changes," what rules apply? What ought to be the basic stance of the Jesuit or the university regarding these confidential conversations? Many questions arise, but note that after establishing that the relationship was not confessional, and therefore not necessarily absolutely sacrosanct, we do not have any guidance about the commonplace, ambiguous settings in which religious frequently find themselves. Subsequently, the Jesuit superior apologized for the breach, but he had no articulated norms nor, for that matter, any written critical insights by Christian ethicists on what norms apply to religious who have access to privileged information.[11]

Consider, for instance, religious on retreat teams in retreat houses and houses of prayer. What norms are in evidence for discussing the spiritual progress of the retreatants? What essays in ethics have been written to guide the exchange of confidential materials by religious in the ministry of retreat giving?

One reason why religious share confidential materials regarding other people without adequate attention to ethical guidelines derives from the habit of a fairly free flow of confidential material about religious among religious. Internal to their lives are few normative guidelines and even fewer ethical essays, or for that matter, discussions or courses about this material. For instance, we have a procedure in the Society of Jesus by which a Jesuit is formally evaluated during his lengthy formation, anywhere between four and seven times, depending on the man and the province. Using a device infelicitously entitled, "informatios," a superior asks about five to eight other Jesuits and other persons to assess the individual Jesuit's living of the vowed life. The individual does not know who the ones are evaluating him nor is the superior required to give him any written report after the informatios are collected and dispensed to the superiors' own circle of consultors. Besides being evaluated by these instruments, many Jesuits fill these informatios out.

There are, to my knowledge, however, no standard instructions about what constitutes disclosable information.[12]

One area of religious life that has examined the practice of maintaining confidentiality regards religious men and women pursuing counseling or psychotherapy. Some of those articles are alarming, however, precisely because they propose to exempt the therapist from the exclusive confidential relationship with the religious client. Sr. Joyce Harris, OSC, argues that it "is simply not so" that a "religious comes to therapy primarily as a single, individual person."[13] Toward this end she proposes that therapy for a vowed religious ought to use a model like the one used in family counseling. In her model, the superior representing the community (though not seeking counseling herself) and the religious client "are equal participants in the therapeutic relationship." This "most critical assumption" leads to "basic assumptions" including that the "therapist ensures the rights and realistic expectations of both parties are respected" and that "[t]he confidentiality of the therapeutic process includes the therapist, the individual religious, and the community representative."

In another article, Mary Ellen Moore holds that the therapist is agent for the religious member only,[14] a position evidently at odds with Harris's therapist who is an agent for the religious member and "the community through its representative." Moore writes that the therapist has the responsibility to "safeguard the confidentiality of his or her client"; Harris refers to the relationship therapy and argues that the (undefined) conscience-matter "is to be safeguarded." Both admit that there are limits to confidentiality, but Moore invokes those limits from those published in the *American Psychologist*; Harris does not make any such reference. She suggests instead that after consultation with the two agents (but one client), the therapist ought to outline the parameters of confidentiality. The differences are apparent and significant. Though Harris looks to the much more ambiguous context of family counseling, she makes no appeals to professional standards even there.

In another journal a similar debate occurred. In this instance, a Jesuit provincial, William Barry, argues somewhat like Harris that the responsibilities of a superior need to be taken into account when a religious sees a therapist, while Janet Dohr and Katherine Mayer address the professional standards of confidentiality.[15]

In all these instances, there is little evidence of those in authority turning to any professional standards regarding confidentiality, nor of those in ministry (aside from some in pastoral counseling courses themselves) being trained in how and to what extent and under what circumstances confidentiality applies to evaluations, therapy, spiritual direction, counseling, and the like. Rather, we see individuals with authority exercising "their own judgment" without recognizing the professional, ethical standards that ought to apply.[16]

Due Process in Priestly Life

Many seminarians learn in both ethics and canon law courses the rights and responsibilities of married persons and the procedures of due process that belong to them; few however study the practice of due process as it affects their employees or themselves.

Concerning due process between pastors and their employees, Anne Patrick reports on two cases (one from the diocese of Brooklyn in the 1930s and another from Key West, Florida in 1989–1990) regarding religious women as employees:

> The first shows women of strong character who made difficult choices that were essentially guided by the patriarchal understanding of what "good sisters" should do. The second case shows women of equal dedication to the church's mission, whose egalitarian-feminist understanding of their moral ideals and obligations led to a dramatically different series of response.[17]

In the two cases, Patrick demonstrates how context affects process.

In the first case, without any due process, the pastor fired the nuns and ordered them not to convey to the people whom they had served in the parish and in the parochial school that they had been dismissed. Leaving the laity with the distinct impression that the nuns were simply abandoning their projects without explanation only compounded the grief of the obedient nuns. Patrick's poignant story includes some very sad interviews with the now-elderly nuns who were involved in that case. Patrick then turns to the later case, when another pastor tried to fire a small group of members from the same religious order by demanding that they remain quiet about his decision. The sisters argued that justice rather than obedience prompted their petition for due process. When they failed to receive any due process, they presented their situation publicly to the parish. The parishioners responded with a full-scale "save the nuns campaign," including full-page newspaper ads ("it is not their choice to leave!").

These narratives highlight how cultures, like religious ones of obedience, enable the conditions for the suspension of due process.

The question of due process and an adequate regard for contractual negotiations is hardly a cumbersome task to understand and embrace. In fact, centuries ago, priests routinely were trained in contracts. For instance, in one of the first Jesuit texts of casuistry, Francisco de Toledo writes about the responsibilities of the confessor and outlines the six issues that all confessors needed to know.[18] The first five were the staple of confessional training from the thirteenth through the twentieth centuries: the difference between mortal and venial sins, the significance of circumstances, the cases that one cannot absolve, the task of restitution, and, finally, impediments. The sixth requirement was to be able to judge the liceity of contracts. This sixth requirement was hardly incidental: Contracts constituted the most significant confessional material in Toledo's manual.[19] These contracts not only applied to businesses but also to church life. If sixteenth- and seventeenth-century clerics learned about the ethics of contracts from manuals like Francesco de Toledo's, they could learn the same today about the ethics of due process.

Internal to ministry, moreover, priests are themselves frequently not treated with due process. Their being treated without normative procedures helps promote a culture that sees little need for ethics in the first place. Here I am reminded of an account told by a pastor in Boston, who as a seminarian twenty years ago asked one of his professors whether the long-awaited, newly revised code of canon law would develop insights into "due process." His professor responded, "We have no need for due process, we live by the law of charity."

In *A People Adrift*, Peter Steinfels attends to this when he identifies three factors that made "serial abuse by priests less likely to come to light."

> First, priest abusers and their superiors operated within an enclosed, self-protective clerical culture. . . . Second, priests moved from assignment to assignment without the open process of inquiry, interview, and evaluation that was characteristic of many other religious groups as well as professional appointments. Third, a powerful aura of being consecrated surrounded the Catholic priesthood.[20]

Steinfels's insights suggest that that aura, in the self-protective clerical culture, made the questions of ethical reasoning and accountability apparently unnecessary.[21]

Strangely enough, the connection between sexuality and due process for priests is more important than one might think. Michael Papesh, a priest from St. Paul, comments at length on how clerical culture rebuffs openness, clarity, and mature responsibility regarding sexuality precisely as seminarians are being prepared for priesthood. He writes:

> Yet the terrible reluctance of the clerical culture as a whole to engage matters of sexuality forthrightly and constructively is a grave impediment to ministry. It is intensified by Catholic moral teaching, fear and anxiety, undergirded by concerns for institutional preservation and self-protection. Consequently, realistic, wholesome and candid discussions of sexuality are silenced. Healthy, balanced formation of ordained ministers is hobbled. Sexuality, for many priests, becomes privatized, solemnized and darkened.[22]

Very pertinent to our conference, he concludes: "Public and private accountability is thwarted."[23] Papesh's claims that the climate that forms yet inhibits seminarians and priests from acknowledging and addressing personal questions of sexuality sets the stage for a climate that forms yet inhibits seminarians and priests from entertaining the rights due to them in other areas of life.

Discourse in Episcopal Life

We need now to examine the ethics of discourse and how it applies to bishops as they treat others and as they are treated. The first and fairly remarkable instance is from an article by the late Bishop of Saginaw, Michigan, Kenneth E. Untener,[24] who reviewed the written responses of five cardinals to two important position papers, one by John Quinn, the recently retired archbishop of San Francisco,[25] and the other by Cardinal Bernardin, who launched "The Common Ground" project.[26] Untener does this because the five statements provide "an unusual opportunity to look in on a discussion among bishops and see not only what we discuss, but *how* we discuss." After noting the respectful tone of all five statements, Untener remarks that their "quality left much to be desired." Specifically he categorized the following issues: making cautionary statements about things the authors never questioned, a low degree of accuracy in reporting the proponents' proposals, the tendency to make generalizations without citing specifics, "the occupational hazard . . . to resolve something with personal conviction and/or opinion rather than available data," ascribing a rather distorted understanding to a fundamental theological concept, that is, "reception," and the issue of actually reporting the substance of another's claim. In each case, the cardinals at least implicitly misinformed their readers about the positions of those whom they critiqued. Untener adds two closing observations. "I want to observe that in critiquing the responses of these five cardinals, I do not cite them as isolated cases, nor point to them as the chief offenders. I simply use the window of this public exchange to offer examples of what we all, myself included, do at times when involved in religious discussions." But, he notes, when bishops speak on behalf of the episcopal conference, or give testimony to Congress, or address important social issues, "I would rate the level of discussion in those cases much, much higher—superb. For some reason we often shift down to another level when we deal with church matters."[27]

The orthodox ethicist Vigen Guroian makes clear that when it comes to ethical normative guidelines, Roman Catholic leaders are no different than other church leaders. Guroian studied a debate in the Armenian Church in 1997, which he describes as a significant moment where "civility failed." He notes two important reasons for the "baseness of the debate." First, it belongs to "a much larger and deeper crisis of moral formation and training of clergy in the Armenian Church." Second, "vital concerns over doctrine and identity were involved."[28] Like Untener's article, Guroian's notes that the tendency to misrepresent and to compromise any basic standards of discourse are more evident when bishops believe that something central to the identity of the church is at stake. As people in other professions recognize, however, precisely when the stakes are higher, there is a greater, not a lesser need to observe at least minimal professional ethical standards of discourse.

dialogue vs conditioned "deception"

Reflecting on discourse in the recent crisis, John Beal notes that "although they are not the only rights of the faithful that have been given short shrift during the current crisis, the interrelated rights of information and expression have been conspicuous casualties of it."[29] Reflecting on how the bishops of Ireland, England, and Wales proceeded in a variety of debates, Gerard Mannion recalls Yves Congar's warning about a "haze of fiction" falling upon us.[30] He reminds us that Hans Kung argued in 1968 "that truthfulness is a basic requirement of the church, a challenge to the church and, indeed, the *very future* of the church." Mannion comments succinctly: "Truthfulness has yet to be embraced as a default virtue in church governance."[31]

In order to understand how bishops treat one another, Timothy Schilling studied the case of Raymond Hunthausen, archbishop of Seattle (1983–1989). His interests were like Untener's: "To me the controversy looked to be a fascinating study in Catholic conversation. How do bishops talk to one another and what does this conversation look like when it is under pressure?"[32] His findings are unsettling. He considers that "the interesting thing about bishops as institutional leaders is the concentration of intraecclesial, legal power in their office. Within a diocese there is no such thing as a separation of powers. The ordinary is the chief executive, the supreme judge, and the guardian of doctrine." In this authority structure, Schilling was able to name nine strategies in which bishops engage; these strategies convey a fairly deceptive culture: showing deference to the structural order and mindset of the episcopacy, associating one's own interests with the best interests of the church, minimizing the appearance of conflict, showing fraternity, practicing courtesy, employing secrecy, recruiting allies, arguing persuasively, and asserting personal identity. He concludes, "In sum, the desire to protect the power and appearance of the church and of the bishops' own position strongly colors how bishops handle conflict." Reflecting on why bishops treat each other this way, he adds, "Moreover, this stance appears not to be something consciously adopted so much as a reflexive behavior the product of social conditioning." Shilling then compares the way bishops handled the Hunthausen case with the sexual abuse/leadership scandal and finds overlapping elements: "the (over)concern with power and appearance, the attempts to deny the problems and then minimize their appearance, the excessive dependency on secrecy, the fear of having real arguments in public and of inviting the broader public to participate in the problem solving, the personal costs and feelings of mistrust and betrayal."[33]

As we have seen, in each instance—confidentiality, due process, and the ethics of discourse—the problem is not simply the absence of professional ethical normative guidance but rather the lack of any social conditioning by those trained in ministry to find any social commitment to professional ethical conduct. The issue is not simply what ministers lack, but more importantly how they are trained. The cultures that form our leadership in itself often resists professional ethical standards.

CONCLUSION

The task of developing a comprehensive program for the professional ethical training of church leaders will evidently require more than the desire to articulate and promulgate norms like a professional code of ethics, though that might be a start. Rather, we need to hear from bishops, laity, clergy, and religious a new mentality that expresses itself in the greater willingness to see just how bereft we are of the foundational mindset for promoting an ethical culture of leadership. We need to hear further admissions that we do not have a grasp yet of what critical ethical thinking in church decision-making processes would look like. That is, before we even attempt to instantiate programs we need first to acknowledge that we have been operating for a long time without them. We need to recognize just how deeply conditioned we ministers are at not considering the ethical within the ambit of our deliberations.

Let me suggest that as we begin to appreciate the tasks before us, that in order to begin a new ethical conditioning we promote among ourselves the habitual inclination to ask the question, "but is it ethical?" whenever a course of action is proffered for a retreat house, a seminary or a house of religious formation, a parish, or a diocese. That question, which keeps people in other professions vigilant about their ethical obligations, could be the first step toward a culture that is at once religious and moral. For us, the issue will be whether the injection of the question is itself a welcoming or marginalizing moment.

NOTES

1. Wayne Meeks, *The Origins of Christian Morality: The First Two Centuries* (New Haven: Yale University Press, 1993), 5.

2. Larry Gostin, "The AIDS Litigation Project," *Journal of the American Medical Association* 263, no. 15 (1990): 2086–93.

3. James F. Keenan and Joseph J. Kotva Jr., eds., *Practice What You Preach: Virtues, Ethics, and Power in the Lives of Pastoral Ministers and Their Congregations* (Franklin, Wisc.: Sheed and Ward, 1999).

4. Martin E. Marty, "Clergy Ethics in America: The Ministers on Their Own," in *Clergy Ethics in a Changing Society: Mapping the Terrain*, ed. James P. Wind, et al. (Chicago: Park Ridge Center, 1991), 23–36, at 23 and 30.

5. Rebecca Chopp, "Liberating Ministry," in *Clergy Ethics*, 84–98.

6. Paul Camenisch, "Clergy Ethics and the Professional Ethics Model," in *Clergy Ethics*, 114–33, at 131.

7. Marty, 23.

8. Richard Gula, *The Ethics of Pastoral Ministry* (Mahwah, N.J.: Paulist Press, 1996).

9. "Court Hears Priest's Testimony in Murder Case Appeal," *CNN.com*, 18 July 2001.

10. "Priest: Jackie Spoke of Suicide After JFK Died," *Associated Press*, 14 Nov. 2003.

11. Lolita C. Baldor, "Jesuit Leader Says Priest's Kennedy Diary is Private," *Associated Press*, 16 Dec. 2003.

12. James Keenan, "Are Informatios Ethical?" *Studies in the Spirituality of Jesuits* 29 (September 1997).

13. Joyce Harris, "Therapy for Religious: The Troublesome Triangle," *Review for Religious* 51 (1992): 282–88.

14. Mary Ellen Moore, "Therapist, Client, and Superior in Relationship," *Review for Religious* 49 (1990): 539–44.

15. William Barry, "A Superior's Relationship with a Therapist," *Human Development* 10 (1989): 11–13 and "Letters to the Editor," *Human Development* 10 (1989): 42–45.

16. I addressed these issues at length in "Confidentiality: Erosion and Restoration," *Review for Religious* 51 (1992): 882–94; for a bibliographical review of issues related to confidentiality see also Keenan, "Truth-Telling, Confidentiality and Fiduciary Responsibility in the Professions," *Theological Studies* 54, no. 1 (1993): 142–59.

17. Anne Patrick, "'His Dogs More Than Us': Virtue in Situations of Conflict Between Women Religious and Their Ecclesiastical Employers," in *Practice What You Preach*, 293–314, at 293.

18. Francisco de Toledo, *Summa Casuum Conscientiae Sive De Instructione Sacerdotum, Libri Septem* (Constantiae: Apud Nicolaum Kalt, 1600).

19. James Keenan, "The Birth of Jesuit Casuistry: *Summa casuum conscientiae, sive de instructione sacerdotum, libri septem* by Francesco de Toledo, (1532–1596)" in *The Mercurian Project: Forming Jesuit Culture, 1573–1580*, ed. Thomas McCoog (Rome: Institutum Historicum Societatis Iesu, 2004), 461–82.

20. Peter Steinfels, *A People Adrift: The Crisis of the Roman Catholic Church in America* (New York: Simon and Schuster, 2003), 46.

21. See also, David France, *Our Fathers: The Secret Life of the Catholic Church in an Age of Scandal* (New York: Broadway, 2004).

22. Michael Papesh, "Farewell to the Club," *America* 186, no. 6 (13 May 2002): 7–12.

23. Papesh, "Farewell."

24. Kenneth E. Untener, "How Bishops Talk," *America* 175, no. 11 (19 Oct. 1996): 9–15.

25. John Quinn, "An Archbishop Speaks Up," *Commonweal* 123, no. 13 (12 July 1996): 5–6.

26. Cardinal Joseph L. Bernadin, "Called to Be Catholic: Church in a Time of Peril," <www.nplc.org/commonground/calledcatholic.htm> (31 Aug. 1996).

27. Untener, 15.

28. Vigen Guroian, "Doctrine and Ecclesiastical Authority: A Contemporary Controversy in the Armenian Church," in *Practice What You Preach*, 252–67, at 261 and 263 respectively.

29. John Beal, "It Shall Not Be So Among You," in *Governance, Accountability, and the Future of the Catholic Church*, ed. Francis Oakley and Bruce Russett (New York: Continuum, 2004), 88–103, at 91.

30. Gerard Mannion, "A Haze of Fiction: Legitimation, Accountability, and Truthfulness," in *Governance, Accountability* 161–77, at 161. Yves Congar's phrase appears in "Power and Poverty in the Church," *Readings in Church Authority: Gifts and Challenges for Contemporary Catholicism*, ed. Gerard Mannion (Burlington, Vt.: Ashgate Press, 2003), 47–48.

31. Mannion, 176. See Hans Kung, *Truthfulness: The Future of the Church* (London: Sheed and Ward, 1968).

32. Timothy Schilling, "When Bishops Disagree: Rome, Hunthausen, and the Current Church Crisis," *Commonweal* 130, no. 15 (12 Sept. 2003): 15–22, at 15.

33. Shilling, 18 and 20.

8: RENEWING THE PSYCHOLOGICAL CONTRACTS OF THE CLERGY AND LAITY

Denise M. Rousseau

". . . invincible blindness in the face of reality,
fierce opposition in the face of privilege,
and a habit of self-protection
are all around us within the Church."

—Father Michael Leo Papesh (2004), 19

"Light's given you to know right from wrong at need.
And free will, so its stuff can stand the strain.
Of its first tussles with the stars, will fight,
If nourished well, to win the whole campaign."

—Dante, Purgatory, Canto XVI[1]

Voluntarily made commitments in the form of psychological contracts are the building blocks of adult relationships and their renewal in the aftermath of conflict or breakdown. Psychological contracts and the processes associated with their transformation and revision are central to restoring trust in relationships as varied as marriage and employment.[2] They have a special role to play in renewing the relationships between clergy and laity in the aftermath of the sex abuse scandal within the Catholic Church in America. Restoring the church's legitimacy and integrity necessitates personal and organizational risk taking and recommitment to create constructive relationships members can rely upon with confidence. This chapter explicates the concept of a psychological contract to promote discussion of how the church in the United States can rebuild quality relationships among clergy and laity. As voluntary agreements, psychological contracts bind parties to values, modes of expression, and conduct that can generate effective mutual support and resilient, sustainable relationships.

PSYCHOLOGICAL CONTRACT

Psychological contracts are beliefs, based upon promises expressed or implied, regarding an exchange agreement between an individual, and in organizations, the firm and its agents.[3] Once formed, psychological contracts motivate individuals to fulfill commitments made to their organizations confident in turn that the organization will fulfill its obligations to them. These obligations can be limited to the instruction a student receives in exchange for tuition or as broad as the generous support and mutual investment community members share. Without agreement, behavior in organizations would be chaotic—as we see when downsizing breaks down the trust surviving workers have in their employer. To make promises that can be kept, the psychological contracts of organizations and individuals need to be consistent with the organization's core mission and the values individuals hold. As I write this I can hear in my head someone saying, "but the Church isn't an organization." That notion is readily countered. The Catholic Church is the quintessential organization if we go by the definition of an organization as a system of patterned activities performed by groups of people whose activities are differentiated into production, support, maintenance, and managerial subsystems.[4] Indeed, the church is an organization of organizations from Cana Conferences to CYO basketball, where its patterns of activities are sustained over time, operating even as leaders and members change.

The notion of a psychological contract can be used to address questions regarding the commitments clergy and laity might need to make to each other in order to restore their relationship while also transforming it in more generative ways. The appropriate set of commitments a psychological contract necessitates varies with the goals the parties have for their relationship (the time frame, short- or long-term; the domain, educational, pastoral, financial, and so on; and the benefits sought, for their own benefit and/or to serve the interests of broader constituencies). It varies also with degree of power and responsibility the parties are capable of exercising. Thus, these commitments would differ depending on whether the parties are children or adults, and on their societal context (rural–urban, traditional–modern, developing–democratic). Relations between clergy and laity also can be expected to take different forms in times of full staffing in an established parish, during a priest shortage, or in transitions as in the case of the start-up of a new ministry to serve AIDS patients or the elderly. Addressing the nature and dynamics of psychological contracts can provide a basis for discussing the obligations clergy and laity each have toward the other.

Six Features of the Psychological Contract

The dynamics of the psychological contract are shaped by its defining features.

1. Voluntariness

Psychological contracts motivate people to fulfill their commitments because they are based on the exchange of promises in which each individual has actively participated. Commitments made voluntarily tend to be kept. For example, a person who agrees to contribute time to a community organization every week is likely to be internally conflicted when an interesting opportunity arises elsewhere. That volunteer is more likely to decline the offer than another person who had made no such commitment. Explicit commitments ("I agree to stay a minimum of a year") have more powerful effects on behavior than implicit ones ("to stay a while"). Voluntarily made commitments are a form of self-persuasion. People committed to a course of action develop attitudes and beliefs that reinforce and sustain that commitment (a colleague of mine says it this way, "behaving is believing"). Participation in church life by individuals, from clergy or lay ministers to active parishioners, involves commitments made in the expectation of some reciprocity or mutual obligation on the part of others. The traditional priest who has spent a lifetime in diocesan service may expect a respectful but passive laity. Lay congregants who contribute financial support to their parish may believe their rector or the larger diocese is accountable to them personally for how that money is used. Such beliefs are part of the psychological contracts individual church members hold as a function of their participation. Note these need not be exactly the terms to which church leaders believe they are obligated to adhere. Rather, these are the beliefs formed as the basis of participation in church-related activities. Creation of obligations that are mutually understood is another matter.

2. Perceived Mutuality

An individual's psychological contract reflects his or her own understanding of the commitments made with another. Individuals act on that subjective understanding as if it were mutual, regardless of whether that is the case in reality. A worker who is told the job requires two to three days of travel a week can interpret that to mean that there will be *no more* than three travel days a week, although the manager who hired her meant there would be no more than two to three days a week *on average*. More experienced people are better at probing for mutual understanding than are rookies and newcomers. The more information available to and shared between the parties the greater the likelihood that perceptions of mutuality will reflect mutuality in fact. Because holding information in common is a prerequisite of mutuality, hierarchical organizations such as the church face great difficulties in creating shared understandings in the psychological contracts held by higher- and lower-level members.[5] Status differences can lead people to interact less, can lead people to communicate seldom or only indirectly, and otherwise can diminish shared perspective and information. What lower-status members believe to be the leadership's obligation to them may differ from those beliefs their leaders actually hold. Lack of shared understanding is one reason why one party violates another person's heartfelt psychological contract.[6]

3. Incompleteness

One inevitable feature of any relationship that continues over time is incompleteness. I use the word "inevitable" because relationships that exist over time are inherently incomplete since parties cannot anticipate or communicate all the demands each ultimately makes of the other. Bounded rationality makes it difficult for parties to recall all relevant details to be shared with another even when they actually know the details. Uncertainty in life and in organizations means that the parties cannot even know all the details. With the exception of short-term, limited transactions (e.g., temporary help), the initially incomplete psychological contracts characterizing relationships need to be fleshed out over time. It is virtually impossible to initially spell out all the details of a relationship that will last a long while.

From the most hidebound bureaucracy to the most loosely structured start-up, incompleteness is endemic in organizations. Realistic preview of what their roles entail can help people make more complete and mutual agreements, fleshing out the details over time in a more consistent fashion. In the case of the church, failure of seminary training to prepare diocesan priests for the lives they would lead—including celibacy, loneliness, and lay expectations—is implicated as a contributing factor in both the current scandal and priest shortage.[7] Moreover, changing circumstances mean that not all contingencies can be foreseen. Few pre–Vatican II clergy anticipated the changing expectations for lay involvement in church decisions. Until the recent sex abuse scandal, the pressure for greater accountability for bishops in personnel decisions was not a widespread lay concern. Thus it is no wonder that the established psychological contracts of both clergy and laity are incomplete guides to action or understanding in the face of contemporary events.

While filling in the blanks along the way, the parties to an agreement can come to have inconsistent understandings over time unless periodic efforts are taken to reinforce mutuality. This reinforcement can take the form of regular meetings, shared social experiences, and collaborative work. In the context of the church, completing the psychological contract in mutual ways is impeded by the traditional hierarchical nature of clergy and laity relations. Differences in status, roles, and the contexts in which clergy and laity perform their roles lead them to have different perspectives, to lack common information, and to draw different interpretations regarding their roles. This lack of complete information and mutual understanding suggests a need to more systematically develop the psychological contracts of clergy and laity. Important understandings to be developed include the boundary conditions regarding the psychological contract (what behaviors are acceptable and which are not), the parties' respective privileges and duties, and ways of resolving potential contradictions and conflicts in their roles (as in the case where personal relationships that constitute pastoral care in the eyes of a priest may appear to be friendships to the laity or vice versa).

4. Multiple Contract Makers

Diverse sources of information shape how people interpret their psychological contract with an organization. For example, church members educated in the Catholic school system can have views different than those from a secular school system. Similarly, for cradle Catholics and those who convert as adults, the sources of information regarding the church, their roles as community members, and expectations of clergy and laity relations may differ as a function of their exposure to various contract makers.

The church, like other complex organizations, has many agents including the senior leadership, formal spokespersons, and in particular, those members with whom people are in regular contact. The immediate people with whom we interact powerfully shape our psychological contracts—so much so that in employment many workers who believe the firm has violated their psychological contract attribute this violation to the fact that their immediate boss left, taking with him or her the shared understandings regarding that worker's psychological contract. For similar reasons, bishops have a powerful influence upon the psychological contracts of individual priests, and changes in bishops can diminish shared understanding. Fellow members also provide information individuals rely upon in determining what they owe the organization and vice versa. Thus, friends and those to whom a person goes for advice in the parish or diocese where one lives and works can have great influence over the psychological contracts of individual clergy and laity. Lastly, formal structures and ongoing practices such as training and social events can signal promised benefits and required contributions. People participating in certain events and not others can draw different conclusions regarding the terms of the psychological contract (one reason why very active members often have dramatically different beliefs than less active ones).[8] When contract makers convey different messages, it erodes the mutuality of the psychological contract. In times of transformation and renewal, it can take considerable time and effort for various contract makers to reinforce comparable messages.

5. Reliance Losses

When a person relies on the psychological contract not only as a guide to action but also in anticipation of future benefits, losses result from failure of the other party to fulfill its anticipated commitments. Losses mean that anticipated (i.e., "promised") benefits fail to materialize, and they are the basic reason why psychological contract violation and change generate strong negative reactions, including anger, outrage, termination, and withdrawal of support. Efforts that both people and organizations take to manage their psychological contract with the other focus both on fulfilling commitments as well as on managing losses when existing commitments are difficult to keep. Employers might offer a challenging assignment when a promised promotion fails to materialize. A worker who cannot attend a critical meeting might make special efforts to follow up with colleagues so that her performance is unimpaired. Psychological contracts established in a mutual fashion lead their parties to behave in ways that reduce the costs to the other from relying on their agreement.

Psychological contracts are a subset of a broader array of beliefs and expectations members and organizational leaders hold. Non-promise-based aspects of organizational life that people find satisfying (e.g., the quality of the physical setting or the camaraderie of colleagues) can over time be viewed as part of the promised *status quo*, necessitating attention similar to that given explicit promises. In times of change in the psychological contract, losses can occur as conditions individuals have relied upon as part of their relationship with organization are eroded or altered.

Reliance losses arise in the context of clergy and laity from the benefits and protections each has come to anticipate from the other. The distinction between church and laity has been fixed since the fifth century, and entertaining even the smallest of changes risks substantial emotional and institutional backlash. In the context of psychological contracts in the church, one aspect of the traditional priestly role, the privileged status as a man apart from others, who exercises unquestioned authority, has become vulnerable in consequence of the erosion of trust and the laity's altered perceptions of clergy. To this end, Bishop Pilla suggests "the priesthood can be special without being privileged."[9] Nonetheless, changes that would diminish the privileges priests have come to rely upon can be a major loss where this privileged status has been an offset for the role's ever-present high demands. On the other hand, lay parish staff and the laity have also experienced losses. As Papesh describes it, they are "newly conscious of how much they do not know about how the Church operates day by day . . . frustrated and vaguely alarmed by the suspicion that they have even less power than they thought."[10] An effective process for renewing and/or revising a psychological contract must anticipate and attend to the losses experienced by its incumbents.

6. Automatic Processes

Once a psychological contract is formed, it creates an enduring mental model of the relationship. This mental model provides a stable understanding of what to expect in the future and guides efficient action without a lot of need to be refreshed or practiced. Think about the way the conventional QWERTY keyboard helps those of us who type or word process in English to compose a document without looking at the keyboard. Having an established (i.e., automatic) psychological contract makes it possible for people to continue to function in the face of uncertainty, ambiguity, and moderate change.

Once a contract is established, subsequent information tends to be interpreted in light of it. For the most part, this is functional since new performance demands can be incorporated into existing understandings of one's role. But sometimes the old psychological contract is too out of line with new reality and a more elaborate change process is required. For example, spillover effects have been reported among managers of information technology (IT) workers when those workers have shifted from being regular employees to independent contractors.[11] Managers continued to believe that their former supervisees should fulfill the duties of regular employees despite the fact that they were now employed by a contracting agency. (Interestingly in this case, the IT workers recognized a difference in their relationship with their former employer and revised their psychological contracts more readily.) Similarly while many pre–Vatican II bishops and clergy continued to think and behave in traditional hierarchical fashion with regard to the laity, those ordained or installed soon after the council held different beliefs and continued to do so throughout their careers.[12] Such effects support the notion of durable psychological contracts not only from the perspective of individuals but across all levels of an organization. The durability of contracts means that they are a source of functional consistency, resistance to change, and building blocks for future renewal.

Types of Psychological Contracts

Psychological contracts can take many forms. Promises can be limited, as in the case of the simple economic transaction entailed by temporary work or fee for service. Or, promises individuals and organization make to each other can involve a host of socioemotional commitments including loyalty and mutual concern. Nonetheless, it can be difficult to gauge a psychological contract at a distance in employment and in clergy–laity relations, much in the same way that is hard to judge a marriage from the outside looking in. To fully appreciate a psychological contract, it is necessary to drill down into the beliefs people hold and the information sources they rely upon rather than relying on general assumptions regarding broad roles or job categories. Nonetheless, despite the fact that the myriad details of a psychological contract can be as unique as each individual, certain patterns do characterize many psychological contracts.

A relational psychological contract includes such terms as loyalty (committing to meet the needs of the other) and stability (an open-ended commitment to the future). This pattern perhaps best befits the historical psychological contract among church members. People with relational contracts are more likely to willingly go out of their way to support the organization, including accepting organizational changes their leaders deem necessary. Although those with a relational contract are likely to be particularly upset when it is violated, the commitment such contracts create often manifest in individual attempts to seek redress or remedy in order to maintain the relationship. Failure to remedy the situation typically leads to abandoning the organization or, should the person remain, to reduced contributions and erosion of the relationship. In contrast, organizations that uphold their relational contracts absorb more of the risk themselves, protecting their members from burdensome costs. An archetypal employer with a relational contract, Malden Mills's CEO Aaron Feuerstein kept his workers on the payroll after his factory burned down to tide them over until a new workplace could be built.[13] Individuals favor organizations that treat them relationally as opposed to transactionally (described below). Organizations in turn offer highly valued individuals more relational contracts than they do others contributing less. In the context of the church, violation of the tenets of a relational contract by abusive clergy is a breach in the eyes of the laity, both as victims and as comembers. The metaresponse of the church to this violation, by evoking the litigiousness characteristic of economic relations, has at a higher level been experienced as violating a sacred trust.[14] To be offered a transactional contract where the norm is a relational one is a signal of one's lower status and worth, warranting treatment suited to a peripheral or less influential member.

A transactional psychological contract includes such terms as narrow duties and limited or short-term duration. Individuals with transactional contracts readily exit when conditions change or when the organization fails to live up to its end of the agreement. Both individual and organization are likely to terminate immediately a transactional arrangement that fails to meet their needs. The archetypal transactional organization is a call center where workers, often anonymous to customers, perform narrow, limited duties, easily substituted for by other workers. Litigiousness can turn erstwhile relationships into arm's-length transactions. One particularly disturbing aspect of the sex abuse scandal has been the involvement of the courts, in particular the church's use of aggressive legal tactics to fend off suits as opposed to making appropriate amends in the context of a relationship with the laity. That the American church has to some extent transactionalized its relationship with the laity is evident in a key condition of transactional contracts, assigning more risk (and costs) to individuals from the uncertainties the organization faces rather than providing them the support and protection characteristic of relational contracts.

Transactional contracts have their strengths in the ease with which new arrangements can be created in highly uncertain environments. However, they are particularly dysfunctional when they are a by-product of violation or poorly managed change in a preexisting relational contract. Under these conditions, a wary arm's length arrangement results from the parties' loss of trust in each other.

The emergence of a hybrid ("balanced") form of psychological contract in recent years combines the open-ended time frame and mutual concern of relational agreements with the performance demands and renegotiation of the transactional contract. Balanced contracts combine commitments on the part of the organization to develop and provide future opportunities for individuals, while anticipating flexible contributions and adjustment on the part of both parties to changing conditions. Balanced contracts entail shared risk between individual and organization and anticipate renegotiation over time as organizational conditions and individual interests and needs change. As such, the building blocks of balanced agreements are shared risks, mutual feedback, and learning. Such arrangements are characteristic of knowledge workers and of organizations offering high value to both members and customers.[15] As we discuss the process of renewing psychological contracts between clergy and laity, the notions of shared risks, mutual feedback, and learning renewal demands may mean that some features of balanced contracts have a role in the church as well.

LEARNING FROM HISTORICAL
PROCESSES OF CONTRACT CHANGE

The need to restore trust has occurred before in church history. In thirteenth-century Italy, there was widespread concern regarding the clergy's materialism and failure to live lives in accordance with their vows. The young man who became St. Francis of Assisi attracted many people to him, clergy and laity alike, through his commitment to gospel poverty and the way of life he offered to others.[16] As with many powerful visions, his appeal was to the better nature of the people who became his followers. This "better nature" reflected heartfelt beliefs—in charity and sacrifice for others—beliefs heretofor unrealized in their day-to-day lives. Indeed it is not uncommon that organizations seeking to radically reshape beliefs and behavior go back to enduring principles that people hold dear yet often believe cannot be realized in their ordinary lives.[17] Popes befriended Francis and supported his rule even though they traditionally discouraged communities such as his because his rule insisted upon avoidance of endowments.[18] Innocent III saw in Francis's expression of heartfelt gospel-based beliefs a way to restore faith and respect for the church.

In St. Francis's time there were two distinct and competing ideological currents reflected in the distinction between the gospels and the institutional church. Each had its own organizing assumptions. Though not necessarily in inherent conflict, human creativity and trial-and-error learning were necessary to sustain the essentials of each. The formation of the Franciscan rule exemplifies an innovation the church with its strong institutional underpinnings used in order to experiment and learn. Without experiments to resolve ideological conflicts, such conflict can give rise to psychological contract violation among organization members that can weaken or destroy their bond.

In contemporary American society a host of ideological currents have come together in conflicting ways, including law, efficiency, fiduciary accountability, moral and social responsibility, and the economics of the marketplace. The contemporary American health-care system is an exemplar of ideological conflict.[19] Health-care professionals, in particular nurses and doctors, are torn between the ideology of caregiving and administrative efficiency. Health-care organizations traditionally have been guardian institutions devoted to the common good, with relatively few hospitals operating on a for-profit basis. With the emergence of health maintenance organizations, Medicare, and other third-party payers as drivers of health-care delivery, concerns for efficiency have raised market factors to a central concern in health-care decisions. Guardian institutions can function quite effectively outside the market and with limited external control. To do so though they must strictly adhere to their own codes in line with the role they hold in society. Such institutions (e.g., the federal and local governments, community and other nonprofit hospitals such as those sponsored by Sisters of Mercy) work best when they foster and honor high trust relationships with their members/public. The breakdown of this relationship in American health care stems from the reluctance of physicians, and, in particular, the American Medical Association, to submit to some degree of price regulation, bringing health-care costs to new levels. Third-party payers have reacted to constrain the autonomy of health-care organizations, making it difficult for caregivers to place clinical concerns foremost in their decisions. In the case of health-care organizations, the disruptions have been multifold, including not only increased regulation by the market but also rising mistrust on the part of the public in response to their instrumental and substandard performance. The power balance has shifted from clinical caregivers to third-party payers, and increasingly in the direction of the public, which has contracts with both health-care insurers and clinical caregivers.

We see health care, risks parallel to those the church runs unless relations among clergy and laity are reformed. The church in America, like all guardian institutions that fail to internally regulate themselves to the highest level of values (their own and those society expects of them), has experienced disruption and greater external control. Its failure is evident in the lack of appropriate responses to instances of pedophilia. The sex abuse scandals teach us that untested assumptions can be dangerous. Bishops when faced with a pedophile priest viewed the behavior as a moral failing rather than as pathology. In the context of the church, moral failures are deemed correctable, requiring commitment on the part of the offender and forgiveness on the part of others. The ways bishops showed their traditional paternal care for priests contributed to the abuse scandal while their neglect of pastoral responsibilities toward parishioners exacerbated it.[20]

The church's failure to regulate itself has prompted imposition of external control. Recent court rulings have created access to the personnel files of accused priests and other church records relating to allegations of child molestation.[21] Declining parishioner donations make it necessary for church organizations to compete for governmental and other public funds, creating closer scrutiny of practices and fiscal records.[22] Breaches of trust and performance failures in guardian institutions lead their stakeholders to demand influence over the institution's practices. It behooves guardian institutions to pay careful attention to the ideological currents they act upon, due to their intrusive effects on thoughts and behavior. This awareness is particularly important in times of stress and challenge where unquestioned and taken-for-granted assumptions can yield conflict, mistrust, and backlash. Those psychological contracts that can be kept are created in organizations where potentially conflicting ideologies are resolved in ways that nonetheless adhere to fundamental and shared principles. As in the time of St. Francis, the church once again is called upon to experiment.

IMPLICATIONS OF PSYCHOLOGICAL CONTRACTS IN RESTORING TRUST

The church's many stakeholders in various clerical and lay roles can hold different psychological contracts, perhaps necessitating different recontracting processes, even while adhering to enduring principles. We need to ask what form an appropriate psychological contract might take. A broken relational contract is like Humpty Dumpty. It can't go back into its old form. Marriages that successfully face fundamental challenges adapt and renew. They don't ossify. The parties learn things about themselves, each other, and their assumptions that in turn foster in this re-creation. Respectful of the active role clergy and laity must play in this renewal, it is not for this chapter to specify the content of a renewed contract. But it can address the "process."

Renewing or remaking psychological contracts requires work, activity by all contract parties in the effort to identify their common, organizationwide and individual, local concerns. One of the hazards in a hierarchical organization is losing sight of the overall vision, instead becoming absorbed in narrow concerns and self-interest. A hierarchical mindset is in danger of assuming that anyone higher in status is a more perfect embodiment of the mission. But all leaders are not good stewards, and even the lowest member can embody the mission's authentic voice.

Michael Papesh suggests that putting all community decisions under a single question—What does God want of us?—can bridge all church levels into a common community. All parties need to be invited in to work out the roles and responsibilities that best respond to this question. Times of change make people more interdependent, their roles shaped by interactions with others, especially because there are fewer preestablished ways of solving the new challenges change brings. Recognizing shared, superordinate responsibility for a common mission can counteract hierarchical blinders. An appropriate model is perhaps found in the imagery of Vatican II, where a vertical church of head and members is overlaid upon a horizontal one of pilgrim people of God.[23] Such a model reflects active participation across all members with those in leadership roles acting as servant leaders, challenging themselves to learn and serve others better.

To renew relationships, particularly when trust is low, each of the parties must have influence. This aspect of the process surfaces another ideological current in American society: "The basic assumptions of the laity are also thoroughly democratic."[24] Parishioners assume that at least some of the authority exercised by church officials, Catholic schoolteachers, and diocesan priests comes from them. Institutional ideology may be otherwise, but parishioners increasingly believe their priests should be accountable to them. The present crisis draws attention to the legitimate use of power, the meaning of clerical and lay roles, and the nature of the relationships between them. Respect for the interests of the other means that each party's concerns receive equal attention, and for that to occur each party must have influence over the nature of this new relationship. In the spirit of giving something to create something new, leaders need to be willing to make themselves personally and organizationally vulnerable, in effect to trust in a process that they cannot fully control. Such trust is often easiest to build step-by-step, taking one interaction at a time. As a wise person once said, "It can be easier to build relationships around tasks."

Tasks around which to renew relationships involve symbolically and morally important decisions. One such task involves decisions regarding finances and church property. For their participation and financial support, the American laity believe they have earned a real say. This belief is exacerbated by the clergy's use of money parishioners had raised for schools to pay off abuse victims instead. How church finances are handled and the creation of transparency prompts concern over how information is best shared and used. The process whereby decisions arise affects their legitimacy by signaling whether the principals have behaved in ways consistent with broadly held values. Decisions taken in secret and without the involvement of affected parties are more likely to look like shady deals, lacking a basis in appropriate values, than are those decisions made in a more public fashion.[25] Common property is a basis for community life, and how that property is used and how information regarding it is disseminated become defining features of the community's values and beliefs. Church property has tremendous symbolic and real value and shared decision-making would constitute a genuinely communal act.

There are 195 Catholic dioceses in the United States, each with its own local dynamics and subculture among the ordained.[26] Reshaping relationships in the face of a myriad of local cultures is a slow, difficult task. Yet there is evidence that this process is already beginning. We see signs of new approaches to sustaining church programs and missions, and these can interject new ideologies such as openness to community concerns and active laity into the life of the American church. In response to falling donations after the scandal, Catholic schools are employing "MBA-style survival plan(s)" to obtain funding. Marketing seminars and capital campaigns make Catholic education conferences resemble business conventions.[27] New data are being gathered to assess the status and needs of traditional Catholic activities such as urban schools. Personnel files of priests and other church records are no longer held to be sacrosanct.[28] Lay ministers play an increasingly important role in American parishes.

Despite these signs of new activity, disillusionment also exists.[29] But some disillusionment from time to time is as normal as uncertainty in times of change. Doubt, an experience many members of faith communities readily acknowledge, can precede new consensus.[30] Even chaos is not a negative feature as long as it provides a step forward in a productive process, a common experience in the transition from old mindsets to new during organizational change. The issue I raise while conducting courses on organizational change is how to get through chaos in expeditious, change-enhancing ways.

Often the first steps toward change fail because people lack the skill and experience to quickly master new demands made of them. Just think about the challenges learning involves. It can be a hassle to have one's young children help fix dinner or wash dishes, since their efforts aren't likely to be successful at first and our control is diluted. Yet over time the children become more active helpful family members, a boon worth the chaos of transition and learning. In the chaos generated as many people step forward with opinion and involvement, we have the potential payoff of a broader range of people able to use their gifts on behalf of the church community. Learning how to cultivate and get through chaos may be a key aspect of servant leadership.

This transition is aided by ongoing questioning of the meaning of roles and notions once taken for granted. Initial efforts don't find their way to a new steady state without challenge and modification. Clergy and laity will both have moments of frustration and confusion when efforts to renew their relationship stumble over newly surfaced assumptions or losses tough to bear. Authority may be vested differently than once was the case, as its nature becomes less hierarchical and more mutual. Authority without endorsement by those whose behavior is affected by it is tyranny. Church leaders will need to build endorsement rather than assume it. Property may be a privilege that divides clergy and laity or a bond they share. Creating a shared understanding of each other's roles and responsibilities can require new shared experiences and a greater sense of a common fate, perhaps as priests live more in the community they serve and less apart from it.

Lastly, there will be a need for feedback and redesign over time as new arrangements are introduced, their strengths built upon, and their limitations overcome. I worry about sustaining a continued willingness to evaluate the effectiveness of changes made in the face of long-standing discomfort with feedback and criticism within the church. Nonetheless, learning how to learn requires a willingness to assess the effects of actions taken and an acceptance that workable agreements require authentic questioning and inspired creativity to sustain themselves over time.

CONCLUSION: CREATING MUTUAL AGREEMENTS THAT ARE KEPT

Information technology, democratic values, and respect for the capabilities of individuals and local communities have created flatter organizations worldwide. Americans in particular are increasingly adaptive to demands for their initiative, learning, and community activity. In this context, the church in the United States has an opportunity to renew itself by inviting members into the process. Some issues to consider in renewing their psychological contracts:

(1) The contract must be both flexible enough to incorporate learning (i.e., able to change with growth and experience, including level of education or competence of members, environmental turbulence, and the like) and consistent in terms of promises, expectations, and obligations so parties know where they stand. We know that experimentation is possible in the context of the church because local parishes already engage in idiosyncratic ways of doing things. Flexibility, for example, exists in the priestly role. Across parishes we can observe priests employing worship styles that suit their personal preferences. Other parishes rely largely on lay ministers with limited priestly involvement. As long as the bishop doesn't intervene, these idiosyncrasies constitute part of the normal variation in parish life. Accommodations the church has made over the ages are not uniformly hallowed from dispensations and indulgences to female altar servers, but there is variety nonetheless. The church is in a comparable position to the employer who learns that flexitime might be a good company policy after discovering the benefits that followed when some local managers granted their workers flexible hours (or when those workers created their own flexible hours with no adverse consequences).[31]

(2) Because there are multiple contract makers, the church needs to attend to the messages sent via its practices and the many people who speak and act on its behalf. This does not mean one size fits all, since the same organization is likely to manage a variety of distinct psychological contracts with its members depending upon their competence, roles, and contributions. Nonetheless, the organization must take responsibility for the messages that it sends via its individual leaders and members, and its array of formal and informal practices. This can be particularly challenging where commitments of transparency and involvement are expressed by some and denied by others. Where experiments are attempted in order to learn, they should be framed as such to promote acceptance of innovation made in good faith.

(3) Despite existence of multiple psychological contracts, organizations need to establish a clear metacontract (i.e., rules about the rules of the contract). This metacontract requires open exchange of information between parties to learn one another's interests, goals, and constraints. It means acknowledging where different psychological contracts exist across hierarchical levels, positions, or functional roles (e.g., teaching versus contemplative) and the bases for these differences. It means that the church's commitment to principles of justice (distributive—fair outcomes; procedural—fair organizational processes, procedures, and decision making; interactional—respectful of persons) must govern its own internal relations. Consistent with the first point above, some degree of experimentation and problem solving is essential in the context of an organization's metacontract.

A metacontract reflects shared values. One such value is reflected in the yearning for a more authentic spirituality and church life.[32] In generative cultures such as the church intends to be, creating community and spiritual growth for its members and the capacity to act for the broader good requires commitment to learn from shared experience in an environment of mutually agreed-upon obligations.

NOTES

1. Dante, *The Divine Comedy, Part 2: Purgatory*, translated by D. L. Sayers (London: Penguin, 1955).

2. Clifford J. Sager, *Marriage Contracts and Couple Therapy: Hidden Forces in Intimate Relationships* (New York: Brunner/Mazel, 1976); Denise M. Rousseau, *Psychological Contracts in Organizations: Understanding Written and Unwritten Agreements* (Newbury Park, Calif.: Sage, 1995).

3. Rousseau, *Psychological Contracts*.

4. D. Katz and R. L. Kahn, *The Social Psychology of Organizations*, 2nd ed. (New York: Wiley, 1978).

5. Denise M. Rousseau, "Schema, Promises, and Mutuality: The Psychology of the Psychological Contract," *Journal of Organizational and Occupational Psychology* 24 (2001): 511–41.

6. Rousseau, *Psychological Contracts*.

7. Michael L. Papesh, *Clerical Culture: Contradiction and Transformation* (Collegeville, Minn.: Liturgical Press, 2004).

8. Guillermo Dabos and Denise M. Rousseau, "Social Interaction Patterns Shaping Psychological Contracts," (*Best Paper Proceedings of the Academy of Management*, New Orleans, August 2004).

9. Papesh, *Clerical Culture*, 9.

10. Papesh, *Clerical Culture*, 10.

11. Violet T. Ho, Soon Ang, and Detmar Straub, "When Subordinates Become IT Contractors: Persistent Managerial Expectations in IT Outsourcing," *Information Systems Research* 14, no. 1 (March 2003): 66–88.

12. Avery Dulles, *Models of the Church* (Garden City, N.Y.: Image Books, 1987).

13. Charles Manz, Karen P. Manz, Robert D. Marx, and Christopher P. Neck, *The Wisdom of Solomon at Work* (San Francisco: Berrett Koehler, 2001).

14. For example, Julie Scelfo, "A 'Shameful' Failure," *Newsweek*, 8 Mar. 2004, 8.

15. Rousseau, *Psychological Contracts*.

16. Adrian House, *Francis of Assisi: A Revolutionary Life* (Mahwah, N.J.: Hidden Spring, 2001).

17. Bernard M. Bass, *Leadership and Performance Beyond Expectations* (New York: Free Press, 1985).

18. House, *Francis of Assisi*.

19. J. Stuart Bunderson, "How Work Ideologies Shape the Psychological Contracts of Professional Employees: Doctors' Responses to Perceived Breach," *Journal of Organizational Behavior* 22 (2001): 717–43.

20. Papesh, *Clerical Culture*, 14.

21. "Court Prevents Blanket Secrecy Orders," *Quill* 92, no. 2 (March 2004): 21.

22. Ron Depasquale, "Business of Survival," *Newsweek* 143, no. 25 (June 2004): 12.

23. Dulles, *Models of the Church*; Papesh, *Clerical Culture*, 59.

24. Papesh, *Clerical Culture*, 82.

25. K. A. Hegtved and C. Johnson, "Justice Beyond the Individual: A Future With Legitimation," *Social Psychology Quarterly* 63 (2000): 298–311.

26. Papesh, *Clerical Culture*, 17.

27. Depasquale, "Business of Survival."

28. "Court Prevents," *Quill*.

29. For example, Scelfo, "'Shameful' Failure."

30. Papesh, *Clerical Culture*, 126.

31. Denise M. Rousseau, *I-deals: Idiosyncratic Deals Employees Negotiate for Themselves* (Armonk, N.Y.: M. E. Sharpe, 2005).

32. Papesh, *Clerical Culture*, 37.

9: ORGANIZATIONAL MORALITY

C. R. (Bob) Hinings and Michael K. Mauws

Hannah Arendt — the banality of evil

"... the organization as a whole is an instrument to obliterate responsibility."

—Zygmunt Bauman, *Modernity and the Holocaust*

Our aim in this chapter is to examine the means by which, and the degree to which, managerial practices suppress individual moral autonomy and 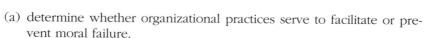 thereby increase the likelihood of moral failure. In doing so, we apply recent developments in moral theory[1] to explore contemporary managerial problems. The objectives in exploring the relationship between managerial practices and moral responsibility are to

(a) determine whether organizational practices serve to facilitate or prevent moral failure,
(b) identify the way in which organizational practices might render individual behavior morally ambivalent,
(c) develop a set of strategies to resist and counteract moral ambivalence within complex organizations.

Our interest in this topic dates back to 1997. At that time, the citizens of Canada were being forced to come to terms with two national tragedies. One of these was the so-called tainted blood scandal, involving the contamination of the national blood supply during the late 1970s and the 1980s. The result of this contamination was the infection of more than one thousand persons with the human immunodeficiency virus (HIV) and the infection of tens of thousands of people with the hepatitis C virus. The other tragedy was the so-called Somalia affair, involving the deaths of two Somalis at the hands of Canadian Forces personnel. These personnel were in Somalia as a result of the Canadian Forces' participation in a United Nations peacekeeping mission in 1992–1993. Commissions of inquiry were commenced to determine the causes of both tragedies, and, in 1997, the final reports of these commissions were delivered to the government and people of Canada.

The two commissions arrived independently at pretty much the same conclusion: that these tragedies were the result of mismanagement. The *Executive Summary* of the Somalia Inquiry, for example, states that "systems broke down and organizational discipline crumbled," "planning, training and overall preparations fell far short of what was required."[2] Similarly, the final report of the Krever Inquiry speaks of "systemic problems" and "shortcomings of the regulator," while repeatedly drawing attention to resource shortages.[3] The conclusion is that, with better organization, these tragedies could have been averted with the explanation being that these tragedies were the product of having failed to put in place the necessary organizational structures and systems.

There is truth to this explanation.[4] For it is clear that, had the identified shortcomings not existed, these events would have been much less likely to have happened. Nevertheless, part of why this explanation has been so readily embraced may be that it is a reassuring explanation to accept. After all, if these tragedies are attributable to organizational shortcomings on the part of the Canadian Forces or the Canadian blood system, the solution is simply to address these shortcomings. And as difficult as it might be to achieve this, it is an appealing solution for the simple reason that it locates the problems to be rectified within the organizations investigated. In other words, it renders them *organizational problems* that can be solved.

There is another explanation for these tragedies that, despite being much more difficult to accept, is equally plausible. Simply stated, the alternative explanation is that the events in question were in fact *made possible* by well-accepted and highly regarded organizational practices. It is because these organizations were as well organized as they were that these events took place, not because they were insufficiently organized.[5] The implication of this explanation is that it applies to the phenomenon of "organization" itself and, thus, to potentially *all* organizations. What they suggest is not that we have failed to organize but, rather, that *organization has failed.*[6] And if this is the case, correcting the identified, specific, organizational shortcomings is unlikely to preclude another tainted blood scandal or Somalia affair. If this is the case, what it suggests is that it is organization rather than the lack thereof that leaves us vulnerable to these sorts of moral failures.

This is the thesis that we think needs to be explored. Influenced as we are by the ethical project of Zygmunt Bauman,[7] we wish to ask whether organizational practices are responsible for the abdication of moral responsibility and, ultimately, for moral failure. And if they are, how do they accomplish this?

Ethical debate has traditionally been situated between the positions of liberalism and communitarianism.[8] In very general terms, those aligned with the former have concerned themselves with finding an ethical code that places the least restrictions on the actions of the individual,[9] whereas those aligned with the latter have sought an ethical code that meets the needs of the community.[10] But despite these differences, both perspectives have an important feature in common. Simply stated, both share the belief that ethics is the precursor of moral behavior; that is, that ethics *produces* morality. And for this reason, the goal in both cases has been the production of a universal code of ethics that can guide those in need of a moral compass.[11]

But as with all grand narratives, the idea of a universal code of ethics became highly suspect toward the end of the twentieth century.[12] The discourse around "postmodernism" has, if nothing else, served to greatly undermine the authority of Reason. It has helped us appreciate that an ethical code cannot be anything more than simply one discourse among many, struggling to make itself heard; that it is an instrument of power rather than an instrument of truth.[13] If there is a difficulty with this, it is simply that it seems to suggest that the ethical project itself is doomed. This is an important reason why so many have been quick to dismiss the claims of postmodernism.

We are quite willing to acknowledge that postmodernism may indeed represent the end of ethics. But we would point out that this need not coincide with the end of morality.[14] For as Bauman notes, "in the same way as modernity went down in history as *the age of ethics*, the coming post-modern era [may] come to be recorded as *the age of morality*."[15] But if we are to understand why this may be, it is necessary that we first fully understand what is meant by "morality" and, in particular, what is encompassed by the idea of "moral responsibility."

In addressing this subject, Bauman refers to the "moral impulse," an impulse through which we recognize our *unconditional* responsibility for the Other.[16] This is an impulse that is *prior to* reason and rational calculation. Reason and rational calculation come *afterward* in our attempts to cope with this responsibility. For our unconditional responsibility for the Other is also an *unlimited* responsibility.[17] Simply stated, we can *always* do more for the Other. And it is the gnawing uncertainty that this creates that is the wellspring of the ethical project.[18] From this perspective, a code of ethics is intended to be that to which one can adhere in an attempt to *know* that one has somehow done enough.

However, the demands of the moral impulse and the accompanying anxiety it creates are also avoided unintentionally on occasion; that is, when our forms of social organization prevent us from recognizing our moral responsibility in the first place. Where this is perhaps most prevalent is in the large, complex organizations that dominate modern society.[19] These organizations are, as Bauman notes, instruments designed to obliterate responsibility, and it is because they do this so effectively that organization is a frequent accomplice in the moral failures that plague our society.[20]

As Bauman's inquiry into the Holocaust makes clear, complex organizations thwart our moral impulses in numerous ways.[21] At the most general level, they accomplish this by facilitating action at a distance. They serve to separate the thought from the deed and, in doing so, they result in decisions being made in relation to abstract entities as opposed to the real Others that those who carry out these decisions must confront.[22] And, conversely, they enable the latter to absolve themselves of responsibility for their actions by virtue of the fact that the decisions that prompted their actions were not their own. Thus, we can see that, by separating decision-making from implementation, the moral impulse is for all intents and purposes bypassed.[23]

One of the common ways organizations accomplish this is through the hierarchical and functional division of labor. Perhaps there was indeed a time when those at the top of the organizational hierarchy arrived there through a slow but steady progression through the organizational ranks; in any case, that time has passed. At best, organizational leaders might now do a whirlwind tour of the lower ranks as part of their preparation for overseeing them. The reality now is that those at the top tend to be recruited from differing sources than those at the bottom and, thus, are limited to *imagining* what life might be like at that level. Nowhere is this more apparent than in management education, which is premised upon the idea of generic managers fit to run whatever sort of organization will have them.[24] Thus, the result is that those at the top are giving orders, the full effects of which they are unaware. To the degree that they have any idea at all, it is at best a detached awareness constructed with abstractions.[25]

The effects of this division of labor rise dramatically when it is effected functionally as well. For with hierarchical division alone, all within the chain of command are engaged in one and the same task. Although those who give the orders may not carry them out, those at the top and those at the bottom agree in their assessment of the task being undertaken. However, with the move to a functional division of labor, the moral significance of one's activities is no longer clear. More to the point, the outcomes of one's actions are multi-final. Whether one is contributing to a morally reprehensible activity depends upon what is done with the *products* of one's labors. Thus, the ability of individuals carrying out these actions to both perceive their moral responsibility and to act on it is severely compromised.

 However, the biggest impact of the move to functional division of labor is the substitution of technical responsibility for moral responsibility that it effects.[26] For no longer can moral standards be employed as measures of success. Instead, it is technical standards that must be referred to. As MacIntyre notes:

Managers themselves and most writers about management conceive of themselves as morally neutral characters whose skills enable them to devise the most efficient means of achieving whatever end is proposed. Whether a given manager is effective or not is on the dominant view a quite different question from that of the morality of the ends which his effectiveness serves or fails to serve.[27]

So within organizations, what we find is that the vocabulary of morality experiences a transformation. In the process, it adopts concepts such as discipline, loyalty, and duty, all of which affirm the authority of superiors and the primacy of organizational as opposed to moral responsibilities. And in this sense, *the triumph of organization is not so much that it thwarts morality, but that it redeploys it toward the pursuit of technical ends.* Within this framing, as Kimberly Elsbach notes elsewhere in this volume, leadership can become a stultifying rather than liberating organizational element.

The vocabulary of organization is also significant in its capacity to dehumanize the objects of bureaucratic operations. By referring to these objects as "enemies," "customers," or "competitors," it renders them different and, in some cases, renders them threatening. In either case, the result is a diminishment in perceived responsibility. Moreover, by creating a "them," it also creates an "us" of which we are a part. And to the degree that we belong, it becomes more difficult for us to resist participation in the group's activities, even if we may suspect their moral quality may be questionable.[28] In Denise Rousseau's terms, there is a fundamental change in the psychological contract at the heart of organizational relationships.

So, our argument is that morality has to be situated before ethics; that the way in which organizational practices substitute their own ends as "moral" require examination. And for this reason, we see a need to return to the "old" organizational question: What are the consequences of the existence of organizations?[29] Examples of this are easily found, and churches are no exception. Large in scale, scattered over many locations, and having authoritative structures and systems that essentially deny individuals per se, the sort of encounter with an Other that might raise the moral impulse seldom occurs. And with extensive power distance between organizational levels that suppresses resistance and dissent, those who are adversely affected are unable to garner the attention of those most able to bring about change. But as we noted above, the churches are not alone in this regard, for the real problem does not lie with particular organizations but, rather, with organization itself.[30]

NOTES

1. Zygmunt Bauman, *Modernity and the Holocaust* (Cambridge: Polity, 1989); Bauman, *Postmodern Ethics* (Oxford: Blackwell, 1993); Bauman, *Life in Fragments: Essays in Postmodern Morality* (Oxford: Blackwell, 1995); Bauman, "On Communitarians

and Human Freedom. Or, How to Square the Circle," *Theory, Culture & Society* 13, no. 2 (1996): 79–90; Bauman, *Postmodernity and Its Discontents* (New York: New York University Press, 1997); see Alasdair MacIntyre, *After Virtue: A Study in Moral Theory* (Notre Dame, Ind.: University of Notre Dame Press, 1981).

2. Commission of Inquiry into the Deployment of Canadian Forces to Somalia, *Dishonoured Legacy: The Lessons of the Somalia Affair*, 5 vols. Vol. Executive Summary (Ottawa: Canadian Government Publishing, 1997).

3. Commission of Inquiry on the Blood System in Canada, *Final Report: Commission of Inquiry on the Blood System in Canada*, 3 vols. Vol. 3 (Ottawa: Canadian Government Publishing, 1997).

4. Arthur Schafer, *The Buck Stops Here: Reflections on Moral Responsibility, Democratic Accountability, and Military Values: A Report Prepared for the Commission of Inquiry Into the Deployment of Forces to Somalia* (Ottawa: Canadian Government Publishing, 1997); see Charles Perrow and Mauro F. Guillén, *The AIDS Disaster: The Failure of Organizations in New York and the Nation* (New Haven and London: Yale University Press, 1990).

5. Danny Miller, *The Icarus Paradox: How Exceptional Companies Bring about Their Own Downfall* (New York: HarperBusiness, 1990).

6. Mats Alvesson, "A Critical Framework for Organizational Analysis," *Organization Studies* 6, no. 2 (1985): 117–38; Barbara Townley, "Foucault, Power/knowledge, and Its Relevance for Human Resource Management," *Academy of Management Review* 18, no. 3 (1993): 518–45.

7. For example, *Modernity; Postmodern Ethics; Life in Fragments*.

8. Scott Lash, "Introduction to the Ethics and Difference Debate," *Theory, Culture & Society* 13, no. 2 (1996): 75–77.

9. For example, Richard Rorty, *Contingency, Irony, and Solidarity* (Cambridge: Cambridge University Press, 1989).

10. For example, MacIntyre, *After Virtue*.

11. Bauman, *Postmodern Ethics*.

12. Jean-Francois Lyotard, *The Postmodern Condition: A Report of Knowledge* (Minneapolis: University of Minnesota Press, 1984).

13. Michel Foucault, *Discipline and Punish: The Birth of the Prison*, translated by Alan Sheridan (New York: Random House, 1979); Foucault, *Power/knowledge: Selected Interviews and Other Writings, 1972–1977* (New York: Pantheon Books, 1980).

14. Thomas McCarthy, *Ideals and Illusions: On Reconstruction and Deconstruction in Contemporary Critical Theory* (Cambridge, Mass.: MIT Press, 1991); MacIntyre, *After Virtue*; Nicholas H. Smith, "Contingency and Self-identity: Taylor's Hermeneutics vs. Rorty's Postmodernism," *Theory, Culture & Society* 13, no. 2 (1996): 105–20.

15. Bauman, *Life in Fragments*, 37.

16. Bauman, *Postmodern Ethics*.

17. Knud E. Logstrup, *The Ethical Demand* (Philadelphia: Fortress, 1971).

18. Bauman, *Postmodern Ethics; Postmodernity*.

19. MacIntyre, *After Virtue*.

20. Bauman, *Modernity*, 163.

21. Bauman, *Modernity*.

22. Foucault, *Discipline and Punish*.

23. Bauman, *Postmodern Ethics*.

24. MacIntyre, *After Virtue*.

25. Bauman, *Modernity*.

26. Bauman, *Modernity*.

27. MacIntyre, *After Virtue*, 74.

28. Bauman, *Modernity*; *Postmodernity*.

29. C. R. Hinings and Royston Greenwood, "Disconnects and Consequences in Organization Theory?" *Administrative Science Quarterly* 47 (2002): 411–22.

30. The ideas presented in this paper are derived from a research proposal funded by the Canadian Social Sciences and Humanities Research Council.

10: ETHICS CODES, INTERVENTION, AND CORRUPTION REFORM METHODS FOR ECCLESIAL PROFESSIONALS

Richard P. Nielsen

"The student of ethics must apply himself to politics."

—Aristotle

"The happiness of others is an end which is at the same time a duty."

—Immanuel Kant

"When bad men combine, the good must associate; else they will fall one by one, an unpitied sacrifice in a contemptible struggle."

—Edmund Burke

According to Massachusetts Attorney General Thomas F. Reilly's investigation and audit of church records of the sexual abuse of children by priests, there have been at least one thousand children abused by more than 235 priests from 1940 to 2000.[1] Even if the abused children not reported to the church and/or not recorded by the church officials are not included in these numbers, if one were to project these numbers across other geographic areas within the United States alone, there are tens of thousands of children who have been abused by thousands of priests during this period. These numbers are large and shocking.

On September 9, 2003, the Roman Catholic Archdiocese of Boston agreed to pay $85 million to settle about five hundred lawsuits to people who were abused by priests when they were children.[2] A jury in Dallas awarded $119.5 million to eleven plaintiffs who had been sexually abused by the priest Rudolph Kos.[3] In California, there have been over one thousand molestation lawsuits in the last five years. If similar financial settlements were made with similar victims across the country, that would represent billions of dollars of financial costs. As a result, educational, social, and medical services to church members, the poor, and the needy have and will have to be cut and continue to be cut. These numerical costs do not of course include the immense psychological and spiritual costs to the thousands of children and their families who were victims of the abuse.

The institutional costs to the church are also very large. For example, since 2002, morale has suffered enormously, five Catholic bishops including the cardinal of the Boston archdiocese have been forced to resign, two bishops came very close to being indicted on criminal charges, and at least a dozen bishops have been subpoenaed to testify at grand jury investigations.[4]

Yet, in the sixty years for which we have records of such extensive sexual abuse and costs of the sexual abuse of children within the church, there appears to have been very little done by ecclesial professionals to protect children and stop the systematic corruption. Much of what has been done in the 1990s to reform this problem has been spurred on by lawsuits stimulated by external whistle-blowing.[5] The issues addressed in this chapter are as follows:

First, do individual ecclesial professionals have ethical obligations to intervene against unethical and corrupt behaviors of other professionals? That is, do we have an ethical duty not only to refrain from sexually abusing children ourselves, but do we also have an obligation to intervene to stop other professionals from abusing children and to intervene to change organizational systems and traditions that permit systematic and extensive abuse, corruption, and cover-up of the abuse and corruption?

Second, can awareness and skills in using ethics intervention and corruption reform methods help empower ecclesial professionals to act as institutional citizens in developing more ethical organizational communities? Can practical knowledge of intervention methods empower ethical individual and organizational character?

Third, what ethics intervention and corruption reform methods can ecclesial professionals use to act and intervene effectively and appropriately to protect children as well as to address other ethics and corruption reform issues?

DO WE HAVE AN ETHICAL DUTY TO ACT AND INTERVENE?

Do we have an ethical obligation to pay attention to the ethical behaviors of others? If we see or hear about unethical behavior, do we have an ethical obligation to act and intervene? One could approach these questions from at least three related ethical philosophical perspectives: Aristotelian, Kantian, and utilitarian cost-benefit analyses.

For Aristotle, "The student of ethics *must* apply himself to politics."[6] What Aristotle means by "student of ethics" is someone who really cares about ethics. That is, if we really care about ethics, then we have to act politically as citizens of a community to address ethical issues in our common community life. Aristotle used a very strong word here. He wrote that we *must* apply ourselves to political action. We *must* act and intervene. It is not enough to live isolated, individual ethical lives when unethical behavior and corruption are going on around us.

Kant seems to concur and builds upon Aristotle's idea of happiness.[7] According to Kant, "That beneficence is a duty results from the fact that since our self-love cannot be separated from our need to be loved by others (to obtain help from them in the case of need), we thereby make ourselves an end for others; . . . hence the happiness of others is an end which is at the same time a duty."[8] We could interpret this from at least two perspectives. One, we have a duty to intervene to help others because we reciprocally need to be helped by others, that is, "our self-love cannot be separated from our need to be loved by others (to obtain help from them in the case of need)." Second, both we and other people acting unethically are unlikely to be genuinely happy. Therefore, for the happiness of ourselves and others, we have a duty to intervene.

In the case of the massive sexual abuse and cover-up of the sexual abuse of children within the church, it appears obvious from a cost-benefit perspective, intervention is required. Tens of thousands of children were damaged spiritually and psychologically. Thousands of priests are unlikely to have been genuinely happy in their abuse of the children. The spiritual, psychological, and financial costs are enormous. The benefits of effective intervention might have greatly reduced these terrible costs.

It appears that we do have a duty to intervene in the ethical, social, and political life of our communities. It is not enough to "mind our own business" and lead isolated, individual ethical lives when around us there are significant and extensive unethical and corrupt behaviors.

CAN PRACTICAL KNOWLEDGE OF INTERVENTION METHODS EMPOWER ETHICAL INDIVIDUAL AND ORGANIZATIONAL CHARACTER?

As referred to above, a problem for many of us is that while we are concerned about ethics, we do not always know how to do (method) ethics in organizational contexts in such a way as to overcome the powerful individual, organizational systems/traditions, and environmental obstacles to build ethical communities and also to care for own personal, ethical development. Method can help us combine and live Aristotle's concepts of *poiesis* (action

poesis - changes external world
praxis - changes the agent

that changes the external world) and *praxis* (action that also developmentally changes the actor). Understanding ethics issues is not the same as the behavioral process of intervening, acting and learning, and sometimes fighting with others in addressing ethics conflicts and problems. We do not always know how to act and learn with others in organizational ethics contexts. When we do not know how to act appropriately, we may not act at all or we may act counterproductively. Both inaction and inappropriate action can hinder individual and organizational ethical development.

ETHICS INTERVENTION AND CORRUPTION REFORM METHODS

There are at least six sets of ethics intervention and corruption reform methods that can help empower us to realize our duty to act ethically not just in our individual work lives, but also to act ethically as citizens of our communities to effectively oppose unethical behaviors and build more ethical communities.[9] The six sets of methods are (1) win-lose forcing methods, such as compliance-based ethics codes and asking for outside help through secret and public whistle-blowing; (2) win-win methods, such as negotiating, reciprocal networking, and even help for the perpetrators; (3) dialogic and participative methods; (4) internal due-process methods; (5) alternative institution-building methods when the corruption within institutions can't be changed or would take too long to change; and (6) social movement methods. There are many more techniques within these six categories. Below are a few examples.

While we might prefer to use a particular type of method such as dialogic participation, which methods will be more and less appropriate and effective often depends on the different types of individual, organizational, and environmental obstacles that characterize the problem situation.[10] For example, some church officials have been unwilling and/or unable to engage in dialogue about the sexual abuse scandals.[11] Ethical and effective ecclesial professionals may need to understand and be able to practice a wide variety of ethics and corruption reform methods including such difficult methods as secret whistle-blowing to realize our duties as professionals and citizens of organizational communities.

1. Win-Lose Forcing Methods

Examples of win-lose forcing methods include top-down, compliance- and punishment-based ethics codes and secret and public whistle-blowing. For the most part, win-lose forcing methods try to establish ethical behaviors through threats of punishment, embarrassment, and exposure. Win-lose methods concentrate on changing behavior unlike some other types of methods that try to change both how people think as well as systems and traditions of organizations that might influence how people think and in turn how people behave.[12]

For the most part, ethics codes are rules and regulations written by top management to control the behavior of lower-level organizational members. Occasionally, codes are more dialogically and participatively developed by people from many layers and parts of an organization.[13]

The top-down compliance codes include punishments for breaking the rules. Organizations that use punishment-based compliance codes tend to be authoritarian, older, larger, bureaucratic organizations and/or organizations that have experienced extensive illegal and unethical behavior.

The older, authoritarian, bureaucratic types of organizations are often characterized by a type of Theory X, win-lose, authoritarian management and leadership where top management acts as if lower-level employees were lazy, irresponsible people who had to be closely supervised and controlled.[14]

Examples of this type of organization are military organizations, government bureaucracies, and older industries such as mining and railroad companies. Some have suggested that the Catholic Church has been and in some important areas may still be similar to these types of authoritarian organizations.[15]

A second type of organization that often uses ethics codes includes organizations that have been caught engaging in extensive illegal and unethical behaviors. Part of the legal settlement with prosecutors and legislators is the establishment of compliance-based ethics codes. For example, this happened in the 1970s when many military and defense contractors were caught taking part in extensive corruption. The government "sentencing guidelines" offered companies lighter sentences and penalties if they established ethics programs with compliance codes and ethics officers to administer the codes.[16] Similarly, in the 2002 settlements between the large U.S. financial services institutions, the Securities and Exchange Commission, and the Justice Department, the financial services organizations agreed to establish compliance-based ethics codes that prohibited the behaviors that the government agencies had found illegal.[17]

Somewhat similarly, in response to the sexual abuse scandals in the church, the United States Conference of Catholic Bishops adopted a nationwide policy for all American dioceses to establish their own protocols for preventing sexual abuse of children.[18] Most of these protocols contain, in effect, ethics codes that forbid the sexual abuse of children as well as requirements to report internally sexual abuse, to stop the sexual abuse, and to punish the perpetrators. While it is unlikely that any authoritarian organization would do so, such codes could also encourage and/or require members of the organization to externally blow the whistle to the press or government if top management does little or nothing about the ethical violations.

A strength of top-down, punishment-based compliance codes is that they make clear that the unethical behaviors are unethical and are forbidden by the organization. A key limitation of such codes is that they can be selectively ignored by the top managers who have the discretion on whether and how to enforce the codes. Sometimes, top management ignores its own codes and refuses meaningful dialogue. In such cases, we may need to ask for outside help through secret or public external whistle-blowing. That is, in authoritarian organizations with top-down ethics codes that top management selectively ignores and suppresses information about, internal change methods are often not politically possible. In such cases, external whistle-blowing is very important. Also, in such authoritarian organizations, asking for outside help through secret whistle-blowing outside the organization to government, the courts, and/or the media may be necessary. The secret part is often necessary to protect the careers and/or the friends of the whistle-blowers from retaliation by the authoritarian top administrators.

For example, the 1993 sexual abuse rules established by the United States Conference of Catholic Bishops, at least with respect to cover-ups and reassignment of abusing priests, did not seem to be well enforced. Perhaps the 2003 rules will be better enforced. Similarly, the ethics codes and ethics officer programs established as a result of the 1970s corruption scandals in the defense industries appeared to have played very little positive role in either exposing or preventing the financial scandals of the 1990s.

Another problem with top-down, punishment-based compliance codes is that at least in some industries such as financial services, the rules tend to prohibit yesterday's unethical behaviors. In organizations that use compliance codes, the belief can grow that if something is not forbidden by the rules, it is permitted, at least until there is another scandal. The rules against the fraudulent junk bond financial reporting of the 1970s did not cover or help much with the fraudulent earnings reporting and auditing of the 1990s.[19]

Given the limitations of top-down, punishment-based compliance codes, it may be essential for organizational members to at least secretly threaten top managers with blowing the whistle outside the organization when top management selectively ignores its own codes and/or suppresses information about code violations.[20]

2. Win-Win Methods Such As Negotiating and Reciprocal Networking

The intention of win-lose methods is to force change through the threat of punishment for violations of ethics codes and/or exposure through external whistle-blowing of perpetrators and top managers who suppress information about code violations. Unlike these threat-based methods, win-win methods try to offer incentives for ethical behavior and incentives for cessation of unethical behaviors.[21]

Two important types of win-win methods are mutual-gain negotiating[22] and reciprocal networking.[23] As with the win-lose methods, the focus of these methods is behavior change rather than cognitive change. For example, a common type of *win-win negotiation* is to offer financial rewards or points toward promotion for ethical behavior, such as a financial bonus for a factory manager who reduces employee accident rates.

It might even be possible to offer alternatives to priests who sexually abuse children that concentrate on changing predatory behaviors rather than on changing minds. For example, a sexually abusive priest might be offered a transfer to a posting that had no children, such as a prison, a military unit, or a retirement home, in lieu of expulsion from the church. Similarly, a sexually abusive priest might be offered treatment in lieu of prosecution. However, the recidivism rates for child molestors are very high and treatment may not be very effective.

Reciprocal networking operates as follows. Person A helps Person B. Person A asks Person B to help Person C. Person A asks Person B and Person C to help Person D, and so on. Person A can do this because Person A is an ethical person who wants to help others or for reasons of selfish self-interest. It works both ways. Through this method, Person A builds a network of reciprocal win-win relationships with Person A at the center of the win-win network. If Person A wants to intervene to stop an unethical behavior and/or increase an ethical behavior, Person A has the political allies to exercise organizational influence.

Reciprocal networking is different than Mafia-type networking in two key areas. First, the network leader is trying to help people rather than exploit others. Two, the network is inclusive rather than exclusive.

A key strength of win-win methods relative to win-lose methods is that most people prefer to be rewarded for behavior change rather than be threatened into behavior change. A key limitation may be that the ethics change agent may not have anything to offer that is an adequate material incentive for stimulating ethical behavior and/or stopping unethical behavior. For example, the financial rewards from high-level corruption are often much greater than the material rewards ethics and corruption reformers can offer the high-level crooks. Perhaps somewhat similarly, a priest who has a sexual disorder for abusing children may not adequately understand that he is doing something very wrong. The ethics reformer may not have any realistic alternative that can substitute for what the priest feels he is receiving from his sexual abuse of the child victims.

3. Dialogic Methods

There are at least three sets of dialogic methods. There are the ethics arguments and criteria that can be used to discuss an issue. There are different methods for structuring conversations. There are different organizational structures for participating in organizational decision-making.

Examples of ethics arguments and criteria include Aristotle's proportionality criterion that emphasizes the appropriate amount of something (neither too much nor too little) rather than its rightness or wrongness, Aristotle's common good criterion, Kant's "treat people as ends in themselves and not solely as means" criterion, Bentham's utilitarian cost/benefit criterion, Derrida's postmodern power bias criterion, and so forth.[24] There are at least twenty different types of arguments and criteria that could be used in an ethics intervention conversation.

For example, with respect to a safety issue, one could reason with Aristotle's proportionality argument that our incidence of accidents relative to the industry is too high. One could reason with Aristotle's common good criterion that unnecessary worker injuries are not good for our organizational community. One could reason with Kant's "treat people as ends in themselves and not solely as means" criterion that allowing avoidable accidents for the sake of profitability is not treating people as ends in themselves. One could consider with Bentham's cost-benefit criterion whether the costs of accidents were greater than the benefits of improved safety. One could reason with Derrida's postmodern criterion that injuries may be occurring more frequently among the least powerful and most vulnerable organizational members.

There are at least six different methods of structuring dialogic conversations.[25] For example, one could use a Socratic method where the interventionist asks questions without advocating positions. One could use Argyris's action-learning method where the interventionist combines inquiry with advocacy and experimentation.[26] One could use Woolman's method where the interventionist inquires about organizational system/tradition forces that may be pressuring organizational members to behave in less ethical ways.[27]

There are many different types of organizational structures for organizing participative decision-making.[28] For example, there are self-managed work teams. There are joint management–employee committees, there are quality circles, there are employee boards and mixed stakeholder group boards that combine internal and external organizational stakeholders in advisory discussions.

4. Internal Due Process Systems

There are at least four different types of internal due-process systems: investigation and punishment, grievance and arbitration, mediation, and employee board systems.[29] Due-process systems are very important because in the emotionality of a scandal and the rush to closure, sometimes top management finds scapegoats rather than engaging in fundamental reforms. Typically, lower- and middle-level employees take the blame either for actions or pressures that come from top management. There is a great deal of variation in the fairness, costs, and flexibility of due-process systems.

In an investigation and punishment system, management does an investigation of an unethical behavior and then announces a decision with punishments if the accused is found guilty by management. This type of system is very fast and relatively inexpensive, but offers few protections to the accused. This is the type of system that is very popular in U.S. business but is illegal in the European Union since it offers so little protection to the accused employee.

In a grievance and arbitration system, several layers of management and employees discuss the case against the accused. If at progressive levels of management and employee representation, agreement can't be reached, a decision is made by an outside arbitrator. This type of system is common in unionized environments and government organizations. It offers a great deal of protection to the accused but is very time consuming and expensive.

In a mediation system, typically a human resources manager tries to mediate and work out some type of win-win agreement between the parties to an ethics conflict. This type of system is very informal, inexpensive, and flexible. However, its fairness depends to a great extent on the individual character and skills of the mediator.

In an employee board system, a jury of employees investigates a potential ethics violation and makes recommendations and decisions about the individual case and/or changes in an organization's policies and procedures that may have contributed to the ethics problem. This system is also very flexible and fair, but it is more expensive and time consuming than a mediator system. This is a relatively rare form of due-process system in American business since top managements are often reluctant to cede power to an employee board.

5. Alternative Institution Building

Sometimes it is not possible or it would take too long for organizational ethics and corruption reform efforts to work. In such a situation, it may be possible to build an alternative institution, such as an alternative school or even an alternative type of church, such as an American Catholic Church that would be independent of the Roman Catholic Church.

For example, in one emerging market country, the state university system was so corrupt that is was not possible to reform it.[30] Professors were often hired and promoted on the basis of political connections. Professors often did not attend classes. Many students did not attend classes. The administrators of the universities often collected kickbacks from university purchases. University resources were spent on nonuniversity activities. There were very few university efforts to help students get jobs after graduation.

Relatively little high-level research (knowledge production) was done in the universities.

For many years, reformers both within and outside the state university system tried to reform the university system, but it was not possible. Instead, the reformers got together to build an alternative private university. Professors were hired and promoted on the basis of research (knowledge production) and teaching (knowledge distribution) achievements. Students were admitted on the basis of their achievements rather than their political connections. Employers were invited to interview and hire students based on their achievements and abilities rather than their political connections. The private university succeeded. Professors who did excellent research and teaching were hired and promoted based on their achievements rather than their political connections. Excellent students were recruited and graduated. There is a 90 percent job placement rate among the students. The university has been growing at a rate of 20 percent a year for the last fourteen years. There is no financial corruption in university purchases and investments. The state universities have begun to imitate some aspects of the ethical private university.

A key strength of this method is that ethical institutions can be created when older corrupt organizations can't be changed. In addition, sometimes when the new ethical organization succeeds and gains prominence and market share, the older corrupt institutions decide to try to change in order to survive in the new competitive environment where before they were protected by their relative monopoly position. Key limitations of this method are that it can take enormous resources to build an alternative institution and that there is often very strong opposition to the new institution that is perceived by the old guard as a threat to their institutional position.

6. Social Movement Methods

Social movement methods are used when the problem is too big for one individual, group, or even organization to address. Examples of social movements include the U.S. civil rights movement, the Swedish Natural Step environmental movement, the U.S. investor capitalist movement, the Korean People's Solidarity for Participatory Democracy corruption reform movement, and the "Voice of the Faithful" church reform movement.[31] Typically, social movement methods combine the resources and efforts of several individuals, groups, organizations, and even associations.

A common series of processes within a social movement include the following:[32]

1. Dialogue among friends about biases in traditions/systems that also discovers political opportunities for reform.

2. Dialogue among friends, reformers, and leaders of established shared interest organizations about their personal values, which may result in alliances between reformers and established organization leaders.
3. Reframing among the leaders of established organizations and members concerning the meaning of membership in terms of active support for reform of biases in traditions/systems.
4. Win-win development of specialized reform organizations and/or alternative institutions.
5. Selected win-lose actions against win-lose opponents to reform.
6. Trailing win-win development of support of the reform movement through instrumental alliances with external support groups.

A key strength of social movement methods is that they are able to help develop large social changes that would have been impossible for individuals, groups, organizations, and associations acting alone. In addition, very important friendships are developed in the long struggle for positive social change. A key limitation of social movement methods is that they require an enormous amount of time from key leaders who are often not compensated financially very much or at all. This requires an enormous personal commitment of a few key leaders, typically taking a great deal of time away from family and normal career endeavors. In addition, social movements require an enormous amount of resources from key supporting organizations and individuals.

CONCLUSION

As illustrated above, there are many effective ethics intervention and corruption reform methods that ecclesial professionals can use to resist corruption and build ethical organizational communities. It is often not enough to "mind our own business" and act ethically in our individual work lives when there are serious unethical and corruption behaviors around us. We have an ethical obligation to act, to ask others inside and outside the organization for help if necessary, and to intervene to help others in resisting unethical and corrupt behaviors and in building ethical organizational communities. Practical knowledge and skills in the application of ethics and corruption reform methods can help enable and stimulate ethical individual and organizational character. As Aristotle observed, "The student of ethics *must* apply himself to politics." And as the Irish political theorist Edmund Burke advocated, "When bad men combine, the good must associate; else they will fall one by one, an unpitied sacrifice in a contemptible struggle."

NOTES

1. Fox Butterfield, "Church in Boston to Pay $85 Million in Abuse Lawsuits," *New York Times*, 10 Sept. 2003.

2. Butterfield, "Church in Boston."

3. Laurie Goodstein, "Lawyer for Church Says He Hid His Own Sexual Abuse by Priest," *New York Times*, 25 Nov. 2003.

4. R. Scott Appleby, "Unheavenly Days," *New York Times*, 7 Sept. 2003.

5. Peter Steinfels, *A People Adrift: The Crisis of the Roman Catholic Church in America* (New York: Simon and Schuster, 2003).

6. Aristotle, *The Nicomachean Ethics*.

7. N. E. Bowie, *Business Ethics: A Kantian Perspective* (Oxford: Blackwell Publishers, 1999).

8. Immanuel Kant, "The Metaphysical Principles of Virtue," in *Ethical Philosophy* (Indianapolis: Hackett Publishing, 1994), 52.

9. Richard P. Nielsen and Jean M. Bartunek, "Opening Narrow, Routenized Schemata to Ethical Stakeholder Consciousness and Action," *Business and Society* 35, no. 4 (1996): 483–519; Richard P. Nielsen, *The Politics of Ethics: Methods for Acting, Learning And Sometimes Fighting, With Others in Addressing Ethics Problems in Organizational Life* (New York: Oxford University Press, 1996); Nielsen, "Systematic Corruption in Financial Services, Types of Capitalism, and Ethics Intervention Methods," *Business and Professional Ethics Journal* 23, no.1 (2003): 1–31; Nielsen, "Corruption Networks and Implications for Ethical Corruption Reform," *Journal of Business Ethics* 42, no. 2 (2003): 125–49; Linda K. Trevino and Katherine A. Nelson, *Managing Business Ethics* (New York: Wiley, 2003).

10. C. R. Argyris, *Overcoming Organizational Defenses* (Boston: Allyn and Bacon, 1990); Nielsen, *Politics of Ethics*.

11. Steinfels, *A People Adrift*.

12. Nielsen and Bartunek, "Routenized Schemata"; Nielsen, *Politics of Ethics*; C. R. Argyris, "A Life Full of Learning," *Organization Studies* 24, no. 7 (2003): 1178–92.

13. Nielsen, *Politics of Ethics*; Trevino and Nelson, *Managing Business Ethics*.

14. D. McGregor, *The Human Side of Enterprise* (New York: McGraw-Hill, 1960).

15. Steinfels, *A People Adrift*.

16. Trevino and Nelson, *Managing Business Ethics*.

17. Nielsen, "Systematic Corruption"; Nielsen, "Corruption Networks."

18. Laurie Goodstein, "Dioceses Are Moving Ahead on Abuse, Audit Finds," *New York Times*, 7 Jan. 2004; Peter Steinfels, "Beliefs: A Professor Offers a Critique of Legal Responses to Reported Cases of Sexual Abuse by the Clergy," *New York Times*, 5 July 2003.

19. Nielsen, "Systematic Corruption"; Nielsen, "Corruption Networks."

20. H. Sender and G. Zuckerman, "Behind the Mutual Fund Prove: Three Informants Opened Up," *Wall Street Journal*, 14 Dec. 2003, 1, 6.

21. Nielsen, *Politics of Ethics*.

22. Roger Fisher and William Ury, *Getting To Yes* (New York: Penguin, 1991).

23. Nielsen, "Systematic Corruption."

24. Kant, "Metaphysical Principles"; J. Bentham, *An Introduction to the Principles of Morals and Legislation* (Oxford: Clarendon, 1879); Jacques Derrida, *Limited Inc.* (Evanston, Ill.: Northwestern University Press, 1988).

25. Nielsen, *Politics of Ethics*.

26. Argyris, *Overcoming Organizational Defenses*; Argyris, "A Life Full."

27. Nielsen, *Politics of Ethics*.

28. F. Heller, E. Pusic, G. Strauss, and B. Wilpert, *Organizational Participation: Myth and Reality* (Oxford: Oxford University Press, 1998).

29. Richard P. Nielsen, "Do Internal Due Process Systems Permit Adequate Political and Moral Space for Ethics Voice, Praxis, and Community?" *Journal of Business Ethics* 24, no. 1 (2000): 1–27.

30. Nielsen, "Due Process Systems."

31. G. F. Davis and T. A. Thompson, "A Social Movement Perspective on Corporate Control," *Administrative Science Quarterly* 39, no. 3 (1994): 141–73; D. McAdam, *Political Process and the Development of Black Insurgency 1930–1970* (Chicago: University of Chicago Press, 1982); Richard P. Nielsen, "The Politics of Long-term Corruption Reform: A Combined Social Movement and Action-learning Approach," *Business Ethics Quarterly* 10, no. 1 (2000): 305–17.

32. McAdam, *Political Process*; Nielsen, "Long-term Corruption Reform."

11: A PROFESSIONAL CODE OF ETHICS REFLECTING THE NATURE OF A CHRISTIAN VOCATION AND AN UNDERSTANDING OF LEADERSHIP IN THE CHURCH

Francis J. Butler

As I began reflecting on this subject, I called several national Catholic leadership organizations to see whether they had published a professional code of ethics. My survey included the U.S. Conference of Catholic Bishops (USCCB), the National Association of Church Personnel Administrators (NACPA), the Association of Catholic Colleges and Universities (ACCU), and the National Organization for the Continuing Education of the Roman Catholic Clergy (NOCERRC). Only the association for personnel administrators was able to report that anything like a code of professional ethics had been developed. And in this case, the code seemed to pertain only to NACPA members and their dealings as members of the association, for example, "I will represent the organization when authorized to do so."

Though the clergy abuse scandal has brought home the systematic, harmful management decisions made by bishops, other clergy, and professional church employees, we still do not see any discernable move outside of implementing the Dallas Charter of the USCCB to take the lessons learned in the last forty-eight months and apply them to the task of church leadership. I know of no committees of bishops, for example, that are taking what we have learned about finances, styles of leadership, personnel decision-making, communications, and so on and incorporating them into a forum for leadership. But as a church, committed to rebuilding trust, more conversation and reflection along these lines are sorely needed.

My reflection here is divided into three parts. First, I will reflect on the need itself for a code of ethics for church leadership. Second, I will offer five aspects of church life that the clergy abuse crisis accentuated and which, in my judgment, might play a very timely role in shaping ethical standards for church leaders right now. Finally, I will propose ten canons that could comprise a Catholic code of ethics for church leaders, whether clergy or lay.

WHY IS A PROFESSIONAL CODE OF ETHICS NEEDED?

Last June, members of the foundation community were shocked to learn from Professor James Keenan, SJ, that in the training for priestly, pastoral, or episcopal leadership there is really little real sustained instruction on the exercise of power. Father Keenan said: "We teach future clergy and ministers everything there is in ethics, except the ethical responsibilities of the personal conduct of the priest . . . no other profession, except those in the Academy, so abstains itself and its leaders from instruction on the ethical exercise of power."[1]

Not only are professional ethical guideposts missing for the clergy but, I would add, the explosion of growth in deacons, lay parish and diocesan staff, teachers and social workers, prison and campus ministers, hospital chaplains, music directors, liturgists, college and university and health-care system administrators reinforces the need for leadership formation programs grounded in Catholic principles and values.

The Center for Applied Research at Georgetown University reported in 1999 that over thirty thousand laypeople were participating in formation programs for some type of full-time or part-time service in the church, running religious education programs, for example, participating in parish liturgy, music and youth ministries, marriage preparation efforts, community and social service programs, and even serving as overseers in parishes without a pastor.[2]

Who are these people? What do we know about them and their professional background? What kind of moral and spiritual lives are they bringing to the church? What do these ministers and future church leaders need to know beyond the competencies of their particular discipline? In their new environment and with their responsibilities how will they exercise power in the name of the church? In what way does the institution that they now serve, damaged so seriously by the harmful practices of its leaders, demand extra care in the behavior and decision-making of all those who aspire to leadership?

AN UNDERSTANDING OF CHURCH AND ITS IMPLICATIONS FOR ETHICAL STANDARDS FOR LEADERSHIP

As I prepare you for the code of professional ethics that I have drafted I would like to offer some short reflections on five areas of contemporary church culture in the United States that explain the particular configuration of ethical norms that I will offer. These include the notion of the church as com-

munion, the role of trust in the functioning of the church, leadership as vocation, authority as empowerment, and, finally, reciprocal communication.

The Church Is a Communion

"The bishop," says John Paul II in the encyclical *Pastores Gregis*, "will
make every effort to develop structures of communion and participation
which make it possible to listen to the Spirit, who lives and speaks in the
faithful, in order to guide them in carrying out whatever the same Spirit suggests for the true good of the church."[3]

This vision, rooted in *Lumen Gentium*, one of the constitutional documents of the Second Vatican Council, recognizes both the equality of baptismal membership and the church's charismatic dimension. The gifts of the
Holy Spirit are manifested in some special way through all of the church's
members. The communion of the church is none other than the inseparable
and dynamic life of the Trinity (Jn 17:21). Our responsibility to one another
flows from an understanding that we, like the Trinity itself, are and should
be a community of love.

This understanding, however, has not replaced an entrenched notion that
the church consists of two very unequal classes, the ordained and those who
are not. The clericalism and caste system that this old division encourages
are robbing the church of the rich sense of belonging to and being responsible for one another.

Trust: Like Air, It Is Necessary for Survival

Membership in the church ultimately is by choice as we are reminded
through the ebb and flow of parishioner attendance each year. Last year's
pew counts in Boston make this point well. Parishes that exhibit vitality in
their liturgical and pastoral life, where an atmosphere of openness and
welcome is fostered, outperform their counterparts in both the level of vol-
unteering and financial support. The church is a trust. Where trust is promoted through honest and accountable leadership, everything else seems
to thrive as well. Leaders cannot rely on a command structure, or appeals
to loyalty, or fidelity to tradition to rebuild trust in their leadership. They
will have to earn trust—and they start with the virtue, honesty, integrity,
and holiness of their lives.

Church Leadership Is a Vocation Not a Job

The church is not an end unto itself nor is it here to serve itself, but rather
it exists as an instrument of communion with God and unity among all

people standing in service to the universal and reconciling mission of Jesus Christ.[4] It is called to the mission of salvation and liberation of humankind from every oppression. Leading this church cannot be reduced to a job or series of postings. It is a calling by God through the Christian community and in service to the Christian community. The church, according to the council, is described in metaphors as the work of the triune God, as a temple of God in the Holy Spirit, and as the Body of Christ. Have we not seen altogether too much careerism driving our church leaders? Is ecclesiastical job climbing and the striving after power that goes with it more consequential in who gets to lead our diocesan communities than integrity, competence, and character?

Authority Is about Empowerment

Authority exercised by leadership is not about dominance but rather service. "I come not to be served but to serve" (Mk 10:45). The church seeks to form servant leaders who encourage collaboration, trust, listening, and the empowerment of others. In the Christian understanding it is "power for" not "power over."

Communication Is Reciprocal

The church is relational in its very nature. According to its self-understanding, it is a living reality in vibrant dialogue with the world and is in constant search of God's presence in the lives of real human beings, most especially the poor. This relational function requires the communication skills of listening and discernment as well as the ability to communicate honestly, openly, and humbly as its founder did. There is no room in the church for spindoctors, one-way communicators, or those obsessed with secrecy.

These five understandings—communion, trust, vocation, authority, and reciprocal communication—speak in some singular way to the current crisis in leadership and the ethical failures which we have all witnessed these past forty-eight months.

The challenge now is to make these principles come alive as we try to imagine canons of ethical behavior that are tailored for a church in such a crisis as ours, as well as one where good leadership will play such a decisive role for the future of the Catholic faith.

TEN PLEDGES IN CHURCH SERVICE: A CODE OF ETHICS

I begin by setting forth the most fundamental aspect of Christian leadership today—that of one's relationship to Jesus Christ. At present we can find an entire bookshelf of essays and analyses probing the crisis of clergy sexual abuse. It reveals a very rich treatment of canonical, historical, administrative, pastoral, psychological, and ecclesial factors contributing to the present chapter in church history. But there is not so much reflection around what leadership behavior has said about the influence of Jesus Christ on the church. We are talking about Jesus Christ who is the love and compassion of God. So I begin my first norm of leadership behavior:

> *I promise to do all in my power to deepen my understanding of the church as a community and, as such, the body of Christ, and I will evaluate my service in the church daily in the light of my relationship to the person of Jesus Christ and his command to love one another as he has loved us* (Jn 15:12).

The second norm is related to the first and addresses integrity of teaching, practice, and understanding of Christian virtues and tradition. Would we be reading about fifty years of systemic abuse in our Catholic dioceses if the church's moral tradition and social principles were applied to its internal life? Large numbers of church workers, especially teachers and hospital employees, are paid scandalously low salaries, there are very high employee turnover rates, no annual reviews for clergy and ministers, few professional standards, and no portability in pensions. Moreover, we all are aware that there is not even a retirement system for the 180,000 Catholic sisters who served the Catholic people with such distinction. Ethical leaders will recognize that actions always speak louder than words. They will pledge themselves to the idea of practicing what is preached. Thus:

> *I will pledge to strengthen my understanding and practice of Catholicism, its teachings, principles, and values on an ongoing basis so as to apply them to church operations and thus to be a credible witness to the faith.*

The culture of secrecy and silence cloaked thousands of bad decisions that gave rise to the present crisis in the church. A culture of secrecy and silence is at odds with an institution that depends on trust and truth. A culture of secrecy and silence cannot be reconciled with a faith that teaches that Baptism rescues us all from the power of darkness. It seems ironic that even now a newly minted code of ethics for diocesan priests of one eastern U.S. diocese lays such emphasis on the control of information: "priests will take the necessary steps to ensure confidentiality by ensuring that offices are properly soundproofed, records are secure and staff members are informed of their duty on matters of confidentiality, and that they will seek legal guidance from diocesan attorneys."[5]

Putting too much emphasis on confidentiality fosters and promotes a culture not unlike that found in a family schooled in a conspiracy of secret keeping. While confidentiality has its proper place, the emphasis should be to form our leaders to be open communicators, to trust the power of truth, and to be good stewards and children of the light. Thus:

> *I will do everything in my power to be accountable and open in my professional and personal life while fostering transparency and openness in the church.*

The church needs to recommit itself to a model of authority that is found in the gospels, recognizing that he who leads, serves. Jesus warned his disciples that they were not to let their authority be felt, that they were not to lord it over others as nonbelievers did, that they instead were to wash the feet of others (Jn 13:14). The *Directory on the Pastoral Ministry of Bishops* reminds each member of the hierarchy that "the bishop avoids everything which smacks of imperious domination as well as paternalism, but rather performs loving service."[6]

Therefore our fourth pledge deals with the use of power. It reads:

> *I will exercise the authority of my office in a way that empowers those whom I serve and work in a collaborative spirit of servant leaders.*

Our next norm is proposed to promote further accountability and professional competency. In a scathing review of church attorneys and professionals, Patrick Schlitz, a former litigator and now professor at a Midwest Catholic school of law, told American Catholic foundations last year that "in too many cases dioceses have received poor legal representation."[7] He maintained that dioceses for far too long have relied on inept legal advice, bad public relations, and shabby accounting. Schlitz makes a cogent observation that is borne up by those of us who have daily dealings with church agencies. In developing a corps of leaders and administrators, the church seems to be doing the minimum to keep the bar high on professional standards, high educational achievement, and sheer talent. Sadly, hiring decisions in many dioceses and church institutions remain penny-wise and pound-foolish while they are often based more on loyalty and conformity than on quality and competency. We come then to our fifth norm:

> *I pledge to observe the highest standards of my profession by regularly seeking evaluation from those I serve, as well as peer reviews. I will work with others to identify and address problems in my profession and will refuse to be silent when I become aware of wrongdoing of any kind.*

This crisis has shown us that many church leaders today seem isolated from human suffering. We have seen a dulled capacity for empathy that is the result of sitting too long behind a chancery desk and board table. It has robbed our leaders of their ability to recognize Christ in the injured and in those who are on the margins of the church's life. As part of their professional life, every bishop, priest, and lay leader in the church should exercise some form of direct personal care for those in human need as an exercise to deepen their capacity to love, to be loved, and to understand the lives of those in their community. Therefore,

I will devote a percentage of my time to public or volunteer service in order to discharge my Christian responsibilities to care for others, especially the poor, in an exemplary manner and to deepen my understanding of the needs of the community.

Establishing more effective communications in the church will require that its leaders learn how to listen and appreciate how actions speak louder than words. The style of meetings of church leaders, especially at the national and regional level, must change. They are remote and exclusive. Bishops appear to gather to parse, to promulgate, and to posture. Would it not be an improvement if such convenings were held to learn and to listen to their clergy and laity as well as their brother bishops? Who is working with our leaders at the moment to help them shoulder their burdens, face their problems, and learn how to interact with other segments of the church with intelligence, integrity, and courage? Thus,

I will seek to be an excellent communicator, developing skills to listen compassionately, to never cease learning, and to speak boldly when necessary.

An empowering leader is one who is eager to consult and to discern the opinion and wisdom of the wider Christian community. The leaders foster a corporate sharing of burdens from everyone and encourage each member of the community to value their particular gifts and perspectives. A leader is careful to respect the legitimate liberty to think differently. Therefore,

I will do all in my power to foster broad participation in the life of the church, to encourage public opinion, and to respect honest differences and the rights of others.

Equality of discipleship through Baptism is the guiding rubric in everyday church life. Yet forty years after Vatican II we are finding that a two-tiered membership is hard to replace not only because of the attitudes of younger priests but because laity also refuse to grow up and to leave the safe and comfortable haven where "Father knows best."

I will oppose anything that encourages clericalism and decisions and actions that foster a caste system of membership and power in the church.

As we will soon be reminded by the National Review Board, the church's secretive behavior in the matter of money has cost the faithful enough money in settlements to build and operate another couple of hundred Catholic high schools. "Sound business practice in the church," the Catholic bishops declare in their pastoral letter *Stewardship*, requires several things: "pastors and parish staff must be open, consultative, collegial and account-able in the conduct of affairs . . . and Catholics ought to have an active role in the oversight of the stewardship of pastoral leaders and administrators."[8]

In this crisis one thing is certain, financial accountability is still at the most primitive stages of development. That brand new code of ethics that I quoted from one diocese earlier reads: "Parish financial records are to be held as confidential unless an appropriate governmental agency or office requires review."[9] Nothing at all is said about the rights of donors to know how their money has been used, nor does it reference contemporary standards of fi-nancial accountability. The shenanigans at Enron, WorldCom, Tyco, and other business giants have reminded America that cultures of financial se-crecy and deceit have enormous potential to destroy trust and human lives. These days there is no justification at all for running things in the dark. The freedom and healthy atmosphere of financial accountability, not to mention its salutary impact on donations and its compatibility with the understanding of the church as a light to the world, suggests that money, how it is raised, used, and accounted for is an area of urgently needed reform today. Dioce-san bankruptcies, chronic parish defalcations, the shameful liquidation of church properties due to legal settlements, and millions of donated dollars lost through the clergy sexual abuse scandals set the stage for my last stan-dard for this proposed code. Thus,

I promise to be a good steward in the use of the church's money, insisting on full public disclosure, independent audits, honesty, and accountability in all fundraising.

Our choice of ten proposed ethical principles for church leaders is condi-tioned by the present crisis, but the principles draw their life from the per-son we follow and who we are as a church community.

Leadership and the exercise of authority in the church during this sad chapter have brought home to us some of the worst aspects of human cor-ruption. The exercise of power and authority in the church must be about service and it must drive wider participation. Today, we see a church in need of a rediscovery of the meaning of Christian leadership. We are yearning for leaders who are truly formed by the Gospel, guided by the council, and pre-pared to exhibit the kind of accountable leadership that the church in the twenty-first century requires.

NOTES

1. James F. Keenan, "The Heart of Virtuous Leadership," in *The Trusted Leader: A Conference on Those We Follow* (Washington, D.C.: FADICA, 2003), 13–22, at 19.

2. Bryan T. Froehle and Mary L. Gautier, *Catholicism USA: A Portrait of the Catholic Church in the United States* (Maryknoll, N.Y.: Orbis Books, 1999), 154.

3. John Paul II, Post-Synodal Apostolic Exhortation, *Pastores Gregis*, October 2003, PG 44.

4. Second Vatican Council, *Dogmatic Constitution on the Church*, *Lumen Gentium*, 1964, n.1.

5. Diocese of Wilmington, *For the Sake of God's Children: Ethical and Behavioral Standards for Church Personnel* (2003), 10.

6. *Directory on the Pastoral Ministry of Bishops* (Ontario, Canada: Canadian Catholic Conference 1974), 36.

7. Patrick J. Schiltz, "On the Quality of Lay Leadership," in *Effective Religious Leadership in an Age of Change* (Washington, D.C.: FADICA, 2003), 41–49.

8. *Stewardship: A Disciple's Response* (Washington, D.C.: U.S. Conference of Catholic Bishops, 1993), 34–35.

9. Diocese of Wilmington, *God's Children*, 11.

12: A PROFESSIONAL CODE OF ETHICS?

Richard M. Gula, SS

To speak of a professional code of ethics for Christian ministers seems redundant. After all, a personal desire to be good and do what is right already seems to be part of the self-image of ministers and their commitment to witness to the gospel. The motivation to love in response to God's call to ministry directs pastoral ministers to live as disciples of Jesus in ways that no code of ethics could ever fully prescribe.

But such a virtuous self-image and saintly commitment run ahead of the reality. Christian ministers are not as good as some people think they are. Even the best intentions of ministers are hampered by human sinfulness. Christian ministers, even morally exemplary ones, need and can benefit from the guidance a code of ethics can give. While we have the Bible and the Code of Canon Law to give us a vision and to set standards, a code of ethics can identify the special obligations that come with the pastoral role along with other moral dimensions of the professional aspects of the ministerial vocation. These special features of a code of ethics also make it a positive resource in the education of ministers.

Moreover, the recent public attention to clerical misconduct has revived interest in finding effective ways to restore trust by increasing accountability within the ministry. Developing and implementing a code of ethics is one possible strategy. Through a code the Catholic Church can show itself, its community of ministers, and the public that we are serious about the quality of our service and conduct and can lay claim to the trust people put in their ministers. In light of the theological vision for organizational reform presented above by Richard Gaillardetz, implementing a national code of ethics may be one way that the church might engage principles of justice to achieve the ecclesial reform that may enable it to be a more efficacious sacrament of salvation.

My conviction inspiring these reflections is that a code of ethics properly developed, personally appropriated, structurally supported, responsibly implemented, and justly enforced can strengthen the ministerial witness to the ministry of Christ and to right moral living called for by the gospel. It may also contribute in a modest way to restoring trust in the church by setting standards for quality, accountable ministerial service.

While every baptized person shares in the ministry and mission of the church as sacrament, to be a sign and agent of the unity of all humanity and creation under God, not everyone needs to be designated a minister nor every service a ministry in order to give authentic witness to Christ. Some of the baptized have been called forth and mandated by a competent authority in the church to minister in the name of the church. These include not only bishops, priests, and deacons, but also all those recognized by their diocese as lay ecclesial ministers. Together these are the ministers who would be covered by a code of ethics. To include provisions for the ordained and lay ecclesial ministers in the same document underscores that there are professional aspects in all forms of ministry that have moral implications, even though there are ecclesial differences in the vocations of these ministers.

Codes of ethics for ministers are emerging all over the world. It is hard to keep up with the trend. The Australian Catholic Bishops' Conference is the first national body to endorse one. Its *Integrity in Ministry* (1999) is a document of principles and standards for clergy and religious, but as yet does not include lay ecclesial ministers. The Canadian Conference of Catholic Bishops has issued a *Statement of Commitment* (1996), but not an official code, reflecting ideals to inspire all appointed ministers, clerical and lay. From Ireland we have *Ministry with Integrity* (2001), a draft document of standards for pastoral ministry. Some specialized ministries in the United States, such as campus ministry and the National Association for Lay Ministry, have issued codes of ethics for their personnel. Some dioceses, in response to the Dallas Charter of 2002 and with the aid of VIRTUS, the National Catholic Risk Retention Group, are presently in the process of developing a code of ethics. The Archdiocese of Baltimore released its *Code of Conduct for Church Personnel of the Archdiocese of Baltimore* in 2003.

While codes of ethics for specialized ministries or individual dioceses are springing up, the Catholic Church in the United States is still missing a shared, national code of ethics. A national code of ethics, while forcing the issue of the ecclesial authority of the United States Conference of Catholic Bishops, might be helpful in fostering a sense of cohesion among ministers by providing a coherent moral framework applicable to all forms of ministry and by fostering cooperative behavior and mutual respect among the community of ministers.

At this point in the life of the Catholic Church in the United States, the question is not whether we should have a code of ethics for ministers. The professional character of ministry requires one. Even morally exemplary ministers need and can benefit from one. The Dallas Charter (Article #12) can be interpreted as requiring each diocese to develop one. And many ministerial communities already have or are forming one. The pressing issues now are what kind of code should we have and how should we get it? To this end, my aim is to be suggestive and not exhaustive of some aspects of the purpose, content, authority, and limits that we need to consider in the process of developing a national code of ethics for ministers.

PURPOSE

To foster authentic ministry is the overarching purpose of a code of ethics. This includes making explicit both the primary values that should govern personal growth in one's professional identity as a minister and the basic moral obligations that mark professional responsibilities in the exercise of ministry. Part of being professionally responsible is to be open to public accountability for one's performance. A code of ethics makes explicit the commonly shared criteria for making this assessment.

The current outcry against bishops and priests for the sexual abuse scandal can be read in part as a desire to uncover what seems to be an implicit code supporting unacceptable behaviors (such as protecting the image of the church more than vulnerable children, transferring problem priests to another parish or diocese without full disclosure, and bishops acting as though they were above the law). The unacceptable components of an implicit code must be replaced with appropriate behaviors in an explicit code that will promote professional responsibility and public accountability.

Although the value of fostering professional identity, personal professional responsibility, and public accountability on the part of ministers seems obvious to many people, my sense is that the way we have overemphasized ministry as a vocation, to the near exclusion of it also being a profession, has been an obstacle for some bishops and priests in accepting a code of ethics as necessary. The chapters by John Beal and Patricia Chang identify some obstacles to the very notion of ministry as a "profession." As a result, they would argue on the basis of other reasons why we may not have fostered the "professional" identity of ministers or considered a code of ethics as necessary for them.

Without a code, a vocational calling too easily becomes the excuse for avoiding professional duties and accountability, and it can breed a sense of isolation, superiority, and, even worse, entitlement. But having a vocation and being professional need not be at odds with each other. In fact, elaborating the core values of a profession and the moral implications of the professional role of the minister in the way codes do can clarify how ministers go about the work of being signs and agents of God's love.

Trust is closely related to authentic ministry. Codes aim to assure the public of the trustworthiness of those accepted into the profession. The implication is that anyone found not to be trustworthy will be dismissed.

Codes can engender trust in at least two ways. One is by serving as a set of criteria for screening candidates for ministry. For example, if the history of a candidate shows a pattern of behavior incompatible with the code's vision, values, and standards, then the code can be used as a reference point for not accepting that person for ministry. Careful screening of candidates and selective admission to protect the church from those unfit to serve as its ministers can be one way to assure the faithful that those in ministry already manifest the character and conduct befitting the ministry. Second, codes can also engender trust by providing the public with an explicit expression of the core values and standards of practice that define the ministerial commitment to the community and, if followed, could serve as a check on any minister's blindness to the misuse of power that violates trust and causes harm.

Codes also provide *a set of standards* that help to define, interpret, and measure responsible pastoral practice. While we can find many standards of conduct for the ordained ministry already scattered throughout the Code of Canon Law, there would be great value in having these brought together in a coherent code of ethics along with standards that would pertain to the nonordained in ministry as well. Assuming the role of a professional minister, ordained or not, entails a commitment to some moral obligations that do not fall on others in the community, or at least they are not binding on others to the same degree as they are on ministers. Among these are matters of maintaining competence appropriate to one's ministry, faithfully representing the church as its public officer, giving a greater degree of preference to serving pastoral needs over one's own, exercising responsible stewardship of the community's resources, and maintaining appropriate boundaries to safeguard against the misuse of power in the pastoral relationship.

In a time when so many unrealistic expectations are placed on ministers, the clarity of a code can support, protect, and liberate them from the social pressures to be and do more than their professional role requires of them. In fact, the feature that I have found most attracts pastoral ministers to wanting a code of ethics at all is the clarity that it can bring both to setting the baseline for the morally appropriate exercise of ministry and to establishing a common set of realistic expectations defining the pastoral role as the public witness of God's care for us. To this end, a code of ethics could serve as a tool in the education of seminarians, priests, and other ministers.

CONTENT

The content of all codes seeks to establish expectations of good character and right conduct in the exercise of the ministerial role. The content focuses primarily on one-to-one pastoral responsibilities along with obligations for personal and professional development. This common content gets elaborated in more or less detail through a variety of literary forms. In trying to fulfill its purpose as an instrument fostering authentic ministry, as a means of assuring trust, and as a set of standards of pastoral practice, the code must instruct as well as inspire, support as well as challenge. One of the great difficulties in writing a code is finding the *right structure and literary genre* to express all of this.

Presently, codes come in a mix of structures and genres, all with some merit though some seem more satisfying than others. The Australian document *Integrity in Ministry*, for example, has inspiring theological visions of church, ministry, and the moral life introducing each of the eight sections organized under the overarching theme of the church as a sign and instrument of communion. It has statements of general principles ("In their lives and ministries, clergy and religious witness God's love for every human person by sensitivity, reverence and respect in their relationships.") as well as specific imperatives ("Never administer corporal punishment to a minor."). By contrast, the code of ethics for pastoral associates and parish life coordinators from the National Association for Lay Ministry does not include a theological vision. It is a list of twenty-one "principles" written in varying degrees of specificity. Some are specific mandates (#7 Pastoral ministers participate in regular, ongoing, quality personal supervision. . . .) and others are ideal aspirations (#8 Pastoral ministers strive for heightened awareness of ecumenical, ethnic, ecological, and gender related issues.). The Canadian document *Responsibility in Ministry: A Statement of Commitment*, while not offered as a formal code of ethics with a set of rules and regulations to be enforced, seems to offer the most attractive structure and genre. It is organized according to five areas of ministerial responsibility: to those receiving ministry, colleagues, the diocesan and universal church, the wider community, and self. It expresses these responsibilities in the genre of ideals to inspire ministers, for example, "Welcome regular evaluation of our ministry by colleagues and the people we serve."

The great challenge in giving content to a code is to distinguish statements of theological vision from prescriptive rules and from the ideals of aspiration and inspiration. Making the appropriate distinctions in semantic forms will be important for the proper interpretation, application, and enforcement of a code of ethics.

AUTHORSHIP

Whether a code of ethics will be effective in achieving its purposes will depend in part on *who is responsible for putting it together*. While the standards of the code ought to rest their moral authority on sound moral argument, the overall credibility of the code will depend on who authors it.

Most codes are written by members of the profession whose behavior the code is to govern. This approach gives a great deal of autonomy to the professional group, but it lacks public accountability by including no one from outside the closed professional circle to check or challenge the group's definition of what it means to act in a professional way. The danger in this mode of authorship is that it can lead to in-house protectionism, since a committee of self-appointed professionals may privilege their own interests and be blind to the interests of those they are to serve. If ministerial codes were developed by a single clerical author, or even a committee of clerics and religious, and then imposed from on high, it may very well not only further damage the morale of ministers but also greatly weaken the code's authority, since it is the product of only those with a vested interest in it. The "code of ethics" authored by Francis Butler, for example, can serve to inspire a conversation about a code of ethics and give direction for its fuller development. As it stands, however, this proposal begs for authority, specificity, and personal appropriation if it is to serve as a corporate instrument of accountability.

So who should write a code of ethics for Catholic ministers? While a national code of ethics will become obligatory only when authorized by the bishops and approved by the Vatican, there may be greater hope of restoring trust in the ministry and achieving accountability from ministers if the code were developed from the *ground up by a collaboration* of those in different types of ministry as well as of the laity.

While clerical misconduct has dominated the agenda for what ought to be in a code, the reason for a code in the first place lies in the need to define the kind of attitudes and relationships ministers ought to have with laypeople and with their fellow ministers on various levels. Since ministers are called from the community, sustained by the community, and entrusted with power and authority to serve the community, I would hope that the whole community (clerical and lay) would be an integral part of the process of defining the ethical standards, shaping the structures of accountability, and supervising the enforcement of the code. This means that the code would not be the product of one author, or a committee of only clerics and religious, or the product of some risk management firm. I would hope that a code emerges as the product of consulting the community by engaging a broad base of collaboration and deliberation. We already have precedent for such a consultative and deliberative process from the Bishops' Bicentennial

Program, *Liberty and Justice for All* (1976), the successive national catechetical directories, and the pastoral letters dealing with peace and nuclear weapons (1983) and the economy (1986).

LIMITATIONS

No matter how broad the base of consultation for developing a code, it will still have some limitations. One is that *a code does not guarantee compliance*. While a process involving a broad base of consultation may make it a little easier to claim ownership of the finished product, we should not assume that those who have knowledge of the code will behave morally. The code itself will not solve the problem of virtue, discipline, and discernment on the part of the individual minister. The experience, knowledge, and skill necessary to evaluate and respond appropriately in a pastoral situation exceed the guidance provided by a code. While codes may be a necessary help to set minimal limits, they are not sufficient to deliver ministers from the ambiguities of the moral dimensions of pastoral ministry. Ministers still need to be virtuous, disciplined, and discerning. So we must remain modest in our expectations of what a code can do to change or direct the behavior of ministers.

Moreover, *a code will not prevent lawsuits*. In fact, in this highly litigious climate, having a code may even prompt more lawsuits by making public clearly defined standards of practice. The code could be used in litigation should one or several statements not be adhered to satisfactorily, even if the breach is not criminal behavior. These legal implications were part of the reason that the Canadian bishops issued a "Statement of Commitment" for those in ministry rather than a formal "code of ethics."

If the other chapters on organizational structures and context teach us anything, they underscore how the church would need to surround a code of ethics with a *culture and structures* that support enforcing accountability in order to make the code credible and effective as a ministerial commitment to trustworthy, accountable service. My experience of working with clerical groups tells me that there is a deep-seated resistance to evaluations and accountability, especially when diocesan administration has a direct hand in it. However, some dioceses are trying to implement pastoral evaluations in ways that might foster a sense of accountability and change the clerical culture of suspicion and resistance.

Without structures to support ministerial colleagues and laypersons in rewarding good performance on the one hand and reporting professional misconduct on the other, the code as an instrument of accountability is an empty promise. For any code to be effective, it will have to be at least accompanied by, if not preceded by, a change in the culture of the church that is more receptive to the evaluation of ministerial performance and has structures that will support reporting violations and applying sanctions. Perhaps a good place to start would be for the bishops themselves to undergo a public evaluation personally of their stewardship, especially in their administration, ministry, presiding, and preaching. The preparation of the five-year reports for Rome could be the occasion for this evaluation if they were made public and given to various diocesan bodies (e.g., Priests' Council, Pastoral Council, Finance Council, etc.) for review prior to submission. A more direct evaluation of the bishops could be included and sent along to Rome and published locally.

Another limitation is that some codes tend to *focus almost exclusively on attitudes and practices of the individual minister* by giving guidance or setting standards to regulate personal development and individual pastoral care. This can give the impression that ministers work totally free from any obligation to their colleagues, to the wider church, and to society at large. It also suggests that ministers are not influenced by ecclesial or social structures that support or limit individual pastoral ministry. But ministers always work within structures. Ministers try to do what is right and be good persons in an environment that often makes it difficult to do both.

Codes generally do not address the social context, culture, or the systemic structures that influence the distribution of power within ministry, such as the way appointments are made or certification is granted, where and with whom ministers must live, the compensation and rewards that are granted, the administrative strategies used for sharing responsibilities, or the environment in which one works, including office structures that influence access to phone and e-mail messages or supervision. An adequate code will have to give some attention to responsibilities to colleagues, to the wider church, to society, and to the minister's own social and ecclesial contexts that greatly influence how ministry is shaped, maintained, and exercised.

A perennial limitation of any set of codified moral standards is their *proper interpretation.* This has a great deal to do with the semantic forms used to express the code. For example, the inspirational ideals of the code can be too vague to be helpful as a guide in complex pastoral situations, while prescriptive rules are too specific to be adaptable to changing circumstances. Moreover, too many rules invite putting the burden of accountability on the code rather than on the individual minister who must decide and act in the midst of so many contingent factors. The proper interpretation of the code may be aided by including some way to distinguish the different weight and degrees of compliance that ought to be given to general principles, inspirational ideals, and prescriptive rules. The Australian document, for example, signifies by a shaded background in the text the standards requiring the highest degree of compliance.

But no matter how carefully we might try to distinguish the degrees of authority and compliance of the various features of the code, having a code at all attracts, and perhaps even encourages, a legalistic and a minimalistic interpretation. Legalists can easily reduce the code to an oppressive means of control; whereas minimalists can cite the code to defend self-interest by claiming that what isn't forbidden must be permitted. Both an excessive scrupulosity and laxity threaten the sound interpretation and enforcement of a code.

In the end, the responsible use of the code calls for the artful discrimination of the weight given to a standard and its prudential application in an ambiguous pastoral situation. *The code will never be able to take us more than part of the way to appropriate pastoral practice.* The possibilities and ambiguities in human and interpersonal ministry are too great for any code to be a definitive summary of what an ethical ministry should be, so that we would only need to consult the code to know whether a particular practice is appropriate. Codes cannot be expected to solve every ministerial problem or guarantee the safe negotiation of a pastoral conflict without fear of false accusation. Codes will have to be subject to ongoing analysis of their implications with the nuance that any moral statement requires, and they will have to be subject to ongoing revision as new ministerial challenges and conflicts emerge.

CONCLUSION

In conclusion, I urge modesty in our expectations of what a code of ethics can do to ensure high quality, trustworthy, and accountable ministerial service. In principle, I support developing a national code of ethics for Catholic ministers. In practice, I say, "Go slowly." If the goal of having a national code of ethics is to foster authentic ministry, to enhance accountability through more public disclosure of what ministers do and why, to restore trust in ministers and the ministry, to facilitate ownership of the highest standards of pastoral practice, and to support ministers in their effort to live committed lives, then the process of developing the code ought to be as inclusive as possible. This means collaborating with grassroots groups representing the diversity that makes up the church. This process should be kept as public as possible with plenty of opportunity for consultation, feedback, and revision. At this time in the life of the church, the process of developing the code, both in its tone and in the mutual learning fostered along the way, may well be more important than the product itself.

13: TOWARD AN ECCLESIASTICAL PROFESSIONAL ETHIC: LESSONS FROM THE LEGAL PROFESSION

Daniel R. Coquillette and Judith A. McMorrow

The sexual abuse crisis in the American Catholic Church has thrust us into a social drama. Where social drama occurs in the United States, lawyers are sure to be present. Adding a few dozen lawyers to any stressful situation inevitably has interesting consequences. The advocacy ethic of lawyers, which is captured in our *Rules of Professional Conduct*, not only encourages but compels the lawyer to function as a zealous advocate for the client. That assures that the client's point of view is strongly presented. From the perspective of some observers, that adversarial ethic encourages distortion and elevation of the interests of the individual over that of the collective. Whatever the challenges of having the legal system—and lawyers—involved in the current crisis, it has had the benefit of identifying individual, and to a lesser extent institutional, failures.

The experience of lawyers may offer assistance beyond the representation of both the victims and the Catholic Church. Lawyers, like clergy, are professionals with professional norms and ethical requirements. There are obviously huge differences in these two professions. But as priests to our secular religion of law, lawyers are "called forth and mandated by a competent authority" to function in a specific and defined role, the specifics of which are reflected in part in *Rules of Professional Conduct*.[1] Lawyers' long and storied history with professional codes offers a cautionary tale to those exploring an ecclesiastical code of ethics.

The rules of the legal profession were originally designed to encourage good conduct. The first set of rules, *The 1908 ABA Canons of Ethics*, was largely aspirational, and spoke generally of loyalty and character. As aspirational guides, the canons were available for review if a lawyer happened to know of their existence. But many of the aspirational provisions were part of the culture of lawyering and did not need a formal code for weight or credibility.

The second effort to codify lawyer conduct occurred in 1969, when the American Bar Association passed the *Model Code of Professional Responsibility* (1969). The *Model Code* contained nine broad canons, such as "A lawyer should assist in maintaining the integrity and competence of the legal profession" (Canon 1) and "A lawyer should exercise independent professional judgment on behalf of the client" (Canon 5). These broad canons were followed by somewhat more specific *Ethical Considerations* (which became known colloquially as "ECs") and very specific *Disciplinary Rules* ("DRs"). The *Ethical Considerations* offered somewhat more guidance, but maintained an aspirational focus. For example, "A lawyer should maintain high standards of professional conduct and should encourage fellow lawyers to do likewise. He should be temperate and dignified, and he should refrain from all illegal and morally reprehensible conduct" (EC 1-5). The *Disciplinary Rules* were designed to be enforced in disciplinary contexts and provided the bottom-line requirements, violation of which could subject the lawyer to professional discipline by the state body authorized to control the admission and expulsion of lawyers. For example, DR 1-102(A)(4) states that "A lawyer shall not engage in conduct involving dishonest, fraud, deceit, or misrepresentation."

The 1969 *Code of Professional Responsibility* did not work well in its dual role of offering both broad ethical pronouncements and specific prohibitions. Some of the *Ethical Considerations* appeared to be inconsistent with the *Disciplinary Rules*, important nonlitigation issues that affect the day-to-day life of lawyers were not addressed, and the code continued to contain provisions, such as limitations on advertising, that were seen as advancing the economic interests of the profession.

The 1969 *Code of Professional Responsibility* was in existence a bare ten years before the lawyers reevaluated the code. Like the current crisis in the Catholic Church, moral and professional failures of lawyers, including Watergate, inspired the return to the drafting table. In 1983 the American Bar Association promulgated the *Model Rules of Professional Conduct*. The *Model Rules* presented, as its name indicates, specific rules of conduct, designed to be clearer and more easily enforced in disciplinary contexts. The natural tendency when crafting a code during a time of crisis is to offer more guidance and direction, rather than less. After all, moral failures arose because the prior guidance was, by definition, insufficient to stop the lapses.[2] As with the current discussions of an ecclesiastical code, using the code as a vehicle to build public trust is an understandable and potentially positive use of a code. That goal, however, also pushes the code in the direction of setting baselines for behavior.

The evolution in the names of the lawyer codes over the last one hundred years reflects this more directive trend. Lawyers moved from broad canons (1908), to a code (1969), to rules (1983). And the focus of these codifications similarly changed from a broad articulation of ethics (1908), to responsibility (1969), to a specific focus on conduct (1983). While the *Rules of Professional Conduct*, recently refined in 2000, are somewhat better vehicles to punish misdeeds through a disciplinary system, no one suggests that they capture the normative whole of what it means to be lawyer. Indeed, the chair of the 2000 revisions panel was quite open that

> Our objective [in Ethics 2000 revision of *Model Rules of Professional Conduct*] was also to resist the temptation to preach aspirationally about "best practices" or professionalism concepts. Valuable as the profession might find such guidance, sermonizing about best practices would not have—and should not be misperceived as having—a regulatory dimension.[3]

As St. Thomas Aquinas observed, punishment does not create high character and virtue, it merely deters evil conduct.[4] Codes, particularly when drawn during times of crisis with an eye to deterring wrongful conduct, have a very specific utility—a vehicle for control and punishment. Presumably an ecclesiastical code would be more receptive to "sermonizing" and a tone that might "preach," but the hydraulic pressure of crisis-inspired codes will be toward specificity.

As codes tend to move to greater level of specificity, the language of values and the broader norms that undergird the specific prohibition often get subsumed into the specific prohibitions. For example, the *Model Rules of Professional Conduct* for lawyers starts out with a preamble that invokes the larger values of the profession. But the weight of the lawyer code focuses on the specifics of prohibited conduct. For example, the importance of the fiduciary relationship, the value of which infuses so many specific provisions, is rarely mentioned in the *Rules* themselves.

Accepting for purposes of discussion that there will be a pressure toward specificity in any ecclesiastical code, with a corresponding danger of losing sight of the fundamental values that drive the code, we can identify some additional challenges and opportunities to a code of conduct. Based on the experience of lawyers, we would predict that the challenges to an ecclesiastical code fall into five broad areas. First, who gets to craft the first draft, quite apart from the complex question of adoption, will reveal much about the goals and likely success of a code. Second, such a code must acknowledge and confront the inherent limitations of all rules: identifying the optimum level of discretion and understanding the role of fact-finding within a code. Third, drafters must understand—as they inevitably do—the necessity of ethical awareness as a precondition for the effectiveness of any code. Fourth, as a code articulates the contours of the role-differentiated

4-   behavior of the professional, it must be sufficiently flexible to reflect the
challenges of role-differentiated behavior. Finally, and perhaps most importantly, a code of conduct by its nature focuses on the function of the individual professional and can be an awkward, and often ineffective, vehi-
5-   cle for addressing the need for changes in the institutional structures within
which the professional functions. Against these challenges sits a huge and
incredibly important benefit—education.

WHO GETS TO DRAFT THE CODE

Who crafts the first draft of a code reveals who is entitled to sit at the table,
whose input is important, and what points of view are most likely to be reflected in the code. Lawyers are regulated at the state level, and these model
versions of the lawyer code and rules also reflect the challenge of who
should have the power of shaping the first draft. By a process largely of default, the "model" versions of the lawyer codes have been crafted by the
American Bar Association (ABA). Since the ABA is a voluntary trade association, it has no meaningful power to regulate lawyers. (Violating the code
would only get you ousted from the ABA. For most lawyers, that would
mean only losing your subscription to the *ABA Journal*.) The real power of
the *Rules of Conduct* is infused when the rules were sent to the state courts,
which then could take the first draft and shape it to reflect the values of the
state. This process has come under increasing scrutiny. Some question
whether the ABA is sufficiently representative of all who are affected by the
lawyer codes.[5] There is concern about capture by the more elitist members
of the bar. There is always the lurking suspicion that the fox is guarding the
chicken coop. As other authors have noted, the same credibility challenges
face the drafters of an ecclesiastical code.

As the *Rules of Professional Conduct* moved from aspirational to regula-
tory, the states increasingly have modified the specific rules to make changes
in the text on issues such as the duty of confidentiality, candor required to a
court, whether lawyers should be mandatory reporters of professional
wrongdoing, and the like. Changes sharpened the differences between those
who proposed the first draft and those who have the power to adopt the final version. This process can provide a vehicle for shared discussion or highlight the differences and tensions between the competing perspectives.

THE INHERENT LIMITATION OF RULES

Professional codes and rules also share the inherent limitation of all rules.
Rules typically have as their goal to identify clear lines of conduct. Their

function is to limit discretion and increase perceived consistency. To achieve that goal, they must become more specific. But the more specific the rule, the less the ability to tailor the rule to new circumstances, and this increases the possibility of unfairness in application.[6]

Even assuming the rule is crafted with an optimum level of specificity, there is still inevitable discretion required. The application of any code or rule requires a decision-maker to analyze what rule applies, engage in fact-finding to see if the circumstances of the case are covered by the rule, and make a decision about remedies.[7] Fact-finding (or self-assessment about facts) is a huge challenge in any ethical deliberation. How many actors in the church crisis did not take aggressive action because they were not sure that wrongdoing was taking place, were hesitant about their competence to find facts, or were uncertain about whether someone else—more properly placed to take action—had intervened? In many cases the factual uncertainty and requisite fact-finding can appear benign. For example, lawyers who are required by both our fiduciary obligations and our *Rules of Professional Conduct* to avoid representing conflicting interests must make factual determinations, such as whether the interest of two clients are "directly adverse" or whether the lawyer's judgment will be "materially limited." The focus on these precise questions can cause the lawyer to lose sight of the important values at stake in this fact-finding.

Rules also tend, over time, to encourage those bound by the rules to take a legalistic approach to their interpretation. The ethical rules for lawyers have become, in many instances, just another tool in the arsenal of lawyers in litigation with an opposing side.[8] There is also a tendency, over time, to see that everything not forbidden is allowed. We are not surprised that lawyers might take a legalistic approach to their own code of conduct. But this tendency is not unique to lawyers. Since accountability is likely to be a goal of an ecclesiastical code,[9] those whose conduct is held up to scrutiny under the code will quite naturally be put in a defensive posture.

All these concerns about the limits of codes are not startling new insights. The Catholic Church has a rich and impressive legal system, including canon law scholars who understand the complexity of doctrinal interpretation and the challenge of words as a constraining force. An ecclesiastical code will not be exempt from these same challenges.

ETHICAL AWARENESS AND THE VALUES BEHIND THE RULES

Rules also require initial cognitive awareness of their possible application. Those bound by the rules need ethical awareness to understand when they are moving into conduct that encroaches on a value behind the rules. But that ethical awareness flows not from the rules themselves, but from the underlying moral values or principles that presumably serve as the foundation for the specific code or rule. Kohlberg's theory of moral development is illustrative. Kohlberg hypothesized six stages of moral development. Choosing to act according to rules because of a concern for punishment reflects a low stage of moral development. Choosing to act according to rules in order to do one's duty, respect authority, and maintain social order rates higher on the scale, but still reflects what Kohlberg characterized as "conventional" approach. More complex moral development requires the person making decisions to understand the values behind the rules and recognize the need to thoughtfully consider the competing claims to right behavior.[10]

Enron is a classic example. With a relentless corporate culture of profit maximization, individual professionals became caught up in the corporate goals. In-house lawyers, who were asked to prepare the paperwork for questionable transactions, often went through the formal process of receiving appropriate corporate approval. They often acted with formal compliance with the rules. But the essence of the transactions was highly questionable. Why didn't more lawyers within the corporation speak out? From what we have gleaned from that experience, they became caught up in a corporate culture that saw legal questioning of a transaction as an indication that the individual lawyer was just not sufficiently clever to figure out how to get the transaction done. That same corporate culture gave tangible rewards to those clever folks who worked around obstacles. There was a slow stretching of what was seen as tolerable. That last clever deal became the median point, not the outer bounds, of what was appropriate.

The corporate culture blunted the ethical awareness of many, but not all, of the lawyers. This was a process of seduction, not a conscious embracing of wrongdoing. It is quite telling that the two high-profile, in-house professionals who most strongly questioned Enron's activities were a lawyer and an accountant who had transferred into a division known for questionable activities. The lawyer and accountant had come from outside that "twentieth floor." They were able to recognize that something was seriously amiss. Because they had not been part of the slow deadening of professional judgment, they could see what was obvious, including what was obvious to outside reviewers during the postmortem of Enron: that is, a few individuals were engaged in serious wrongdoing, and a large number of other individuals acquiesced, either through active assistance or a decision to stay silent.

The parallels between Enron and the crisis in the Catholic Church are striking. Both the executives at Enron and the abusive clergy were engaged in clear wrongdoing. Both criminal and corporate law had ample provisions to prohibit the worst of the activities in Enron. Similarly, both criminal law and canon law provided ample support to censure the wrongdoing of the individual church actors. No code of ethics will prevent such knowing wrongdoing. As we are well aware, in both Enron and within the Catholic Church, the most painful failures were systematic failures that flowed from tunnel vision of many of those around the wrongdoers. A culture of silence impaired ethical decision-making. A code of conduct does not magically create ethical awareness. Education is required to achieve that goal.

→ see Reinhold Niebuhr's critique of "education" towards ethics!

ROLE-DIFFERENTIATED BEHAVIOR

Professional codes purport to identify rules of conduct that are specific, that cannot be derived from general moral principles applicable to all. Often called *role-differentiated behavior*, the notion is that lawyers and priests and others who function in a professional role have specific obligations that flow from their professional roles.[11] For example, the strong obligation of confidentiality shared by both priests and lawyers derives from the professional role. We expect both priests and lawyers to maintain confidentiality, even in the face of competing claims that right behavior for nonpriests and non-lawyers would require disclosure. The professional obligation is grounded in an assessment that the greater good is achieved by maintaining confidentiality. While the duty of confidentiality is often the subject of dramatic television shows, the reality of the life of most lawyers—and priests—is that the duty of loyalty and ethic of care that flow from the fiduciary obligation causes the greatest ethical challenges.

We all engage in role-differentiated behavior, whether as a spouse, parent, lawyer, doctor, or minister. The challenge comes when the individual sees the role (like compliance with rules) as a complete identification of how they should behave. Role-differentiated behavior was a significant culprit in both Enron and the Catholic Church crises. Many individuals saw questioning as outside their role, sometimes understandably so. There was, in both cases, an assumption that others were in a superior position of both power and fact-finding.

Role-differentiated behavior is an endemic challenge. For example, one of our students was standing on a station platform of the "T," the public subway, in Boston. To his surprise, a twelve-year-old kid grabbed the purse of an old lady. There were fifty people on the platform, but no one intervened. The student reported that, inspired by a class discussion about Aristotelian responsibility, he unsuccessfully rushed after the purse-snatcher. When the student finally found a policeman at the top of the station stairs, the officer pointed out that he was a City of Boston policeman, and that the student would have to call the MBTA police. Too many rules, too much occupational specialization, as Max Weber observed, can get in the way of seeing your true responsibility in a clear way.

THE RELATIONSHIP BETWEEN CODES AND
THE SYSTEMS WITHIN WHICH THEY FUNCTION

An ecclesiastical code of conduct may have an important role in sharpening values important in professional functioning. But codes of professional conduct are directed toward *individual* misconduct, and their utility can drown under conflicting signals sent by the institutions and structures within which the professional functions. As Professor Richard Nielsen notes, "external environments and internal organization systems and traditions can support and encourage unethical behavior."[12]

Again, the lawyer codes are illustrative. They prohibit the individual lawyer from overbilling, lying to the court, fabricating evidence, representing conflicting interests, and the like. But all the punishment is directed at the individual lawyer. A few jurisdictions have flirted with the eight-hundred-pound gorilla in the room: structural systems, such as law firm policies and the adversary system itself, that tolerate and sometimes even encourage unethical behavior. For example, it is a violation of the lawyer's code to state to your client that you have put in one hundred hours when, in fact, you have worked only fifty. That false statement involves both lying to, and stealing from, your client. Lawyers are occasionally sanctioned, some quite seriously, for such misconduct. But law firms that require twenty-two hundred hours per year by associates—a work level that strongly pushes toward padding of time sheets—receive no disciplinary scrutiny.

The problems of the American Catholic church demonstrate, as so many chapters in this volume attest, that the systems within which the professional functions can have a huge impact on professional choices. Certainly we do not want a defense that "the system made me do it." Such defenses have been decried since Nuremberg. But the systems within which both lawyers and clergy function can blunt ethical awareness or, more often, create a sense of powerlessness on the part of the individual professional.[13] And many aspects of the system are not addressed in the professional codes.

This problem is shared by all professionals. Physicians, nurses, and other health-care professionals struggle with the tension between their professional ethic and the reality of managed care and limited resources. Teachers struggle with professional obligations, in the face of increasing expectation of schools to solve complex social issues with inadequate resources. Business managers must confront the relentless pressure of profit maximization. A code of conduct can highlight norms and values, but as all authors who have touched on this subject recognize, it cannot cure institutional failures.

The *Rules of Professional Conduct* for lawyers could not function against the corporate culture in Enron. It is difficult to envision rules, certainly more specific rules, that would have stopped the professional failures. Similarly, an ecclesiastical code could not have corrected the numbing of ethical awareness, the discounting of the possibility of recurrence, and the awareness of the effects on victims. Professional codes cannot function in isolation. To be effective, a code must interact and be harmonious with the aspirational goals of the systems in which the professional functions. As Bob Hinings and Michael Mauws have shown, organizational structure, such as the adversary system of justice, can either facilitate or prevent ⟵ moral failure. Specialization by function and occupational hierarchies can be both highly desirable and dangerous. In their words, "our form of social ⟵ organization [may] prevent us from recognizing our moral responsibility in the first place."[14] This is great danger. *(Niebuhr, again)*

THE VALUE OF CODES

Codification of ethical norms can offer some advantages. To achieve those advantages, drafters must approach the process with great humility and caution. The process of crafting the rules, if inclusive, can facilitate a conversation about shared norms. Rules can help clarify best practices in recurring situations. If reinforced by the corporate culture, rules can be part of the norm setting within the institutions. Rules can be one part of a larger educational process.

But we must recognize that rules can, as many of the essays in this volume suggest, occasionally get in the way of virtue. Here is an example we use in class. It is an ethical dilemma drawn from life, not a sterile hypothetical. A corporate client authorized $800,000 to settle a terrible accident in which it was clearly at fault. The victims, a poor immigrant family, could not speak English. The victim's lawyer demanded "$400,000, and not a penny less." He was incompetent and did not know the value of his own case. What should the client's lawyer have done? The usual answer, in light of the confidentiality and zealousness rules, is to offer "$250,000, and not a penny more!" Now our students are good young men and women. Many are religiously devout and know well the Sermon on the Mount and the Talmud. But occupational rules, which enforce professional minimums, get in the way of their better intuitions. For them law school is like a bramble bush. As Karl Llewellyn observed, they jump in "and scratched out both [their] eyes."[15]

We often take that blindness, the role, as inevitable. But we forget the rest of the poem that inspired Karl Llewellyn's famous book. "[A]nd when he saw that he was blind, with all his might and main he jumped into another one and scratched them in again." A professional may be guided by a code of conduct, even sanctioned for failure to comply with it. But such a code must be constantly examined in light of larger moral principles. Those larger principles have been developed, under the inspiration of the church, by some of the greatest philosophical minds. Hopefully, efforts to develop an ecclesiastical profession will be more successful than the legal profession in fully embracing this moral foundation.

THE VALUE OF EDUCATION

culture
2 d.

The dominant theme of this collection of essays is that the root of effective reform is cultural, not technical or legal. And culture is about education, both for the clergy and the laity. We are not experts on seminary education, but our hope for the legal profession is that, through education, we can improve the professional culture. We spend much of our professional lives working with the lawyer codes and can appreciate the important, but limited, utility of rules. We have no faith in rules alone. They are a small part of the much larger question of the exercise of discretion.

Formal education within a law school or seminary, or for the laity, is one part of the educational process. That education must include not simply analysis of the norms, but much more rigorous and thoughtful education about how to facilitate conversation and exercise discretion. Too often formal education treats the professional with an ethical dilemma as an autonomous individual with no communal support in assessing right behavior. We must teach students the skills of outreach in ethical discussions. We must constantly remind ourselves that the greatest risk comes from cultures that silence discussion about right behavior.

We also need education in context. This is the case for casuistry—a context-driven decision-making that brings moral theory to life.[16] Education in context recognizes a role for deductive decisions from larger moral theory and virtue ethics, but validates the messiness of real-life decisions. We need to be constantly teaching each other how to deal with the real-life pressures to stay in role, ignore uncomfortable facts, and embrace deliberate ignorance. This education does not end when the diploma is granted. It is a lifelong necessity. A final example might bring this into sharper focus. One of the authors of this chapter adheres to a religious tradition of pacifism, yet actively supports the education of commanding officers at the Naval War College in Newport through the Naval War College Foundation and participates in its programs. Why? Because in an era of terrorism, where there are no neat uniforms to mark combatants, the first line of defense against evil conduct, genocide, or war crimes is, at least on our part, the culture of our professional military. That culture is based on their professional education. The War College teaches its graduates critical judgment, the judgment necessary to abstain from evil conduct and not to tolerate it in others, regardless of the provocation or justification. The same should be true of lawyers and for the church as well.

NOTES

1. See Richard Gula's essay in this volume.

2. See Richard Nielsen's essay in this volume.

3. E. Norman Veazey, "Ethics 2000: Thoughts and Comments on Key Issues of Professional Responsibility in the Twenty-First Century," 5 *Del. L. Rev.* 1, 4 (2002).

4. Daniel R. Coquillette, *Lawyers and Fundamental Moral Responsibility* (Cincinnati: Anderson, 1995), 90–96.

5. Charles Wolfram, *Modern Legal Ethics* (St. Paul, Minn.: West, 1986) §2.6.2; Andrew L. Kaufman, "Ethics 2000—Some Heretical Thoughts," *Professional Lawyer* 1 (2001).

6. Fredrick Schauer, *Playing by the Rules: A Philosophical Examination of Rule-Based Decision-Making in Law and in Life* (New York: Oxford University Press, 1991).

7. Larry Alexander and Emily Sherwin, "The Deceptive Nature of Rules," 142 *U. Pa. L. Rev.* 1191 (1994).

8. David B. Wilkins, "Legal Realism for Lawyers," 104 *Harv. L. Rev.* 469 (1990).

9. See Richard Gula's essay in this volume.

10. Lynne L. Dallas, "A Preliminary Inquiry into the Responsibility of Corporations and Their Officers and Directors for Corporate Climate: The Psychology of Enron's Demise," 35 *Rutgers L. J.* 1, 13–17 (2003).

11. Richard Wasserstrom, "Lawyers as Professionals: Some Moral Issues," 5 *Human Rights* 1 (1975).

12. See Richard Nielsen's essay in this volume.

13. See Richard Nielsen's essay in this volume.

14. See C. R. Hinings and Michael Mauws's essay in this volume.

15. Karl N. Llewellyn, *The Bramble Bush* (New York: Oceana, 1960), iii.

16. Paul R. Tremblay, "The New Casuistry," 12 *Geo. J. Legal Ethics* 489 (1999).

14: TURNING PRO: THEOLOGICO-CANONICAL HURDLES ON THE WAY TO A PROFESSIONAL ETHIC FOR CHURCH LEADERS

John P. Beal

theologically — priests not "employees" of church — how then to make a professional code of ethics?

FRAMING THE CANONICAL ISSUES

At the conclusion of a brief news story on the recent *nolo contendere* plea by the Archdiocese of Cincinnati to five charges of failing to report sexually abusive priests to Ohio law enforcement authorities, *America* magazine reported that the district attorney believes that the archdiocese no longer *has in its employ* any active priests who have been accused of sexual abuse of minors.[1] While this news may be reassuring to the faithful of the Archdiocese of Cincinnati and to the citizens of Ohio, the district attorney's reported remarks are a bit unsettling for canon lawyers. The decision to paraphrase the district attorney's statement makes it impossible to know whether he himself spoke of the archdiocese having priests in its employ or whether the phrasing came from the reporter. Nevertheless, the fact that this phrasing survived the careful scrutiny of the editors of *America* suggests the extent to which the view that priests are employees of the church has become conventional wisdom, even among educated Catholics and at least some priests. Throughout its history, canon law has characterized the relationship between a priest and the particular church or institute of consecrated life for whose service he was ordained in a variety of ways, but it has never characterized it as an employer–employee relationship. The fact that, in less than two decades, the forces unleashed by the priest sexual abuse scandal have overwhelmed centuries of canonical and theological resistance to the idea that a priest can be adequately characterized as in "the church's employ" may prove to be, for good or ill, its single most significant outcome.

This ongoing crisis in the Catholic Church, prompted by revelations that numerous priests had sexually abused minors and vulnerable adults and that

169

bishops, when apprised of these crimes, had dealt with them in a less than responsible manner, has led to a call for the articulation of a clearer and more stringent professional ethic for church leaders. The crimes themselves, involving, as they often did, abuses of ministerial relationships with the victims by perpetrators, were morally and ethically reprehensible. Moreover, the nonfeasance, and sometimes malfeasance, of church authorities in the face of complaints about these crimes by their subordinates undoubtedly constituted ghastly violations of their own moral and ethical responsibility. In light of these horrible abuses of ministerial authority, the call for a clearer and more stringent professional ethic is certainly understandable. Indeed, the crisis has already sparked efforts to formulate an ethic for church ministers and to reinvigorate thinking about ministerial ethics.[2] These initial and tentative efforts can provide a basis for further discussions and developments. However, efforts at elaborating a *professional* ethic for church leaders and, more importantly, enforcing it once it is formulated and accepted can be successful only to the extent that church leaders can be accurately described as professionals and identify themselves as such.

While there is a long tradition of including the ministry among the learned professions, neither canon law nor the official theology underlying it view the church's ordained ministers primarily as professionals in any ordinary sense of that term. Moreover, it is not clear that ordained ministers view themselves primarily as professionals. This self-assessment of ordained leaders, encouraged and legitimized by canon law and its underlying theology, that they cannot adequately be described as professionals in the church's employ has had a long history and has been accepted and more or less consciously internalized by the faithful. Indeed, the vehemence of the popular reaction, both Catholic and non-Catholic, to revelations of clerical sexual abuse and episcopal irresponsibility is comprehensible only when these offenses are seen as terrible betrayals of trust much deeper and more serious than any breaches of professional ethics.

From an objective point of view, of course, Catholic Church leadership can be considered a profession inasmuch as it involves a full-time occupation, is entered into after completion of formation at a specialized training institution, and, to a considerably lesser extent, joins together those engaged in the same calling in professional associations. However, while it would be inaccurate to say that church leaders are bound by no code of ministerial conduct, it cannot be said that this ethical code is, at the present time at least, one that professionals have developed for and enforced upon themselves. In this respect, church leaders are in a markedly different situation than other professionals who elaborate and enforce internally their own codes of professional ethics.[3] From a subjective or attitudinal point of view, Catholic Church leaders are professionals in that they generally have a strong sense of calling to their field of endeavor and are deeply dedicated to service to

those who entrust themselves or are entrusted to their care. However, the use not (yet)
of a professional organization as a primary reference point, self-regulation, defined
and professional autonomy, which are the hallmarks of other professions, as
are notably lacking in the ministerial experience of ordained Catholic Church career
leaders. As Provost pointed out,
↓
see
172-173

> A profession normally sets its own code to which the professionals bind them-
> selves. There is nothing directly comparable in the Church. Official ministers are
> bound by the teachings of the Church as well as the code of law imposed on
> them by the hierarchy. They do not have an active role in determining these,
> and . . . even their life style is set for them.[4]

While the elaboration of a professional ethic for church leaders is a worth-
while, indeed an indispensable, project, this project will have little impact
beyond academe unless the church's official theological and canonical, as
well as its popular, understanding of official ministry can be nudged in a direction that creates a climate in which ministerial professionalism and an accompanying professional ethic can flourish. I will limit myself to identifying
three longstanding tensions in the understanding of church leadership in
canon law and the theology that underlies it, which stand in the way of ap-
preciating church leaders as professionals: the tension between status and
function, the tension between public and private life, and the tension between bureaucracy and professionalism.

THREE ENDURING TENSIONS IN THE OFFICIAL UNDERSTANDING OF CHURCH MINISTRY

The Tension between Status and Function

By the early second century, the functions of bishop, presbyter, and dea-
con, as well as others, had clearly emerged as stable ministries in the church,
and those who performed these functions on an ongoing basis were organized into orders, or *ordines*. Although induction into one of these *ordines* no
doubt gave individuals a certain personal status in the community, the differentiation was primarily functional and did not call into question the fundamental equality of all the baptized in the community of faith. However, as
the early church's *ordines* were integrated into Roman cultural and political
structures with their stratified system of castes or statuses distinguishing various groups, they gradually took on not only the trappings but the substance
of the Roman stratification of society into castes. As a result, basic inequality became the cornerstone of the ecclesiastical structure even to the extent
that the caste difference between clergy and laity was claimed to be based
on divine institution.[5] Although the resulting theology and the canon law

based on it did not ignore the function or service that clergy performed in and for the church, this function was often subordinated to the status clergy enjoyed in the church and to concern for maintaining this status. Consequently, many, if not most, of the rights and privileges of clergy in traditional canon law had less to do with the benefit to the individual cleric who enjoyed them than with the preservation of the dignity of their state. Thus, clerics enjoyed the right to decent support not so much because sustenance was due them as a human right but because it would dishonor the clerical state if clerics were seen begging. Of course, structured inequality and the privileged caste system it entailed led inevitably to the sort of clericalism that has been so much in evidence during the current sex abuse crisis in which concern for maintaining the public image of the clergy too often trumped the physical, emotional, and spiritual well-being of the people of God, especially its most vulnerable.

The teaching of the Second Vatican Council, especially its teaching on the equality of all the baptized, its insistence on ministry and hierarchical authority as service, and its not always consistent attempts to shift the emphasis from the life (i.e., status) to the ministry (i.e., function) of the ordained, marked a conscious effort to redress a long-standing imbalance in the church's official understanding of ordained ministry. This teaching has been substantially incorporated into the revised Code of Canon Law, but, as the revelations of the past few years have demonstrated, this teaching and the discipline based on it are either insufficient in themselves or have not yet sufficiently filtered down into ecclesial praxis to achieve the sort of balance between ordained minister's status and function to permit the development of an effective professional ethic. Indeed, an overriding concern for the honor of the clerical state is still much in evidence in the recent but belated efforts of bishops to purge sexually abusive clerics. Having failed to maintain the honor of the clerical state by keeping the crimes of clerics out of the public eye, bishops seem to have decided to achieve the same goal by disappearing any cleric who has tainted the honor of his state by becoming subject of an accusation of sexual abuse (or, for that matter, of sexual immorality of any kind whether it constitutes abuse or not), regardless of any evidence of repentance and reform or even of any clear evidence of guilt.[6]

A professional ethic cannot be effective in a system that values status over function. As Richard Gula has pointed out, part of being professionally responsible is to be open to public accountability for one's performance. A code of ethics makes explicit the commonly shared criteria for making this assessment.[7] Long before the eruption of the sexual abuse crisis, Catholic clergy, bishops, presbyters, and more recently deacons stubbornly resisted the introduction of standards and procedures for holding them publicly accountable for their ministerial performance.[8] This resistance has been rooted in what Gula calls a long-standing overemphasis on ministry as a vo-

Tom Reese, Archbishop: Inside the Power Struc of Amer Cath Ch.

cation, to the near exclusion of its also being a profession. As a result, a vocational calling then becomes the excuse for avoiding professional duties and accountability, and it can breed a sense of isolation, superiority, and, even worse, entitlement.[9] What Gula calls the overemphasis on vocation at the expense of profession is the priority of status over function dressed in ecclesiastical garb.

vocation + status opposed to profession + function

The Tension between the Public and Private Life of Church Leaders

One of the corollaries of the traditional emphasis in the church's official theology and canon law on the status of ordained ministers is that the line between the public life and the private life of church leaders is not a very bright one, if indeed there is any such line at all. Of course, church ministers are not the only public figures for whom private morality impinges on fitness for public office. The long agony of the Clinton impeachment proceeding should disabuse us of any naive idea that the private and the public spheres can be hermetically sealed off from one another. What is unique about church ministers is the extent to which their private life is a public issue and their personal lifestyle is subject to public expectations and regulation. As Provost has noted,

> The celibacy issue is an obvious point of conflict that has been a major occasion for several recent sociological studies about priests. But questions of clerical dress and personal living quarters have also been points of conflict between what priests consider their professional autonomy and what they perceive to be bureaucratic efforts to control their [private] lives.[10]

how to separate public from private in the variety of relationships

Less visible but perhaps more insidious is determining when an official minister is acting in his or her ministerial capacity and when he or she is acting as a private person and identifying the appropriate professional boundaries to be maintained by church ministers in a wide variety of interactions with others. Most ordained ministers have discovered that they are never completely off duty, even when they are with their own families, and that they never know when they will be called upon to act as representatives of the church in the midst of the most private occasions. In addition, even within a clearly ministerial setting, the variety of roles ordained ministers are expected to play with the same people depending on the circumstances stretches any sense of professional boundaries to the breaking point. As John Gonsiorek has pointed out:

> clergy roles are inherently more complex and fraught with boundary strains [than those of other professionals]. The role of a typical clergy member involves liturgical activities, spiritual direction, pastoral and other counseling, fund-raising, group leadership, and social activities, all with the same group of individuals.

Health care professionals generally have much more circumscribed roles. In fact, some health care professionals, such as psychologists, consider such a complex role to be inherently unethical, because of dual relationships. In effect, some health care professionals have determined that the extraordinary diversity of roles that clergy routinely play are simply impossible to manage appropriately, because of boundary strains.[11]

This blurred line between a minister's private and public lives poses a serious problem for the development of a professional ethic for church leaders. If a professional ethic is to be anything different than a special form of personal morality writ large, there must be some way of distinguishing a person's public life from his or her private life. Distinguishing public and private life, however, will require explicitation and renegotiation of the complex web of psychological contracts that bind church ministers with those they serve and with those with whom they serve in the ecclesial organization.[12] Until such explication and renegotiation are underway, it will not be clear whether ordained ministers have or are entitled to anything that can be accurately described as a private life or whether a minister's own attempts to satisfy his or her need for intimacy can be, from an ethical perspective, anything but exploitive.

The Tension between Bureaucracy and Professionalism

Church leaders in the Catholic Church are situated in a theological and canonical context that, to some extent at least, encourages them to behave and think of themselves as professionals. However, the predominantly bureaucratic mode of organizing official ministry in the Catholic Church creates tensions with and obstacles to genuine professionalism in ministry. The situation was well described by Provost:

> As bureaucrats priests are subject to a centralized leadership, while as professionals they respect leadership based on expertise. As representatives of the institution they must emphasize and support standard procedures, whereas as professionals they seek to adapt procedures to the needs of individual parishioners. From a bureaucratic point of view, they look to simplify tasks so that they can be done piecemeal and routinely; as professionals, they seek a comprehensive grasp of the total work. Little initiative is fostered in a bureaucracy, whereas broad initiative characterizes professionals. Corporate responsibility is emphasized in their corporate mode, with obedience the primary virtue; personal responsibility is the most prized dimension of their professional work. As a bureaucrat the priest is expected to deal equally with all sorts of other priests, somewhat impersonally, so that he can be transferred to wherever the institution needs to place him; as a professional he seeks close colleague relationships with priests of like mind or challenging talent. Priests enjoy a certain prestige and status from office, an ascribed status; as professionals, many priests desire

to be respected for their competence and not merely because they are pastors or officials of some agency.[13]

The bureaucratic system of the church into which official ministers are inserted is not the ideal type described by Max Weber[14] but, in tune with its Roman roots, one in which organization for efficient operation of the institution is combined with paternalism and achievement is harmonized with class ascription.[15] This mixed type of bureaucracy had disastrous results for the economy of the Roman Empire, as the centralization of power to assure domination allowed concern for domination to replace concern for production as the rationale for the bureaucracy itself.[16] There is ample evidence that the centralization of power in the church, both at the diocesan and at supra-diocesan levels during the last forty years has had the effect, even if not necessarily the intent, of assuring domination. Provost asked:

> With the present reliance on bureaucratic organization for official ministry, is there evidence that domination is replacing concern for the care of souls, as it did in the Empire? Certainly it has not replaced it in principle or in official policy. But neither did domination replace the ideology of efficient production that surrounded the bureaucracy of Imperial Rome.[17]

This centralized bureaucratic structure does not create a climate hospitable to the stirrings of professionalism among underclass ministers. Bureaucratic authorities may be amenable to imposing a code of ethics on their underlings and enforcing it themselves, but such a tactic would not result in the self-regulation characteristic of other professions.[18]

The situation of official ministers in the church is also different from that of other professionals who find themselves employed in a business or government bureaucracy. The difference seems to be that priests are in a closed system, a profession that cannot be exercised outside the church without violating the faith commitment that constitutes the essence of their call to be a priest in the first place.[19] Thus, unlike many other professionals, an official minister does not have the option of transferring, changing firms, or going into private practice. Moreover, practitioners of this encapsulated profession do so in the context of an organization that exhibits all of the telltale symptoms of a lazy monopoly, in which an extremely high price is exacted for exit from the system and voice as a mean of expressing dissatisfaction and effecting change is ignored, delegitimized, or stifled.[20] In short, this is not an atmosphere in which professional attitudes can flourish.

CONCLUSION

The elaboration of a professional ethic for Catholic Church leaders or official ministers would certainly be a welcome development. However, to be

effective in enforcing professional standards of behavior for official ministers, there will have to be simultaneous developments in the church's official theology and canon law that recognize the professional character of its
ministers and in the perception of the their identity as professionals both by
official ministers themselves and by the faithful they serve. These developments were encouraged by the teaching of the Second Vatican Council and
the revised Code of Canon Law. Nevertheless, the conciliar teaching and revised law has not yet nudged the official understanding of ordained ministers sufficiently away from an emphasis on their status rather than their
function, provided a clear line of demarcation between their private and
public lives, or overcome the predominantly bureaucratic organization of
their life and work in the church to open the way for an appreciation of
church leaders as genuine professionals. Nor has this teaching and law yet
succeeded in promoting the *novus habitus mentis* that is necessary for the
ministers to view themselves primarily as professionals. However, in just a
few years, the sexual abuse crisis has overcome centuries of resistance to
the idea that ordained minister could be properly considered to be in the
church's employ. Perhaps this crisis can also encourage a willingness to
think of these official ministers as professionals.

NOTES

1. "Cincinnati Archdiocese Pleads No Contest on Failure to Report," *America* 189,
no. 19 (December 2003): 4. Italics added.
2. See the discussion of various proposed codes of ethics for ministers in Richard
Gula's essay in this volume. See also the discussion of the need for renewed and critical reflection on ministerial ethics in James Keenan's essay in this volume.
3. See Robert Hall, "Professionalization and Bureaucratization," *American Sociological Review* 33 (1968): 92–104; Harold. L. Wilensky, "The Professionalization of
Everyone?" *American Journal of Sociology* 70 (1964): 137–58; and James H. Provost,
"Toward a Renewed Canonical Understanding of Official Ministry," *Jurist* 41 (1981):
457–68.
4. Provost, "Toward a Renewed Canonical Understanding," 461. Similar reserva-
tions from the social science perspective are voiced in Patricia Chang's essay in this
volume.
5. Provost, "Toward a Renewed Canonical Understanding," 455.
6. For a discussion of the ways in which organizational dynamics can blunt the
sense of moral and ethical responsibility see C. R. Hinings and Michael Mauws's essay in this volume.
7. See Richard Gula's essay in this volume.
8. Thomas J. Reese, *Archbishop: Inside the Power Structure of the American
Catholic Church* (San Francisco: Harper and Row, 1989), 251: Everyone agrees that
the weakest part of the priests' personnel system is the lack of any systematic evaluation. In most archdioceses there is no real evaluation of a priest's work. See also Kevin
McDonough, "Diocesan Bureaucracy," *America* 177, no. 10 (October 1997): 12–13.

9. See Richard Gula's essay in this volume.

10. Provost, "Toward a Renewed Canonical Understanding," 463.

11. John Gonsiorek, "Assessment for Rehabilitation of Exploitive Health Care Professionals and Clergy," in *Breach of Trust: Sexual Exploitation by Health Care Professionals and Clergy*, ed. John Gonsiorek (Thousand Oaks, Calif.: Sage Publications, 1995), 154–55.

12. See the discussion of psychological contracts in Denise M. Rousseau's essay in this volume.

13. Provost, "Toward a Renewed Canonical Understanding," 459. See also Joseph Fichter, *Religion as an Occupation: A Study in the Sociology of Professions* (Notre Dame, Ind.: University of Notre Dame Press, 1961), 224.

14. Max Weber, *Economy and Society* (New York: Bedminster Press, 1968) 3: 956–1006.

15. Provost, "Toward a Renewed Canonical Understanding," 464. See Robert. J. Antonio, "The Contradiction of Domination and Production in Bureaucracy: The Contribution of Organizational Efficiency to the Decline of the Roman Empire," *American Sociological Review* 44, no. 6 (1979): 905.

16. Provost, "Toward a Renewed Canonical Understanding," 468–69; Antonio, "Contradiction of Domination and Production," 905.

17. Provost, "Toward a Renewed Canonical Understanding," 469. For a somewhat different perspective on the economic analysis of church practice, see Michele Dillon's essay in this volume.

18. See Patricia Chang's essay in this volume.

19. Provost, "Toward a Renewed Canonical Understanding," 458. See also William R. Headley, *The Departure of a Priest: Management of a Deviant Identity* (New York: New York University Press, 1974), 4–16.

20. See Albert O. Hirschman, *Exit, Voice, and Loyalty: Responses to Declines in Firms, Organizations and States* (Cambridge, Mass.: Harvard University Press, 1970). For an application of Hirschman's concept of a lazy monopoly to the Catholic Church and its clergy, see John Seidler, "Priest Resignations in a Lazy Monopoly," *American Sociological Review* 44, no. 5 (1979): 763–83.

15: REFLECTIONS ON ETHICS, ORGANIZATIONS, AND CHURCH CULTURE

James E. Post

The Catholic Church has endured, and survived, many moral crises and catastrophes over two millennia. The clergy sexual abuse scandal certainly qualifies as a tragic, historically significant addition to this list. What can we learn from this crisis? How can lessons from this experience be transformed into actions that heal the church, repair damage done, and chart the course for institutional change that will ultimately benefit the mission of the church? The answers, I believe, are to be found in a deeper understanding of how the culture of the church affected the organizational and ethical safeguards that might otherwise have deterred such widespread abuse.

LESSONS LEARNED

One of the most important lessons is that a moral mission is not sufficient to protect an institution from the deviant behavior of its members, including the most trusted and respected of those members. This lesson is understood when applied to business, government, or other nonprofits, but seems somewhat startling when applied to churches. Sadly, churches—and in this case, the Catholic Church—often behave in a manner that is similar to other institutions in modern society. This reality sets the stage for considering the lessons to be learned from the sexual abuse crisis in both a specific organizational context and a more general institutional context.

Culture, organizational life, and ethics are entwined like a ball of string. It is difficult to understand or discuss one of these elements without discussing the others, and it is impossible to change one of these elements in an institutional setting without affecting the others. The clergy sexual abuse scandal in the Catholic Church illustrates, and exemplifies, the interdependence of culture, organizational life, and ethics.

Culture

We live in a culture that is rapidly being transformed by new developments in communication, transportation, and commercial activity. These factors are transforming much of the world into a secular and material culture, divorced from religion and religious values. This tends to isolate religious institutions on the one hand, but strengthens their determination to survive on the other hand. The conflict between modern culture and religious values in the United States is manifested in a range of current issues that stretches from the role of faith-based institutions as partners with government in meeting social needs to the endorsement of political candidates by religious leaders. The culture of the Catholic Church in turn, has become a clerical culture. Clericalism is, by definition, a culture state characterized by privilege, power, and secrecy. (I am indebted to the late Rev. Robert Bullock for this definition. Fr. Bullock was a cofounder of the Boston Priests' Forum.)

Throughout the clergy sexual abuse crisis (2002–2004), privilege, power, and secrecy have been repeatedly cited as contributors to the protection and relocation of abusive priests by church authorities. The pivotal role of culture was prominently cited by the National Review Board of the USCCB in their report (February 27, 2004). Culture was also cited as contributing to the "re-victimization" of survivors of abuse who, when they reported the abuse to church authorities, were shunned and dismissed.

Organizational Life

Culture shapes human and organizational behavior. Protecting abusive priests and systematically ignoring the claims of victims is traceable to core elements of clericalism. Culture also shapes ideas. Thus, it was psychologically and pragmatically necessary for church authorities to behave in this manner to protect the institutional church. The dominant features of organizational life and governance in the Catholic Church also contributed to the abuse crisis. Authority rests with the bishop who, in turn, exercises virtually unchecked power to administer the affairs of the diocese as he deems best. Canon law provides few constraints on episcopal authority and most often supports the bishop in his exercise of discretionary authority. Only the Vatican can exercise real influence on a bishop's behavior, and, in practice, that only sparingly.

The laity has a minor authoritative role in most aspects of church life. Clergy have a degree of authority, and some autonomy, especially at the parish level. There are, however, very few arenas in which the laity's influence is primary or where their decisions carry the day. This imbalance of power and authority affects many facets of Catholic life in communities around the nation and world.

church property

One area of internal and public controversy involves the ownership of property. Property is often owned in the name of the bishop through the legal device "corporation sole." This "corporation" is an artificial legal person embodied in the person who holds the church title of bishop or archbishop. Diocesan assets are thereby owned by the bishop in the form of the corporation sole, which conveys the many practical rights of corporate status. (Interestingly, there appears to be some variation across American dioceses in the details of parish ownership as revealed in the bankruptcy filings of the Archdiocese of Portland, Oregon, and the Diocese of Tucson, Arizona, in 2004. In Boston, Massachusetts, however, where more than one-fifth of all parishes are being closed and hundreds of millions of dollars of assets liquidated, the archdiocese has argued that all parish property is owned by the archbishop as corporation sole, thereby entitling him to suppress parishes and seize all of the assets.) In this arena, the clash between the clerical and secular cultures is stark.

Corp. sole

Ethics

Legal norms are not the same as ethical norms. Much of the current conflict between the hierarchy and laity involves a definition, or redefinition, of legal rights and responsibilities. But the ethical relationship amongst bishops, clergy, and laity is more textured, complex, and, I believe, important to the long-term health of the church. Fundamental moral understandings were violated in the sexual abuse crisis. Children were abused; the most innocent of God's human creation were violated by adults who ostensibly devoted their lives to Christ. A horrible wrong had occurred. The Catholic Church is one of the world's great contributors to ethical thinking. That has made the abuse crisis more shocking and more painful, and has encouraged many Catholics to insist that norms and standards of behavior be codified as a way to better prevent future abuses. In the course of this debate, sexual abuse has led people to expand the zone of concern to encompass church finances, parish life, and personnel practices. In short, the entire scope of church life is ripe for reexamination.

There is a clash of cultures (secularism versus clericalism) within which Catholic institutional life occurs for clergy, hierarchy, and the laity. The pressures of culture and organization clash in ways that require, but also call into question, the presence (or absence) of ethical norms and standards. Gaps develop between the expectations of these constituencies and the realities of the institution. Closing those gaps is a task—perhaps the mission—of managers and administrators.

ACCOUNTABILITY AND TRANSPARENCY

These are difficult times for American bishops. Each month brings additional allegations of clergy sexual abuse within the Catholic Church, often accompanied by charges of cover-up and deception by members of the hierarchy. In addition, serious charges have been made against a half-dozen sitting bishops.

- In Phoenix, Arizona, Bishop Thomas O'Brien was convicted in a case of "hit and run" driving that resulted in the death of an Arizona man named Jim Reed. Bishop O'Brien was sentenced to serve time for this crime.
- In Springfield, Massachusetts, Bishop Thomas Dupre's resignation was accepted by the Vatican one day after he was confronted with a credible accusation of sexual abuse. In September 2004, Bishop Dupre was indicted by a grand jury on criminal charges of rape.
- In Albany, New York, Bishop Howard Hubbard was charged with two incidents of sexual molestation dating back to the 1970s. Following months of public investigation and discussion, Bishop Hubbard was exonerated.
- In Rockville Centre, New York, Bishop William Murphy is accused of shielding abusive priests while serving as an auxiliary bishop in Boston. The head of Parents for Megan's Law, a child protection group, accused Murphy of nearly a dozen specific actions in which he concealed, deceived, and misled authorities. The group argues that Murphy is unfit to oversee the welfare of two hundred thousand children in the diocese.
- In Manchester, New Hampshire, Bishop John McCormack is living under a negotiated agreement with the State Attorney General that orders the diocese to undergo annual audits. The bishop now claims that the agreement is nonbinding and that the Manchester diocese will not comply or assume the costs of such an audit.

Would a code of professional ethics have prevented these actions? Could a code, or any statement of professional responsibility, have provided the moral compass that appears to have been missing? Each of these cases raises the public question of whether American bishops—the institutional church—are playing straight with their priests, parishioners, and public authorities.

In the world of public affairs management it is accepted that "perception is reality." Some might argue this point, but it is practical "gospel" among lawyers, public relations experts, marketers, and other professionals whose work involves the image, reputation, and credibility of a person or organization. If you are a leader who deals with the public, you must operate on the assumption that perception is reality.

As Kimberly Elsbach notes in her paper, "effective perception management appears to require organizations and their leaders to resist inclinations to confirm the stereotypes of strong leadership" (namely, the illusion of control, escalating commitment to a failed course of action, and the refusal to admit mistakes). This paper rightly points to the essential responsibility of leaders to preserve the credibility and legitimacy of the organization or institution.

In 2003, a reporter in Arizona, who had followed the sexual abuse issues for many months and who was covering the O'Brien trial, posed this question: "Does the O'Brien case . . . have any bearing whatsoever on the church's efforts to regain credibility lost as part of sexual abuse scandal? Is anyone saying this is just another case of a bishop gone amok? Are Catholics anxious to put O'Brien and the sex scandal behind them?" These questions seemed quite reasonable at the time, and in retrospect, they are even more reasonable. I responded to the reporter:

> Catholics are eager to put the scandal behind them. I think there is a certain kind of "outrage fatigue." Americans like quick fixes and short wars. But this tragedy does not lend itself to either a quick fix or a speedy resolution, and I believe more Catholics are recognizing that truth every day. . . . Cleaning up the Catholic Church is more than spring cleaning—it requires the most serious reassessment of a clerical culture that has run amok.

In the world of perceptions, the Catholic Church is drawing a lot of "bad press," but it is also seething with pressures for change. As Jean Bartunek has written, people are engaged in trying to make sense of what they are observing, hearing, and learning. This is "sensemaking," in academic language, but it is also "making sense" in the vernacular. People recognize that something is very wrong with the Catholic Church today and it needs to be fixed. Recent polls show high levels of support for change from Catholics across the political spectrum.

The "social drama" that Bartunek describes communicates the story of our effort to save an institution that is afflicted with a serious disease. But the story line of this drama has changed over the course of several years. Two years ago, the story line was the drama of victims of abuse coming forward to tell their stories to an audience that previously did not want to know the facts. That story was followed, in turn, by the drama of bishops and other members of the hierarchy refusing to either tell the truth or surrender their authority. Then, the story shifted to the emergence of laywomen and laymen as activists, and the drama of a new movement of laity—the Voice of the Faithful.

VOICE OF THE FAITHFUL

The social drama of the survivors remains the most powerful and central theme in this story. It has a singular consistency about it—I have never heard a survivor of sexual abuse say they are better off because of that experience. There is always a gap between what they perceive to be a "normal" life, free of abuse, and the reality of their lives, which have been marked by abuse.

There is always a psychological gap, and their perception is always their reality. Two years ago, I could not have imagined being asked to comment on
such matters. But so much has changed since 2002. The need to speak out
about the "great disconnect" between Catholic values and Catholic administrative practice cannot be denied by thousands of ordinary Catholics. The
birth and growth of Voice of the Faithful symbolizes a sharp cry of pain from
innumerable decent, middle-of-the-road Catholics whose faith is challenged
by the revelations of a culture we never really understood.

This points us toward a conclusion. As Denise Rousseau has so beautifully
written in this volume, there is a vital psychological contract among members of our church. It has been very dysfunctional of late, but it is the psychological framework we must understand if we are to appreciate the full
consequences of this tragedy. Mutual expectations were established and understood. Today, the special quality of that relationship has crumbled in the
face of scandal. It is credibility lost, legitimacy lost, and trustworthiness lost.
Remedial action is essential, and that is where a professional code of ethics
or other systemic means may play a useful role.

Metaphorically, the "genie is out of the bottle." There is no going back to
the old ways. We do not know the future, but we must walk into the unknown. It would be well to do so together. Organizational behavior scholars, such as Jean Bartunek, have written of the first-order, second-order, and
third-order effects that flow from organizational change. Today, the Catholic
Church is being challenged, and changed, by the first-, second-, and third-
order effects of the sexual abuse crisis.

The first-order effects are profound: admission of guilt, acknowledgment
that the church's culture and administrative systems perpetuated the problem and that thousands of the most vulnerable were exploited. The second-
order effects are equally harsh: public disgrace, the outrage and disgust of
church members, embarrassment and loss of face in virtually every public forum. Now, it is time to assess the third-order effects, including changes in the
structure, systems, and procedures of the institution itself.

I doubt that we could have had much of a discussion of an ecclesial professional ethic two or three years ago. But today, the time is ripe to consider the
"relational and psychological contracts" that Denise Rousseau has described.
We have peeled away several of the first-order and second-order layers of the
proverbial "onion" of this great tragedy. Today, we are reaching to explore a
layer of still deeper issues of ecclesial personal and professional responsibility.

CONCLUSION

This chapter began with two central questions: First, what can we learn from
this crisis? Second, how can lessons from this experience be transformed into

actions that heal the church, repair damage done, and chart the course for institutional change that will ultimately benefit the mission of the church?

As to the lessons learned, we have certainly learned that culture, organization, and ethics are entwined. That makes the causal analysis more complicated and the shaping of practical interventions more difficult. But we now understand that the pattern of clergy sexual abuse has deep, complicated roots. The John Jay College study of the scope and scale of sexual abuse in the Catholic Church in the United States over the past fifty years provides a sweeping picture of the scandal and some of the factors that contributed to it. Further research studies, to which the National Review Board and the USCCB are committed, will explore the causal relationships further.

How do we build on the lessons learned? Throughout this collection, thoughtful scholars and practitioners have suggested at least five ways to do so.

1. Recognize the importance of leadership. From today's vantage point, we recognize at least three types of leadership failure in the sexual abuse crisis. First, there were a small number of church leaders directly involved in sexually abusive conduct. Second, there were leaders who covered up, concealed, and deceived others regarding the facts of clergy abuse in their parish, diocese, or order. Third, there are church leaders who, while cognizant of the magnitude and consequences of the crisis, have been reluctant to "over-invest" in responding. Their concern seems to be that too many changes, or changes that have far-reaching effects, will prove ill-advised in the long term. They hew to an incremental, go-slow approach. This, it seems to me, is a failure of vision.

2. Accept that "perception is reality." The public face of the church is not a public relations problem, but one that expresses core values and conduct that conforms to principle.

3. Acknowledge that we are engaged in "sensemaking" and in making sense of our situation. We are involved in the social construction of images, stories, and meaning.

4. Grasp the magnitude of this great social drama. It is a drama in which we all have an essential part to play.

5. Acknowledge that the psychological contract among lay Catholics, clergy, and the institutional church is shattered and that we are unsure whether it can be repaired or whether (and how) we are to shape a new contract.

These questions, and lessons learned, still leave many disturbing questions unanswered. I close this reflection with a blunt and serious question for readers: Is the Catholic Church a "lost cause"? Given what we have learned to date, can the institutional church be repaired? Given the sordid truth of the matter, do we have any basis to conclude that the institutional church is a not a lost cause? What is the source of hope?

We must recognize that, as they say in the military, "hope is not a method." What method, then, do we propose as a way to join hope with reality? Hope, in my opinion, must be built on three organizational legs: First, the institution must recognize its problems and their causes, fully and accurately. Second, the institution's leadership must make the unambiguous commitment to transforming the institution through change in the structures and systems that contributed to the original problems. Third, processes of participation will be created to provide meaningful lay involvement. The absence of any one of these elements will undermine the reform process that is essential in the modern Catholic Church.

The development of an ecclesial professional ethic may provide a method or an approach through which hope and reality can be joined. Such an ethic must link culture, organizational life, and ethical norms in ways that remind bishops, clergy, and laity of the essential connection between mission and practice. For the Catholic Church, there can be no other course.

code of ethics must include notion of priest / bishop as relationship — & work in what the laity are

16: AN ETHICAL CHURCH CULTURE

Patricia M. Y. Chang

In the wake of unfathomable decisions made by church leaders, it is not surprising that each of us reaches for a solution that seems accessible to our talents, interest, and training. In this I am no different. My area of expertise lies in the area of organizational sociology and so I turn my attention to the proposal of an ecclesial code of ethics as a scholar of institutions.

For me, the scandalous behavior of the church has not been the result of miscalculation, misstep, or procedural misbehavior. Rather it is the result of a flawed institutional culture that cannot easily be corrected by the replacement of personnel, decision leaders, or even the implementation of a new set of operating instructions. Culture, unlike operational procedures, is not easily changed. It is the result of established understandings, ways of thinking, and unexamined assumptions that by their very nature are difficult to root out and expose to new light.

Sadly, the seriousness of the crimes and their widespread nature has issued the kind of wake-up call throughout the American Catholic Church that makes this kind of soul-searching now commonplace. This book has been one result of this soul-searching, and while no one in this volume believes that our ends will be accomplished by simply issuing a new set of behavioral expectations, each of us believes that these dialogues must be held in some form as part of a series of cumulative acts of change.

As an organizational scholar I would like to examine some of the institutional implications of this dialogue. Because the behavior of priests is largely seen as one cause of the current crisis, many people have been quick to assume that the priests must also bear the responsibility of bringing about the necessary changes. In the first part of this chapter I examine the kinds of organizational structures that are needed to generate an ethical change in the culture of the church and argue that the diocesan priesthood, lacking the essential ingredients of professional autonomy and oversight, are perhaps in the weakest position to do so. In the second part of this chapter I examine the organizational culture of the church more closely and question the taken-for-granted assumptions that permitted the abuse of children to be dealt with so ineffectively. This culture worked consistently to protect the reputation of the church and the status of the priests largely because the institutional culture had come to be defined so closely with the interests of the priesthood. The response to this problem I argue is not to form stronger professional associations among priests, but to attempt to change the organizational culture within the church so that self-interest is more broadly defined to include the interests of the laity, as well as the priests, and the reputation of the institution.

CAN ONE HAVE A PROFESSIONAL CODE OF ETHICS WITHOUT A PROFESSION OF PRIESTS?

While clergy and priests have long been considered one of the oldest and most honored of the so-called professions,[1] this title reflects a traditional understanding that references the status and the prestige of the occupation rather than any underlying theoretical category or organizing principle. This understanding has shifted in the light of systematic analyses of "professional occupations" by social scientists in the past fifty years who have looked into the historical development of these groups and the distinctive characteristics that set so-called professions apart from other occupations.[2]

These analyses have found that one of the characteristics that make professional occupations distinctive is an institutional autonomy and social power that allows them to exercise power and control over their work and their working environment, especially in relation to the organizations that employ them. Most often their success in making these claims to power lies in their ability to make strong claims to a specialized body of knowledge. This power is enhanced to the extent that a professional body, as a semiautonomous entity, is able to control access to this knowledge and also to certify practitioners. In exchange, the profession takes a certain responsibility that practitioners will have a standard level of competence and be guided by uniform codes of ethical conduct. In this way, the code of ethics has become an external symbol of professional status. It represents a set of ethical values and standards that professionals agree to hold themselves up to in a self-regulating manner, over and above any situational ethic that they may face in the organization in which they work.

The primary example of a strong profession is the medical profession.[3] The American Medical Association controls, through its entrance exams, who gets into medical school, how many doctors are licensed, the content of the curricula, and what knowledge is required for board specialization. Through certification limits, it even controls how many doctors can specialize in each field. In turn, doctors take responsibility for almost all aspects of medical practice—managing the hospitals in which they work, disciplining doctors who are no longer competent, and training future doctors.

While the Catholic priesthood, like the medical profession, has no difficulty in making claims to a specialized knowledge base, it cannot make the more important claim of an expertise-based independence from the institutions that employ them. Therefore, it has no basis of autonomous power. The role of the priest is defined and constituted by the traditions and institutions of the Catholic Church. Unlike doctors, they are agents of the organization, but not independent professionals. Groups of priests cannot take it upon themselves to discipline one another on the basis of a violation of some transcendent professional norm, they can only complain to those within the hierarchy who have the power to take disciplinary action. Nor can they collectively organize to change the conditions of their work or work environment if they are dissatisfied with the ways that the church treats them. In sum, priests, as an occupational association, can exert very little leverage vis-à-vis the church because their roles are constituted by the church and they cannot exist independently of the organization of which they are a part.

This relationship creates problems for the priesthood in creating and maintaining a self-regulating code of ethics. Indeed, the idea of such a code is at first glance contrary to the role we associate with priests as the arbiters of morality in our communities. On one level, it would seem that priests should be the group that is least likely to require a code of ethics since laity turn to them for moral guidance. If people perceive that the priesthood needs a code of ethics to tell them right from wrong, then the moral authority and legitimacy of the priesthood comes into question. At a second level, if such a code is in fact necessary, but can only be implemented if adopted by the bishops and then imposed from above, then this structure undermines one of the chief characteristics of a professional code of ethics, which is that it is an internalized set of norms and values instilled by the practice of the profession.

A code of ethics is thought of as a set of standards and values that transcends obligations to the organization in which one works. It is a calling to a higher standard of behavior, which is what gives professions their status. How can priests, whose primary oath of loyalty is to God and the church, make such a pledge? For a professional ecclesial code of ethics to have force it must have a basis that can claim some autonomy from the church and its hierarchy. Yet for most priests, and for diocesan priests in particular, the authority of the bishops who control their careers, possibility for advancement, and indeed their very lifestyles makes this scenario highly unlikely.

In sum, for a code of ethics to have an independent moral force, capable of regulating the behavior of priests, it must be based in an autonomous, normative, professional culture that has an independent power to regulate and sanction its own members. The priesthood by its nature and constitution lacks these characteristics. As agents of an organization that is bureaucratic in nature, priests are subject to the rules and laws of that organization. How then can members of the priesthood seek to change the organizational rules by which they are governed?

THE FORMATION OF A MORAL VANGUARD

Given the questions about the professional status of priests, how can priests work to improve the current situation? Despite the aforementioned arguments, a code of ethics still appears to be a common place to begin. If you Google the words "code of ethics" on the Internet, you get over three million listings. Rakesh Khurana, a professor at the Harvard Business School who is currently looking at the professionalism of managers, has documented over two thousand occupations that have a code of ethics. My own search shows that everyone from antiquarian booksellers to industrial hygienists has a professional code of ethics. The reason for the ubiquity of these codes lies less in their effectiveness for promoting moral behavior than that they act as a signaling device to the larger social environment of its legitimacy and social status.[4] In the case of an ecclesial code of ethics, serious attention will have to be paid to what such a code would signal to the larger environment. It is likely that the normative signal that will be received is that priests who subscribe to such a code have agreed that they have responsibilities to their professional identity that transcend their loyalty to the church. Given the serious implications of such a claim, this should certainly be considered with care.

Since there is no mechanism by which priests can agree to such a code as a condition of their priesthood, and at the moment there is no obvious national association of priests with the power to implement such norms, subscription may very well be decided on a voluntary individual-by-individual basis. But such a code need not be universally adopted to have its desired moral effect. There are frequent examples by which a vanguard of practitioners have declared their allegiance to a higher standard and become moral exemplars in their field. If this vanguard is highly visible and influential either by numbers or influence, what often happens is that the rest of the environment is forced to adopt this standard or risk losing their legitimacy in suffering by comparison.

This model of a moral vanguard is frequently used in political affairs with a small group of powerful nations gathering to agree to certain environmental protections, for example, and then using moral suasion and other means to get other countries to comply. The trick of the moral vanguard is to artic-ulate a stance that is prima facie appealing so that when announced, those who do not comply are viewed with suspicion. The grassroots campaign to get universities to divest from holdings in companies doing business with South Africa is an example of a moral vanguard that eventually gained wide-spread momentum and ultimately helped bring about political changes in that country.[5] Similarly, if visible and influential groups within the Catholic Church were to step forward and adopt an ecclesial code of ethics, the effect could conceivably snowball into change.

While it is institutionally challenging for diocesan priests to lead such a moral vanguard because of the high degree to which priests are dependent upon their bishops, religious order priests, such as Benedictines, Francis-cans, and Jesuits, would appear to have a greater ability to play this role. While there is structural variation among the religious order priests, the lives of order priests are organized in a much more democratic and cooperative fashion than diocesan priests. This makes them stronger candidates to posi-tion themselves as a moral vanguard within the Catholic Church.

Priests who are members of religious congregations operate within a provincial structure headed by provincial superiors who are often democrat-ically elected by the members of the congregation. These provinces in turn participate within a larger body headed by a superior general who is also elected by representatives of the provincial congregations. There are repre-sentative bodies both at the provincial and the national level that offer op-portunities for priests to gather and make collective decisions about their or-der that does not exist within the diocese. They may even collectively discuss and amend certain parts of their constitution and bylaws in accor-dance with canon law.

This kind of structure makes it possible for some orders to discuss and for-mulate a code of ethics. While such a code would not be binding upon those outside the order, it would serve as a highly visible and symbolic declaration of an ethical moral standard, implicitly issuing a challenge to other Catholic institutions to follow in their example.

Of the various institutions in the Catholic Church, the orders seem best po-sitioned, by their structural organization and by their visibility, to be able to collectively formulate such a code, to win voluntary compliance from a large and influential segment of the priesthood, and to do so with a degree of au-tonomy from the hierarchy.

CHANGING THE ORGANIZATIONAL CULTURE

Even if a moral vanguard strategy is successful, I believe it only addresses a small part of the problem. There have been many analyses and opinions of what conditions and decisions led to the sex abuse scandals, and like everyone else I have my own perspective to add to the conversation.

As an organizational sociologist, one of the interesting features of the scandal has been the operation of the church as a bureaucratic organization. In one sense the church operated very efficiently. Early on it developed a routine for handling abusive priests and it stuck to that routine despite startling evidence that the routine was ineffective in stopping abusers and immoral in its treatment of victims. It did not seem to make a difference who was in the role of the decision-maker, the same policies were carried out over and over again over many years. Functionally, this is precisely what bureaucratic structures are designed to do.[6]

We know from studying organizations and the people in them that creating new routines can change the outputs of the organization, and there has been some attempt to do that in the wake of these scandals. But the goal of a code of ethics attempts to do far more than this. It is trying to change the sense of responsibility of the actors involved in these decisions; this is a much deeper problem and one that a code of ethics is unlikely to actually address.

Sociologists and economists have been among those who argue that behaviors are governed in part by individuals and organizations seeking to maximize their own self-interest.[7] Thus the best way to change someone's behavior is to change that person's perception of his or her self-interest. This is most commonly done by changing the incentive structures within the organization. To give a mundane example, if an organization wanted their employees to stop smoking it would be more effective for them to raise the cost of health insurance for smokers than it would be to put up a sign that said "No Smoking" or to prohibit smoking in the workplace. While the former creates a financial interest in the worker to stop smoking that will have widespread effects on his or her disposable income and therefore the lifestyle choices he or she is able to make, the latter simply tries to govern a particular behavior in the workplace.

In hindsight, it seems that the organizational culture in the Boston archdiocese was one that was very common within bureaucratic organizations. The culture basically sought to preserve the status quo and had a high level of structural inertia. Leaders saw their primary goal as preserving the authority and reputation of the institution and their secondary goal as taking care of what they perceived to be its closest members, that is, the priests.

While many laypeople can understand and forgive the church's desire to limit the damage to the church's reputation caused by the abuse, and can perhaps even understand and forgive the church's ignorance that led to the mistaken belief that abusive priests could be rehabilitated, what they cannot forgive and indeed struggle to understand is the church's neglect and callous treatment of the victims of sexual abuse. An organizational interpretation suggests that this failing came about because the diocesan leadership identi-fied the interests of the church solely with the priests and the hierarchy. They did not include the laity in their definition of the church. I sincerely believe that the priests involved in this scandal, and by this group I include the abu-sive priests, the decision-makers on the bishop's staff, and the priests who stood by silently in suspected cases of abuse, felt they were working in the best interests of the church. The problem was that they did not include the ⟵ laity in their definition of the church.

To prevent the reemergence of similar problems in the future, I do not be-lieve it will be enough to issue and monitor the safe environment guidelines, as the United States Conference of Catholic Bishops has done. I also do not believe that it is enough to replace the decision-makers, as the pope has done with the Boston archdiocese. Rather, I believe that for real change to take place, the organizational culture of the decision-makers must change.

For this reason, like John Beal earlier in this volume, I believe that a code of ethics that reinforces the idea of the priesthood as a separate profession may be a problematic strategy. The church does not need yet another insider group of ordained priests, even if it creates an autonomous voice against the hierarchy in its decision-making. For the organizational culture of the church to change, ordained leaders within the church need to see their interests as being broader than that of the institution and the hierarchy, they need to identify their interests with the laity and truly see the church as a unity of priests, vowed religious, laity, tradition, and institutions. Only when the or-ganizational culture shifts toward seeing the laity as part of "us" rather than "them" will the bureaucratic culture begin to reflect the interests of the entire church rather than simply the ordained. *need to see laity as "church" before change can occur*

CONCLUSION

relational ethics

What then, can we do now? Combining the strategy of both cultural change and the moral vanguard, what Catholics can do now is begin conversations about a (relational ethics) that includes all the peoples of the church—priests, vowed religious, laypersons, hierarchy, lay ministers, and religious workers. These conversations can and should take place everywhere, and simultaneously—in local congregations, in orders, in priest associations, at universities, and in dioceses, and each of these independent bodies should take it upon themselves to formulate a code of ethics that is not focused on any single group within the church but on the ethics that should govern ap-propriate relationships within the church and the people in it. This can in-clude discussions about what is appropriate in relationships of authority, respect, and power sharing; what the function is of each group within the body of the church; how they are related to one another in the life of the church; and what kind of church they want to share in their collective future. They should decide among themselves, independent of the hierarchy, what kind of ethic they want to govern their personal behavior as Catholics.

This strategy, of letting a thousand conversations bloom, will perhaps do more to change the cultural climate that currently exists than any strategy that any one group can enact alone. As the taken-for-granted assumptions and understandings of each group surfaces and are shared, we can hope that new moral vanguards will take shape on multiple levels within the church. We can also hope that a precedent will be established for ordained, religious, and laity to work together on an important project that directly affects the future of their church. The mere act of sitting down together and thinking through their fundamental relationships to one another will begin a process that can only lead to a better understanding of one another's position and develop a more integrated and shared vision of the church.

Let us provide spaces where parents and priests can sit down together and discuss what each of them fear the most. Let us have conversations that allow Catholics to express their fears and begin to heal. Let us develop new models for community and conversation that can eventually be used to build local governance structures built upon mutual understanding and trust. Let us begin at the bottom. Let us begin now.

NOTES

1. Donald M. Scott, *From Office to Profession: The New England Ministry, 1750–1850* (Philadelphia: University of Pennsylvania Press, 1978).

2. Andrew Delano Abbott, *The System of Professions: An Essay on the Division of Expert Labor* (Chicago: University of Chicago, 1988); Eliot Freidson, *Profession of Medicine* (New York: Dodd and Mead, 1970); Magali Sarfatti Larson, *The Rise of Professionalism in Sociological Analysis* (Los Angeles: University of California Press, 1977).

3. Paul Starr, *The Social Transformation of American Medicine* (New York: Basic Books, 1982).

4. John W. Meyer and Brian Rowan, "Institutionalized Organizations: Formal Structure as Myth and Ceremony," *American Journal of Sociology* 83 (1977): 340–63.

5. USCC, *Divestment, Disinvestment, and South Africa: A Policy Statement of the United States Catholic Conference* (Washington, D.C.: Office of Publishing and Promotion Services, 1986).

6. Max Weber, *Economy and Society: An Outline of Interpretive Sociology*, ed. Guenther Roth and Claus Wittich (Los Angeles: University of California Press, 1978).

7. James Samuel Coleman, *Foundations of Social Theory* (Cambridge: Belknap of Harvard University Press, 1994).

INDEX

bishops: Carroll on, 33; and discourse, 92–94; ideological fortress and, 19–20; and public involvement of Church, 46–47; and response to crisis, 6–7; strategies of, 93. *See also* hierarchy
Bishops' Bicentennial Program, 152–53
Boston Archdiocese, 181
Boston College, xiii
Boston Priests' Forum, 180
boundary issues, in clergy roles, 173–74
Bourdieu, Pierre, 51
breach, in social drama, 23; and sexual abuse scandal, 24
Buffet, Warren, 77
Bullock, Bob, xv, 180
bureaucracy, versus professionalism, 174–75
Burke, Edmund, 123, 133
Butler, Francis J., xiv, 137–45, 152

Call to Action coalition, 48
Camenisch, Paul, 86
Canada: codes of ethics in, 148, 151; organizational morality in, 115–16
canonical issues: in ecclesial professional ethics, 169–77; framing, 169–71
capital, types of, 52
Cardman, Francine, 8
Carroll, John, 32–33
casuistry, case for, 166
Catholic Charities, 46
Catholicism in America: sociological perspective on, 43–56; stages of, 31–41
Catholic population, changes in, 34, 39
Catholic Rural Life Movement, 36
Catholic School of Social Service, 36
Catholics Speak Out, 48
Catholic Trade Unionists, 36
Catholic Workers, 36
Catholic Youth Organization, 36
centralization, 8, 13; John Paul II and, 14
certainty: Kerry on, 78; as leadership trait, 70; as trap, 74–75

Chang, Patricia M. Y., 187–94
character, intervention methods and, 125–26
Chopp, Rebecca, 86
Christian Family Movement, 36
Church: future of, 185–86; and kingdom of God, 60–61; nature of, and code of ethics, 138–39; as organization, 98; participation in life of, and code of ethics, 143; as sacrament, 59–60; as visible sign of gospel justice, 63–67
Church culture, 179–86; changing, 191–93; ethical, need for, 187–94
"The Church in the 21st Century," xiii–xiv
circuit priests, 32
civil discourse, crisis of, 65
clerical culture, 179–86; deceptiveness in, 93; and sexuality, 91
clericalism, 9; definition of, 180; opposition to, and code of ethics, 143
code of ethics: authorship of, 152–53, 160; Butler on, 137–45; content of, 151; Gula on, 147–55; importance of, 165–66; interpretation of, 154–55; limitations of, 153–55, 160–61; Nielsen on, 123–35; profession question and, 188–90, 193; purpose of, 149–50; rationale for, 138, 147–48; requirements for, 190; and system, 164–65; values and, 161–63
Colish, Marcia, 8
communication: and code of ethics, 143; as reciprocal, 140
communicative action theory, 11–12
communion, Church as, 139
communitarianism, and ethical debate, 117
community, understanding of, and code of ethics, 141
competence: as leadership trait, 70; as trap, 73–74
compliance, code of ethics and, 153
confidentiality, in religious life, 87–89
Congar, Yves, 10–11, 57
conscience, Vatican II on, 45, 47–48

ABOUT THE EDITORS AND AUTHORS

Jean M. Bartunek, RSCJ, is the Robert A. and Evelyn J. Ferris chair and professor of Organization Studies at Boston College. She is also a past president of the Academy of Management and a fellow of the Academy of Management. Her most recent book is *Organizational and Educational Change: The Life and Role of a Change Agent Group* (2003). Her research interests center around intersections of organizational change, cognition, and conflict. She is a member of the Society of the Sacred Heart.

John P. Beal was ordained to the presbyterate for the service of the Diocese of Erie, Pennsylvania, in 1974. From 1984 to 1992, he served as judicial vicar of the Diocese of Erie. Since 1992 he has taught canon law at the Catholic University in Washington, where he is now associate professor. He was coeditor of and major contributor to *A New Commentary on the Code of Canon Law* (2000). He has contributed articles to several scholarly journals.

Francis J. Butler is the president of Foundations and Donors Interested in Catholic Activities, Inc. (FADICA), a national consortium of fifty private philanthropies. FADICA functions as a forum for the discussion of church-related needs and effective philanthropic practices. He is the editor of *American Catholic Identity* (Sheed and Ward, 1994), is a contributing writer to *Governance, Accountability, and the Future of the Church* (2004), and has widely published on subjects related to religious philanthropy.

Patricia M. Y. Chang is an associate research professor in sociology at Boston College, specializing in the study of religious institutions. Her past work has focused on the career mobility of Protestant clergy, the role of denominational hiring strategies in reducing wage inequality among male and female clergy, and the political structures of American Protestant denominations. She is currently working on a project that examines the role of the family in the transmission of religious faith. She is also the assistant director of the Boisi Center for Religion and American Public Life at Boston College.

Daniel R. Coquillette is the J. Donald Monan University Professor at Boston College Law School. He has served on the Committee on Ethics and Professional Responsibility of the American Bar Association (ABA) and the Special Task Force on Model Rules of Professional Conduct of the Supreme Judicial Court of Massachusetts. He is also a reporter to the Standing Committee on Rules of the U.S. Judicial Conference. He has served on numerous committees that have tried to deter bad conduct by lawyers.

Michele Dillon is professor of sociology at the University of New Hampshire and past chair of the American Sociological Association section on the Sociology of Religion. Her publications include *Debating Divorce: Moral Conflict in Ireland* (1993), *Catholic Identity: Balancing Reason, Faith, and Power* (1999), *Handbook of the Sociology of Religion* (editor, 2003), and *Lived Religion* (with Paul Wink, forthcoming).

Kimberly D. Elsbach is associate professor of management and Chancellor's Fellow at the Graduate School of Management, University of California, Davis. Kim's research focuses on the perception and management of individual and organizational images, identities, and reputations. She has studied these symbolic processes in variety of contexts ranging from the California cattle industry and the National Rifle Association to radical environmentalist groups and Hollywood screenwriters. Her work aims to build theory about the cognitive and emotional processes organizational members use in perceiving their organization, their coworkers, and themselves.

Richard R. Gaillardetz is the Murray/Bacik Professor of Catholic Studies at the University of Toledo. He has authored or edited six books, including his most recent, *By What Authority? A Primer on Scripture, the Magisterium, and the Sense of the Faithful* (2003) and *Readings in Church Authority: Gifts and Challenges for Contemporary Catholicism* (2003). He is currently a member of the U.S. Catholic-Methodist ecumenical dialogue.

Richard M. Gula, SS, is professor of moral theology at the Franciscan School of Theology at the Graduate Theological Union in Berkeley, California. As a Sulpician priest, Rich has devoted his ministry and academic interests to the education and continuing formation of seminarians and priests. He has lectured widely to ministerial groups on interests in moral theology and professional ethics.

C. R. Hinings is professor emeritus in strategic management and organization in the School of Business at the University of Alberta. His primary interests are in organizational design and organizational change. His is a Fellow of the Royal Society of Canada and a Fellow of the Academy of Management. He attends St. Paul's Anglican Church in Edmonton.

Mary Ann Hinsdale, IHM, is associate professor of theology at Boston College, where she teaches courses in the doctrinal areas of Catholic theology, with special emphasis on the use of critical social theory. Her current research focuses on the role of women theologians in the Catholic Church. Her most recent book (coauthored with Helen Lewis and Maxine Waller) is *It Comes From the People: Community Development and Local Theology* (Temple). She is a member of the Sisters, Servants of the Immaculate Heart of Mary Sisters (IHM), Monroe, Michigan.

James F. Keenan, SJ, is professor of theological ethics at Boston College. He is on the boards of the Society of Christian Ethics and Theological Studies and the editor of the *Moral Traditions* series. Among his writings are about a dozen works illustrating the need for more ethical reflection on church practices and governance.

Paul Lakeland is professor of religious studies and chair of the Religious Studies Department at Fairfield University in Connecticut, where he teaches courses on ecclesiology, religion and culture, and religion and literature. He researches and writes in the areas of ecclesiology and religion and culture. He is the author most recently of *The Liberation of the Laity: In Search of an Accountable Church* (2003).

Michael K. Mauws is an associate professor of business strategy and entrepreneurship at Athabasca University. His research revolves around the effects of language on how we organize and understand social reality. Currently, he is exploring the managerial implications of precognitive perspectives on morality.

Judith A. McMorrow is professor of law at Boston College Law School. She is coauthor, with Daniel R. Coquillette, of *The Federal Law Of Attorney Conduct (Moore's Federal Practice)*, serves on the Massachusetts Supreme Judicial Court Committee on Judicial Ethics, and has served as chair of the Association of American Law Schools Section on Professional Responsibility.

Richard P. Nielsen is a professor of organization studies at Boston College. He works as a participatory action researcher, educator, and consultant in the areas of organizational change and negotiating methods applied to ethics and corruption reform problems in different types of political-economic systems. His publications include *The Politics of Ethics: Methods for Acting, Learning, and Sometimes Fighting, with Others in Addressing Ethics Problems in Organizational Life.* He serves as senior editor for ethics articles for the journal *Organization Studies.*

James M. O'Toole is professor of history at Boston College. His work focuses on American Catholic history, and he is currently writing a general history of the American Catholic laity. He is the author of *Militant and Triumphant: William Henry O'Connell and the Catholic Church in Boston* (1992) and *Passing for White: Race, Religion, and the Healy Family* (2002).

James E. Post is president of Voice of the Faithful, an organization of more than thirty thousand lay Catholics formed in response to the sexual abuse crisis. VOTF's mission is "to provide a prayerful voice, attentive to the Spirit, through which the laity can participate in the governance and guidance of the Catholic Church"; its goals are to support survivors of abuse, support priests of integrity, and shape structural change in the church. Jim is professor of management at Boston University where he teaches strategic management, business ethics, and public affairs. He is the author of many books and articles on the role of business in society.

Denise M. Rousseau is the H. J. Heinz II Professor of Organizational Behavior at Carnegie Mellon University, jointly in the Heinz School of Public Policy and Management and the Graduate School of Industrial Administration. Her research addresses organizational change with an emphasis on changing employment relations and how workers actively contribute to creating flexibility in contemporary firms. During 2004–2005 she is president of the Academy of Management. She is a fellow in the Academy of Management, American Psychological Association, and Society for Industrial/Organizational Psychology; and editor of the *Journal of Organizational Behavior.*